Poor People's Politics

Poor People's Politics

Peronist Survival Networks and the Legacy of Evita | *Javier Auyero*

DUKE UNIVERSITY PRESS | DURHAM & LONDON, 2001

© 2000 Duke University Press
All rights reserved
Printed in the United States
of America on acid-free paper ♾
Designed by Rebecca Giménez
Typeset in Monotype Garamond
with Franklin Gothic display by
Tseng Information Systems, Inc.
Library of Congress Cataloging-
in-Publication Data appear on the
last printed page of this book.

A LA MEMORIA DEL VIEJO

A MAMÁ

A GABRIELA

Contents

Acknowledgments

"My desk had become a sanctuary, and as long as I continued to sit there, struggling to find the next word, nothing could touch me anymore. . . . For the first time in all the years I had been writing, I felt as though I had caught fire. I couldn't tell if the book was good or bad, but that no longer seemed important. I had stopped questioning myself. I was doing what I had to do, and I was doing it in the only way that was possible for me. Everything else followed from that. It wasn't that I began to believe in myself so much as that I was inhabited by a sublime indifference. I had become interchangeable with my work, and I accepted that work on its own terms now, understanding that nothing could relieve me of the desire to do it. This was the bedrock epiphany, the illumination in which doubt gradually dissolved. Even if my life fell apart, there would still be something to live for" (Auster 1992, 112). While I was working on the doctoral dissertation on which this book is based, I came across these beautiful lines written by Paul Auster in *Leviathan*. They nicely encapsulate the *economy of feelings* through which I traveled while writing this work: a mix of anxiety and pleasure, a feeling of overcoming obstacles and accomplishing what I struggled for during the last three years.

At the same time, those lines misrepresent the *economy of effort* that contributed to my dissertation and, later, to this book. This is not the product of a lone writer, working in isolation. On the contrary, and paraphrasing Auster, I have to admit that, while I "caught fire" writing this work, I was "touched" by many, many people. With their contributions, their criticism, or simply their interest they encouraged me to follow the set of intuitions with which I began when conducting the research on which this book is based.

First and foremost, I thank the people of Villa Paraíso. Had they not given their time to, extended their patience to, and encouraged this "guy who asks so many questions," this book would not have been possible. The team of social workers assigned to the municipality of Cóspito provided me with key insights into the workings of local politics for which I am extremely grateful. Paraíso and Cóspito are real places with real people, but their names have been changed to ensure anonymity.

I am also genuinely indebted to the members of my dissertation committee at the New School for Social Research—Charles Tilly, Deborah Poole, and José Casanova—for their criticism, support, and encouragement. José was extremely helpful in guiding this foreign student during his first steps at the New School and in making me reckon with the larger issues implied in this case study. Coming from different disciplines and sometimes warring traditions, Debbie and Chuck were extremely attentive and encouraging readers. Their detailed and challenging queries and comments throughout the long process made writing this work a pleasant learning experience, and I have no words to thank them. Those who know Debbie and Chuck know how generous and intellectually stimulating they are.

Dozens of friends, colleagues, and students read drafts of the book or heard and critiqued portions of some chapters. Although not all their comments were incorporated into the final text, their feedback was extremely helpful and supportive. In this vein, I especially thank Lucas Rubinich, Loïc Wacquant, Daniel James, Diana Taylor, Robert Gay, Elizabeth Jelin, José Nun, and Ricardo Sidicaro for their comments and support. At the New School for Social Research, William Roseberry, Deena Abu-Lughod, Joel Stillerman, Xavier Andrade, Kumru Toktamis, and Ann Mische gave me insightful criticism at early stages of this project. Tulio Halperín, Michael Kimmel, Judith Hellman, Carlos de la Torre, and Takeshi Wada also read and critiqued versions of chapters 2 and 5. I am thankful to them, as I am to the participants in the panel "Still the Century of Peronism?" at the 1998 annual meeting of the Latin American Studies Association in Chicago. We spent three days "talking and talking" about issues central to this book. I thank Mark Healey, Moira Mackinnon, Pierre Ostiguy, and Steve Levitsky for their careful reading and excellent suggestions. The CECYP (Centro de Estudios en Cultura y Política), at which I presented and discussed early versions of chapters 4 and 5, provided a very stimulating atmosphere. I am very grateful to its members: Lucas Rubinich, Alejandro Grimson, Jorge Elbaum, Pablo Semán, Marcela González, Daniela Soldano, Claudio Benzecry, Marina Farinetti, and Carlos Belvedere. Earlier versions of some chapters were published in *Theory and Society,* the *Journal of Contemporary Ethnography,* the *International Journal of Urban and Regional Research, Qualitative Sociology,* and the *Latin American Research Review.* I would like to thank these journals' anonymous readers as well as Chandra Mukerji, Loïc Wacquant, and Robert Gay for their trenchant criticism. I also extend grateful acknowledgment to the members of the Contentious Politics Seminar at Columbia University.

There is much badly needed work that the scope of the present project does not permit me to undertake but that I hope to be able to complete in the coming years. Knowing of work in progress—that of Steve Levitsky, for example—has made it easier for me to live with the limitations imposed by circumstances. I am truly indebted to Steve, with whom I have held many, many conversations over the past two years on the extremely complex and enigmatic practices of the Peronist Party. I also thank my friends in Cóspito, Hector Mazzei and Sandra Gallegos, and my friends in San Cristóbal, Gabriela Michetti and Eduardo Cura. They know why.

In addition, I thank the Social Science Research Council and the New School for Social Research for their financial support. My gratitude also to Jacqueline Kay and Elizabeth Zack for many helpful suggestions and careful editing. I am very grateful to Valerie Millholland, Miriam Angress, and Patricia Mickelberry at Duke University Press for their highly competent and helpful editorial assistance. Very special thanks go to Joseph Brown for his detailed final editing.

Opportunities to present summaries or sections of this book have been provided by the American Sociological Association, the Latin American Studies Association, the Janey Program for Latin American Studies at the New School for Social Research, the Contentious Politics Seminar at Columbia University, the Seminario General at the Casa de Altos Estudios en Ciencias Sociales, the Instituto Torcuato DiTella, the University of General Sarmiento, the Graduate Social Sciences Department at the University of Buenos Aires, the CECYP at the Fundacion del Sur, the Latin American Center at Duke University, and the Latin American and Caribbean Center at the State University of New York at Stony Brook.

My new academic home, the Sociology Department at the State University of New York at Stony Brook, has provided a wonderful environment in which to write this book. All my colleagues, my graduate students, and the administrative staff here made my first steps as an assistant professor an incredibly enjoyable and stimulating experience. When leaving New York for his graduate studies in Iowa, Facundo Montenegro gave me the first book I ever read on political clientelism as a farewell present (he was the one leaving, but that's not the point here). Over the phone, here in New York, or in Iowa City, Facundo constantly reminded me of that decisive fact while pointing out that he deserved a paragraph in the acknowledgments. Well, Fac, here it is.

Gabriela Polit patiently tolerated both my long absences from home while doing fieldwork and my apprehensive presence while writing. She also encouraged my "looking elsewhere" when the answers I was seeking were not in the limited (and limiting) boundaries of the discipline of sociology.

Gabriela, my mother Ana, my brother Gustavo and his partner, Majo, and that wonderful trio (Tuqui, Pablo, and Esteban) were especially supportive during the extremely difficult times since the death of our *compañero más querido,* my father, Carlos Auyero. No words can describe how much we all miss him. No words can depict the political and intellectual inspiration that "El Pelado" has been to me. He loved doing (another kind of) politics. This work is dedicated to his memory.

Who Is Who in the Peronist Network

MATILDE: Councilwoman of the municipality of Cóspito. Owner of the UB called Three Generations, and main political broker in Villa Paraíso and nearby areas. Former press secretary of the Peronist Party, and former secretary of social welfare of the municipality of Cóspito.

ADOLFO: Matilde's husband. Undersecretary of public works at the municipality of Cóspito

PEDRO, PACO, AND LUIS: Matilde's sons. Pedro is a public employee at the municipality of Cóspito and private secretary to his father, Adolfo. Paco is the president of the cultural center Jauretche, located half a block from Matilde's UB in front of her two-story home. He is married to Mimi.

MIMI: Matilde's daughter-in-law. Coordinator of the largest state-sponsored food program in Cóspito City—the Plan Vida. The Plan Vida distributes milk, eggs, cereals, and sugar in poor neighborhoods of Buenos Aires on a daily basis through block delegates. These block delegates, mostly women working for free for the program, are known as *manzaneras* of the *Plan Vida*. Mimi coordinates the twenty-three *manzaneras* in Villa Paraíso.

BRIGITTE: Matilde's cleaning lady. Secretary of the cultural center Jauretche, and a *manzanera* of the Plan Vida.

MARCELA: Matilde's private secretary.

RAFAEL BIANCO: Known as "Cholo." He has been working with/for

Matilde for the last four years. He is a Peronist activist and local broker. He owns a UB in the Fifth Road, the poorest area in Villa Paraíso.

JUAN PISUTTI: Known as "Juancito." A public employee of the municipality of Cóspito, and president of the UB called The Leader. He is also a political broker in Villa Paraíso and was, in the past, secretary of the main neighborhood association (Sociedad de Fomento).

ANDREA ANDRADE: A public employee of the municipality of Cóspito, secretary of the UB Fernando Fontana at the center of Villa Paraíso.

JUANA MEDINA: She is in charge of a recently opened UB called "Chacho Peñaloza" in Villa Paraíso.

RODOLFO FONTANA: Publicly known as "Rolo." He is the mayor of Cóspito City and president of the Peronist Party of Cóspito.

HILDA "CHICHE" GONZALEZ DE DUHALDE: The governor's wife. Director of the food-distribution program Plan Vida and other social assistance programs. President of the Consejo Provincial de la Familia y Desarrollo Humano.

EDUARDO DUHALDE: Governor of the province of Buenos Aires.

The Day of the Rally

Complaining about T-Shirts on Perón's Birthday

Perón's Birthday

It is Thursday, 8 October 1996. In the city of Cóspito, located in the Conurbano Bonaerense, Argentina, some people of the Peronist Party, led by the mayor, Rodolfo Fontana, are organizing a rally for tonight.[1] They are commemorating the 103d anniversary of the birth of the leader of the Peronist movement, General Juan Perón, or, as one of the organizers told me: "We are celebrating Perón's birthday." For the last twenty-two years, since the death of Perón, the Peronist Party of Cóspito has been organizing this sort of political ritual. However, tonight is a special night because the mayor, "Rolo," considered the "last *caudillo*" by many Peronists in Cóspito, is under political attack: one of the most important television channels has accused one of Rolo's closest friends, a political associate, of corruption. This friend, an official in the city government, was caught on tape by a hidden camera discussing the mayor's participation in "the whole business." The political opposition in Cóspito is trying to take advantage of this sudden and unexpected turn of events. They will attempt to impeach the mayor at the next local council meeting.

At 10:30 A.M., I stop by the Unidad Básica (UB) "Three Generations" —the grassroots office of the Peronist Party—located on the border of Villa Paraíso, in Cóspito. Although its name suggests the contrary, Villa

Paraíso is a densely populated, destitute shantytown (*villa*) located on the outskirts of the city of Buenos Aires. More than 60 percent of its potentially economically active population is unemployed or underemployed; violent petty crime, drug trafficking, and shoplifting are standard survival strategies here, and most of the inhabitants are affected in some way. By official standards, more than 50 percent of the population of this stigmatized *villa* has "unmet basic needs"; that is, the people are poor, and approximately 70 percent have incomes that are below the official poverty line.

The UB "Three Generations" belongs to Matilde, former press secretary of the Peronist Party, secretary of social welfare of Cóspito until last year, and currently a councilwoman. Juan, twenty years old, is at the UB fixing a drum, the traditional *bombo peronista,* that he is going to play tonight at the rally. I ask him what he is up to. "You see, I'm fixing this for tonight," he replies. "What are you celebrating?" I ask. The answer: "I have no fucking idea [*no tengo ni puta idea*], but there's gonna be a lot of people [*un pedazo de gente*]."[2] Juan is unemployed, but he has been showing up at Matilde's UB for the last four months; he expects to obtain a municipal job soon ("Espero que pronto pinte algo"). There are two other youngsters at Matilde's UB. One of them holds a public job but spends his working hours at Matilde's UB. The three of them are part of "the Band of Matilde," a group of approximately seventy men (mostly youngsters) who play the drums and carry the party flags and banners displaying Rolo's and Matilde's names during the political rallies. None of the three knows exactly what they are commemorating tonight, but they fix their drums with a luthier's precision and dedication.

Walking through the shantytown is safer in the morning than in the afternoon, when on almost every corner there are youngsters drinking beer or smoking pot, acting as human tollbooths, asking for change in exchange for safe passage. But in the morning there is no fare to be paid. "They are sleeping, you know," one of the older Paraíso residents tells me.

I traverse the shantytown from Matilde's UB to Cholo's UB, located on the "Fifth Road," one of the streets bordering Villa Paraíso. This sector has the worst reputation in the shantytown: all the drug traffickers are said to live there; the "Little Pirates" gang, whose members climb on trucks and buses as soon as they stop and rob the passengers, is said to take refuge there during police raids. Residents point to the Fifth Road to deflect the stigma of living in a shantytown; its inhabitants are defined as the real *villeros* (shantytown dwellers). This sector is the poorest in Paraíso: some streets remain unpaved; there are very precarious shacks, open sewers, and little functioning running water (especially during the summer).

At 11:30 A.M., a small truck from the secretariat of public works of the municipality of Cóspito—driven by one of Matilde's sons, Pedro—stops at Cholo's UB. Pedro knocks at the door of Cholo's house, located half a block from his UB. Together, Cholo and Pedro unload thirty bottles of beer, thirty bread rolls, thirty *chorizos* (meat sausages), packages of noodles, polenta, powdered milk, sugar, rice, and *yerba mate* from the truck. They deposit everything in the UB. Pedro also gives Cholo fifteen T-shirts and fifteen caps with the emblem "Fontana Leadership: The Band of Matilde" (*Fontana Conducción: La Banda de Matilde*). Later in the afternoon, two hours before the rally, Cholo will organize a barbecue—with beer, bread, and *chorizos*—for those who attend the public gathering. After the rally, he will give them the food that Matilde sent him.

Pedro is "in charge of me," Cholo tells me. Matilde's son is the one who sends the buses to every UB that works with Matilde and makes sure that every *puntero* (party broker) fulfills the busload quota that has been assigned him or her. Cholo usually gathers forty people for the rallies. Assuming that he will do so again tonight, Pedro sends enough *chorizos,* bread, beer, etc. for forty. The T-shirts and the caps, Pedro tells Cholo, were to be distributed tonight among "his people" before they make their way to Matilde's UB—where they will all meet the rally. After Pedro leaves, Cholo realizes that fifteen T-shirts and fifteen caps are not enough: "You know, if there are forty people on the bus, I have to give them forty caps and forty T-shirts or twenty caps for some of them and twenty T-shirts for the others. But, with fifteen T-shirts and fifteen caps, what am I supposed to do?" So he decides not to distribute the T-shirts and caps until he and "his people" reach Matilde's UB. That is where, later tonight, the trouble will begin.

Cholo has been working with Matilde for five years now. He defines himself as part of "Matilde's group," as a representative of Matilde in this sector of Paraíso. Cholo holds a part-time job with the municipality, with a contract that must be renewed every three months with the approval of Matilde. He earns $300 a month but does not actually do any work for the municipality. He is what in Argentina is known as a *ñoqui,* a party activist who collects a paycheck as a ghost employee of some public dependency. Cholo also works for Plan Vida, a food-distribution program run by the governor's wife. From 4:00 to 9:00 A.M. every day (except Sundays), Cholo accompanies the truck on its route within the shantytown and through the different shantytowns and other poor neighborhoods of the area adjacent to Villa Paraíso. He and two other men distribute the milk, cereal, and eggs to the block delegates (known as *manzaneras*) of Plan Vida. He also spreads news concerning Plan Vida (an upcoming rally that will launch the program at which the governor or his wife will be present, the program's newspaper will be distributed, etc.) and other news related to the Peronist Party (the time of tonight's rally, the invitation for the barbecue, etc.). He reports any problem that a *manzanera* might have (a new member of the program, a dropout, a complaint about shortage of food) to Mimi, Matilde's daughter-in-law, who is the area's program coordinator. He earns $50 a week for this second job.

Cholo is a lifelong Peronist, and he has been living in Paraíso for the last thirty years. Some neighbors consider Cholo the one who "has done the most for the improvement of the slum." Some of those who live in the area deem him responsible for the pavement of the streets, for the improvement of the sewage system, and for the leveling of the soccer field. A couple of days before the rally, Cholo told me that it was "through Matilde that everything was done here . . . she really delivers. Since I started working in the party, I've seen that Matilde has done the most. She sent the pipelines for the sewage system and the cement for the pavement of the streets. Adolfo [Matilde's husband, who is the undersecretary of public works] sent the machines to do the job."

Not far from Cholo's UB, Mónica — one of the *manzaneras* of Plan Vida — spends her mornings distributing milk, eggs, cereal (once a week), and sugar (one kilogram once a month) to the more than 150 mothers and children on her block. Cholo invited her to become part of the program. At first, having no experience whatsoever, she was "very nervous," but then she "got used to it": "I really like the program; it's a real help." In between distributing the milk and the eggs, Mónica cleans her precarious one-bedroom house, bathes her two children, and prepares their breakfast and lunch. After twelve, she leaves the house and visits her mother-in-law, Victoria, another Plan Vida *manzanera*. Victoria also became part of the program through Cholo. Her husband, Mario, works at the health center of Villa Paraíso in a full-time public job that he got six months after joining "Matilde's Band." "Playing the drums [*los bombos*], you know?" Catalina—Mario's stepdaughter—tells me, "but it was for free, *ad honorem,* as they say." Victoria explains that Mario "went after Matilde, becoming one of the drum players in her band. She [Matilde] promised Mario a job. After six or seven months he got it; he has been working there for two years. Matilde really delivers. . . . She also sends powdered milk to the UB around the corner [Cholo's]."

Mónica and Mario will go to the rally tonight with Cholo. "I really like going to the rallies. . . . It is also a way of thanking Matilde for everything she does for us," Mónica tells me. Victoria will stay home because "I have to take care of the house, you know?" Catalina would love to go—"I hardly miss a rally," she comments. But she has just had an eye operation, and she needs to rest. As she is unemployed, she has no health insurance (*obra social*); a friend with insurance allowed Catalina to have the operation under her name.

At 2:00 P.M. I meet Toni, who is the porter at the Ateneo Parroquial, a social club associated with the local Catholic church. He works as a part-time garbage collector for the municipality of Cóspito. He got this job when he was working at the UB "Perón-Perón," another UB in Villa Paraíso. Juan Pisutti is the president of the UB and a close friend of Toni's. I spend four hours with Toni talking about the history of Villa Paraíso, which he knows pretty well. Villa Paraíso, Toni notes, is the site where *Detrás de un largo muro* (Behind a long wall), one of the first realist Argentine movies, was shot. The movie portrays the lives of those recent internal immigrants who, in the 1930s and 1940s, moved to the city of Buenos Aires and chose Villa Paraíso as a place to live. At that time, Toni tells me, the place was almost a lagoon, and "we filled it, we made this *barrio,* you know?" During the 1950s, the national government had walled in the shantytown so that tourists on the adjoining main road (which at that time provided the easiest access to the international airport) would not have their impressions of the beauty of Buenos Aires spoiled by the living conditions in Paraíso. Behind that long wall, thousands of people were building a place of their own.

Villa Paraíso, Toni tells me, is the place where Sandro—one of Argentina's top pop singers—first performed, where Acavallo—a world boxing champion—used to train. It is the place that inspired the novelist Bernardo Verbitsky to write *Villa miseria también es América* (1957)—although Toni is not sure on this point. And it is also, according to Toni, the site where many of the members of the "Peronist Resistance"—a clandestine union-based movement that fought for the return of Perón to Argentina during the 1950s and 1960s—used to hide. "This guy, Don Mario, was the mailman of the Resistance. . . ." Villa Paraíso, Toni observes, is a "very politicized place."

"See those buses? They are going to Matilde's UB . . . because tonight there's a rally," Toni points out. Although he defines himself as a "Peronist . . . but a Peronist of Perón" and he knows that today is "Perón's anniversary," he will not go to the rally. "I don't like people messing around, smoking pot and drinking wine, and playing the drums. . . . We have nothing to celebrate. . . . Perón is dead, and it would be nice to remember him in another way, not shouting as crazy people and drinking and smoking. Besides, I don't want anybody to *take me* to the rally. If I want to go, I'll go by myself." Before I leave the Ateneo, Toni tells me that, if I am interested in what is going on in Villa Paraíso, I should attend tonight's rally because "a lot of people from the *villa* will go." He adds a very harsh remark about Matilde: "She calls people whenever there is a rally; she uses those guys, who are idling around. She takes them to paint walls. She uses them for the rallies to play the drums, and, when the day is over, she gives them a packet of food or a joint. . . . That has nothing to do with social justice."

It is almost dark when I leave the Ateneo and head for Matilde's UB, arriving there at 6:15 P.M. Pedro is inside, handing out the T-shirts with the slogan "Rolo Conducción: La Banda de Matilde" to groups of youngsters. Most of them come from Villa Paraíso, although others come from nearby shantytowns and poor neighborhoods. A youth is rolling a joint. Pedro warns him: "Hey, man, there's not gonna be anything for you later." The others laugh. Another youth from the band, who works for the municipality in the secretariat of public works, tells me: "I am here because I have to work; I'd rather be at home, watching TV and drinking *mate*."

Outside the UB, Matilde's two other sons—wearing the T-shirts with the slogan—direct the people who approach the UB to one of the seven buses that are lined up on the street. Mimi—Matilde's daughter-in-law and coordinator of Plan Vida—is wearing a T-shirt on which is printed a photograph that shows Matilde and Rolo together, smiling for the camera. She, together with Coca—Matilde's other daughter-in-law and the coordinator of Plan Vida in the nearby Villa Tranquila—who is also wearing the T-shirt with the photograph, are chatting with some *manzaneras,* telling them about the upcoming rally launching the program that will take place a week from now in another neighborhood of Cóspito City: the governor's wife is going to be there. They are also distributing T-shirts and caps.

The Jauretche Cultural Center is located half a block from Matilde's UB in front of Matilde's two-story home. Paco, Matilde's other son, is its president. At this time of the day the center is open, and Briggite—Matilde's cleaning lady—is attending to the people who ask for medicine or food. An old woman asks Briggite for some sedatives; Briggite, carrying a bag full of T-shirts and another bag full of packs of cigarettes, tells her: "Not now, *mamita;* why don't you come back tomorrow? Now I am in a rush, you know? We have an *acto* tonight. . . . Do you wanna come?" "Not today," the old lady answers, "I have to take care of the children, but next time, sure. . . ." She leaves, without her pills.

The cultural center is jammed with photos of Eva Perón, Juan Perón, Governor Duhalde, Matilde, and Rolo. There is a pile of Peronist Party newspapers, with a front-page photograph of Duhalde and the phrase "To govern is to create jobs." Dozens of soccer trophies stand in the center's glass showcase. There are also diplomas in recognition of Matilde's various social activities. At 7:00 P.M., Matilde, a bleached-blonde, forty-five-year-old woman, very well dressed and wearing light makeup, shows up. She greets everybody, me included, and asks me: "Are you coming to see the way the Peronist masses mobilize?"

Outside, Pedro tells the youngsters from Matilde's Band (numbering by now nearly seventy) to look for the drums in the garage of the UB. In no more than five minutes, the seventy "musicians" are rhythmically playing their drums. He gives them packs of cigarettes and chewing gum. Pedro tells me that they hope next year to "incorporate trumpets into the band. If it [Matilde's bid for provincial deputy] turns out good, we will surely have trumpets."

By 7:15 P.M. the seven buses are full. Matilde's band is playing amid a cloud of marijuana smoke. Matilde's sons and daughters-in-law are waiting for the other buses to show up. Half an hour later, seven more buses, coming from the Fifth Road and from Villa Tranquila and Barrio Rioja, show up. Fourteen buses and around five hundred people are ready to go.

Cholo, Matilde's *puntero* in the Fifth Road, is arguing angrily with Mimi and Paco. "My people deserve the T-shirts and the caps! You gave me only fifteen T-shirts and fifteen caps, and you know that I usually move forty people. What am I supposed to do? I didn't distribute them because I didn't know what to do. . . . Now you go and tell them that there are no T-shirts or caps." Mimi replies: "You can't complain. Come on, give me a break; other groups got only ten T-shirts." Cholo would later recount the discussion in the following terms: "And I am not stupid. How could she tell me that every group got only ten T-shirts if I, and my people, saw that everybody was wearing a T-shirt?"

More than half of Cholo's people get off the bus as Mimi and Paco look on in astonishment. Matilde and her husband have already gone to the church where, before the public rally, a mass is being held in honor of "El General." Together with Cholo, twenty people head back to the Fifth Road, in Villa Paraíso. Tonight, they are not going to the rally. The other half stays, among them Mónica and Mario. As Mónica later tells me: "I won't dirty my hands over a T-shirt [*No me voy a ensuciar por una remera*]."

The square where the rally is being held is located a short fifteen-minute drive from Matilde's UB. The police have blocked traffic, so we easily make it to where the other buses are parked. The group is quite large: five hundred people on a cold evening in Cóspito City, wearing white T-shirts and caps, with seventy people in front playing the drums and two big banners—one of them held by Mario—at the head of the contingent.

Photographs of Perón, Evita, and Rolo decorate the stage, which is already surrounded by approximately four hundred people, most of them dispersed in groups of different sizes carrying Peronist flags and banners with the names of Rolo and other local *punteros*. Matilde's group represents more than half the whole crowd.

As soon as the mayor, Matilde, and other municipal officials leave the church and come onstage, the *acto* (rally) is officially opened by an announcer, who welcomes everyone. The audience sings both the national and the Peronist anthems. Afterward, the announcer introduces the first speaker, Susana Gutierrez, the mayor's adviser to the Social Welfare Area and president of the UB "Cuca Gutierrez" (Cuca was the nickname of Susana's mother). Susana is a forty-two-year-old bleached blonde, very well dressed; she addresses the audience, saying, "Today is a day of glory for the Peronist people. Perón meant the happiness of the people; he meant social justice. . . ." She then recites a poem that she has—in her own words—"written for the occasion," a poem that "the *compañeras* [comrades] have asked" her to recite, a poem that "expresses my feelings" and that is worth quoting:

Hombres y mujeres de mi humilde patria
quiero yo contarles a la juventud
y contar la historia, la historia de un hombre
que le dió a su pueblo todo lo mejor.
Les brindó trabajo, viviendas honestas
lucho por los niños y el trabajador
muchos más felices fueron los ancianos
y una vida digna a ellos les dió.
Tuvo a su lado alguien que lo quizo,
entregó su vida y todo su amor,
fue mujer de lucha, de sangre guerrera,
que le dió al humilde, justicia y honor.
Juntos siempre juntos, lucharon unidos,
le dieron al pueblo la paz y el amor,
lucharemos siempre, somos peronistas,
hijos bien nacidos de Evita y Perón.

Men and women of my humble motherland,
I want to tell something to the young people,
to recount the history, the history of a man
who gave the best to his people.
He bestowed jobs, honest dwellings on them.
He fought for the children and the worker,
the elderly were much happier,
and he gave a dignified life to them.

He had someone who loved him at his side,
who offered her life and all her love,
she was a woman of struggle, with warrior's blood
who gave to the humble honor and justice.
Together, always together, they struggled united,
they gave to the people peace and love,
we will fight forever, we are Peronists,
well-born children of Evita and Perón.

She ends her ardent recital amid an ovation given by the close to a thousand people in the square. Cheers, applause, and the sound of the drums mark the transition to the next speaker: Rolo. At this time, I lose sight of Mónica. She is in the nearby park, supervising her children, who are playing with other children, none of them paying attention to what is going on in the *acto*. She is still wearing her T-shirt and cap.

The announcer presents Rolo's multiple credentials: "In order to talk about General Perón—undisputed leader, the man who transformed the doctrine of this time, and the man who created Peronist doctrine—Rolo Fontana will speak. He is the president of the Peronist Party of Cóspito, political secretary of the Peronist Party of Buenos Aires Province, member of the National Council of the Peronist Party, five-time mayor, and the last Peronist *caudillo*." Rolo is a seventy-two-year-old man who has serious health problems and whose voice is increasingly difficult to understand. His twenty-minute speech is dedicated to lauding the image of Perón and Eva and to deriding the opposition, which, according to him, is conspiring to bring the Peronist government down. He emphasizes that the *pueblo peronista* must keep the Peronist flame alive:

> We are Peronists from the heart, Peronism is a sentiment, and we are used to fighting, we are used to sacrifice, and if they [the opposition] want to fight, we will fight. We all know that there are various plots to break the constitutional stability of Menem's government. We have to think that he is the man that we appointed as our president. . . .
> If the Peronist government falls, all of us will fall, and we will lose everything. . . . We have to keep defending what Juan Perón and Eva Perón gave to us, and we are going to make the *pueblo argentino* happy, as we made it with Juan Perón.

He finishes his speech with an implicit reference to the political scandal going on in the municipality, the "hidden-camera issue," saying, "Thanks for coming; in these days, I need your affection."

The people cheer him, the drums play for ten more minutes, and the different groups head back to their buses. Mónica comes back from the nearby park with her exhausted children. We all get on the bus and return to Villa Paraíso.

The rally has had different—although not necessarily mutually exclusive—meanings for its participants: for some the rally was a party of sorts, an opportunity to get together with friends, to drink a free beer and smoke a free joint, to play the drums and dance *al compás del tamboril* (to the rhythm of the drums). For others, the rally was part of their job, part of their day's work. Others took advantage of the free ride to take their children to play in the nearby park, a rare treat. Others went to the rally for the bag of food offered. For the political brokers, the rally was, apart from elections, probably one of the most important forms of political objectification, *the* way of making numbers visible and "showing the mayor how many people you have." For others, some of whom were not even present, the purpose of the rally was simply to pay homage to the "great man." For some members of the press and some progressive politicians who will report and comment on the rally, this was a clear manifestation of "political clientelism"; for others, among them some social scientists—more attached to an understanding of politics that is based on what it should be and not on what it actually is—the rally was a holdover from the past with no bearing whatsoever on contemporary politics.

Clientelist Exchanges?

"The other day, I was watching TV," Cholo tells me two days after the rally, "and a politician . . . I don't remember his name . . . was saying that the *punteros políticos* [party brokers] *use the people*. He was saying that the officials use the *punteros* and that, in turn, the *punteros* use the people. And I think to myself, 'That's me, I use the people' . . . because I give food to the people, and the officials play their game . . . because Matilde didn't send enough T-shirts and caps, she didn't even send enough *chori-*

zos. . . . She has helped with the pavement of the street, but since then she is not really delivering. I am still waiting for the sewage pipes for the Fifth Road, and she hasn't sent the machines to level off the ground for the soccer field. . . . *She is not giving me the air that I need.* I am tired, you know?" Abruptly, Cholo becomes what Goffman (1963, 111) would call *situation conscious,*[3] and his comments about Matilde suddenly change. He complains about his fixed-term contract: "I am worth more than $300 . . . because I *always* move forty people, and they know that . . . and if they know that, why did they send only fifteen T-shirts and fifteen caps?"

In front of Cholo's UB, there is a large tract of land that used to be part of one of the biggest military factories in Greater Buenos Aires. The factory was closed down in the early 1970s and is now abandoned, a skeleton where the Little Pirates hide themselves. Cholo has been trying to construct a soccer field on this public land: "You know, if Matilde sends the machines, I'll level off the ground, I'll put up two goals, and I'll surround it with a wire fence. . . . I can get $150 a month from the rent of the soccer field . . . but Matilde still owes me the machines. . . . She hasn't shown up much in this area recently." Matilde is not sending the "oxygen" he needs, he repeats, "because, you know, today people do not go to the rallies for Perón and Evita, they go for interest. . . . How does she think I'm gonna manage with only fifteen T-shirts and fifteen caps? That's not possible."

Cholo is highly indignant about the whole "trouble with the T-shirts," and he is thinking about backing out of his informal arrangement with Matilde. "I am really tired, you know?" he repeats. But he will not leave Matilde's group. A week from Perón's birthday, he and "his people" are in front of the municipal building of Cóspito City celebrating the Day of Loyalty — the founding day of Peronism — together with Matilde's Band and another twelve hundred people. Rolo and Susana are, again, the keynote speakers.

Cholo's understanding of why people show up at the rallies is surprisingly close to that of many progressive politicians and journalists. For them, as for Cholo, people attend these and other rallies for "interest." They go because they get a bag of food, a pair of sneakers, a barbecue, T-shirts. Yet opposition politicians and the progressive press will report and comment on this and on the dozens of rallies organized by the Peronist Party during the year as "acts of manipulation," as the expression of "political clientelism." Although they agree with Cholo's diagnosis, they will denounce these practices as bribery (exchanging food for support), as antidemocratic, as the exact opposite of the way in which a democratic civil society—as they understand it—should function.

Probably unconsciously, much of the academic discourse on the subject also agrees with Cholo: interest is the driving force behind much of the support that political patrons and brokers obtain from their "clients." In contexts of extreme material deprivation, so the tale runs, clients are not blind followers, dupes in the grip of clientelist politics: their support is calculated, a way to improve their lot by aligning themselves with the brokers and patrons who have the most to offer. In the more optimistic scenarios, instrumental calculation comes with "resistance" to the domination exerted by patrons and brokers alike. Clients, like the Mónicas and Marios who abound in the poor neighborhoods and shantytowns, are seen as crafting a "hidden transcript," that is, a "critique of power spoken behind the back of the dominant" (Scott 1990, xxi) that allegedly vents their profound, visceral discontent with this way of doing politics.

It is true: food, favors, beer, and drugs circulate in one direction (from patrons and brokers to clients), and support—and sometimes votes—circulates in the other (from clients to brokers and patrons). But do such exchanges actually cause the practices that we see? A view strictly concerned with the undemocratic character of the exchange of food for votes—or with the morality of such practices—fails to grasp one essential element: the rally dramatizes the *already existing* informal networks and shared cultural representations. These networks and these representations are key elements in the everyday lives of many shantytown dwellers and many among the urban poor. These networks and these representations are the subject of this book.

Neither the political/journalistic discourse on the subject of Peronist political clientelism nor the usual tools provided by studies of clientelist exchanges in other parts of the world will help us understand what is going on during the rally days organized by the Peronist Party in the contemporary Conurbano Bonaerense. They will not facilitate our understanding precisely because the explanation of why people go to those rallies—organized by the official party during times when the conditions of existence of those attending them are further deteriorating—is to be found, not in the rally itself, but in the underlying ties expressed, strengthened, and sometimes even renegotiated at the rallies and in the memories shared and future plans made there.

The Plan of This Book

Most of the people who gathered on 8 October 1996 had five things in common: they came from Villa Paraíso; most of them were poor; they knew Matilde or her counterpart in other poor neighborhoods or shantytowns; they defined themselves as Peronists; and they clapped furiously when Susana shouted: "We will fight forever, we are Peronists, well-born children of Evita and Perón." In other words, those who supposedly went there for a bag of food share a network of relationships and claim a common—although multifarious—identity.

Through a serious exploration of these five elements, this book will show that the rally described above is one constitutive element, among many others, of ongoing informal problem-solving networks meant to ensure material survival and of shared cultural representations. The rally, the T-shirt dispute, the expressions of gratitude to Matilde, Susana's Peronist performance, the daily distribution of milk, the barbecue, and the "affection" that the mayor confessed he needs—all are important parts of the everyday relationships that make up the political culture(s) in which the lives of the urban poor are embedded. The rally, the T-shirt dispute, and the poem recited by Susana are thus dramatizations of intricate networks, of competing histories, and of multiple identities.

The analyses presented in this book are based on the first ethnography of *clientelist networks* ever carried out in urban Argentina.[4] Chapter 1 examines the fate of the urban poor in contemporary Argentina, with special emphasis on the structural forces that affect the everyday lives of thousands of *bonaerenses,* depriving them of their usual means of subsistence. Deepening inequality, hyper-unemployment amounting to outright deproletarianization, the increasingly casual nature of the wage-labor relation, and the related retrenchment of the populist-welfare state are examined as the processes behind the further impoverishment of the urban poor during the last decade. The result of this profound deterioration in the material conditions of existence is a transformation in the mainstay of subsistence of the urban poor: the lack of monetary consumption in a growing number of households determines the increasing relevance of informal consumption, and of domestic and self-help activities, as ways of satisfying principal subsistence needs.

Chapter 2 explores the forms that the processes described in the previous chapter take in a particular geographic and social setting: the stigmatized and destitute shantytown Villa Paraíso. One can hardly think of a space that is located lower than this in the symbolic hierarchy of places that compose the Conurbano Bonaerense. Middle-class neighborhoods in decline, working-class *barrios,* squatter settlements (*asentamientos*), projects, all stand above the shantytown and distance themselves from it.

Chapter 2 reconstructs the lived experiences of shantytown dwellers through an exploration of the history of the ways in which they have been solving their major subsistence problems. As we will see, Paraíso does not have a founding day—as some squatter settlements do—because it has grown gradually, through accretion, since the mid-1940s. More than 50 percent of the land that it now occupies was covered by lagoons. Paraíso also grew through a landfill process. And, as they improved it, the inhabitants constructed a series of neighborhood institutions and a set of cultural understandings about life in Paraíso. They constructed a *place in which to live.* The shantytown's increased isolation and the concomitant sense of abandonment make the inhabitants feel that "the future is no longer what it used to be." What used to be a place in which to live has become simply another *space in which to survive.* Chapter 2 therefore explores the way in which the shantytown's inhabitants understand what has happened to it.

Against the background of the transformation in the mainstay of subsistence in Paraíso, chapter 3 explores some of the problem-solving networks available to residents. Church charity and reciprocal networks among neighbors are still important ways of satisfying basic needs, and underground activities (drug dealing, shoplifting, petty crime) are increasingly important means of obtaining cash. After a brief description of these underground activities, the chapter thoroughly explores the different problem-solving networks that, with a political broker as their focal point, abound in the slum. Within Villa Paraíso, there are four major problem-solving networks over which the Peronist Party has a decisive influence; the chapter explores those networks' different resources, variable extensions, and similar forms and functions. Information hoarding and resource control are the key functions of brokers. The problem-solving networks can be envisioned as concentric circles surrounding the brokers; in every case, a network consists of an inner circle of everyday, ubiquitous relationships central to the problem holder's life and an outer circle of more casual and intermittent ties. When the focal points of the network are not competing with each other in the local political arena, the networks overlap: a member of one inner circle can get his or her problems resolved through the intervention of a broker at the center of another circle. In contrast, when the focal points compete, the networks are mutually exclusive.

Chapter 3 examines the differences and similarities between the various brokers, illustrating the ideal-typical trajectories of political brokers's careers. Brokers can be classified as *beginners, declining, consolidated,* or *potential,* depending on their links to third parties and on their own ability to garner and maintain support. The chapter also examines the functioning of Plan Vida, the largest food-distribution program currently carried out by the government of the province of Buenos Aires. The workings of this food program embody the "Peronist way" of solving survival problems among the urban poor.

Chapter 4 elaborates on the poem recited by Susana at the rally, treating it as an indicator of the cultural tradition enacted by Peronist brokers each time they grant a favor or hand out a bag of food. In the same way in which chapter 3 explores the resources distributed by brokers (i.e., the "whats" of the Peronist networks), chapter 4 examines the "hows" of this distribution (i.e., the way in which brokers publicly present their favors). It analyzes brokers' practices as performances, as public presentations, and as a form of symbolic labor in which a representation of the relation between problem solver and problem holder is proposed and a particular version of Peronism (as a cultural tradition) is re-created. This chapter explores the solution of problems, not only as a veiled form of doing politics, but also as a way of "doing gender," reproducing gender differences within the local political arena.

Chapter 5 problematizes the notion of clientelism by taking into consideration the way in which so-called clients feel and think about the "interested exchanges." It analyzes the different points of view that the shantytown dwellers have on the distribution of goods by political brokers, the various evaluations that they make of political brokers, and the competing views about politics and its particular role in the history of the neighborhood. In order to avoid a disembedded "recollection of voices," this chapter locates these points of view in the cluster of relations traced in chapter 3. It also returns to some of the issues explored in chapter 2, casting new light on the different narratives that exist in the shantytown concerning its history.

Chapter 6 further elaborates some of the issues explored in the previous chapter. Specifically, it examines the different meanings that "being a Peronist" has to the shantytown dwellers and anchors these diverse meanings in the problem-solving network. This chapter also examines Peronism as a public narrative and explores what is left of what Daniel James (1988) calls *the populist Peronist heresy*. It analyzes both the way in which the mayor, the governor and his wife, and local officials—such as Matilde—*talk* about Peronism, its historical mission, and its promise to solve the poor's problems and the varied ways in which Peronism is remembered by shantytown dwellers.

The conclusion reflects on certain personal experiences that I had while carrying out my fieldwork. Such reflection allows me to construct a final cultural hypothesis concerning the dynamics of the political culture(s) of the urban poor in contemporary Buenos Aires.

An Invitation to Read: Lessons from Villa Paraíso

Poor People's Politics developed out of my doctoral dissertation. The last question posed during my dissertation proposal defense was reserved for my adviser. I do not recall his exact words, but the question went something like this: "Eventually, your dissertation will turn into a book. If we go to the library, where are we supposed to look for it? In the urban history section, in political sociology, in Latin American studies, in cultural studies?" The question caught me off guard. It was not—I am sure—a blunt attempt to reduce my work to the province of one discipline at a time when boundaries between disciplines are crumbling. On the contrary, it was keen advice intended to guide my future work: "Do not spread yourself too thinly." On a deeper level, it was an elegant way of asking me why people who care neither about Villa Paraíso nor about Argentine politics should read my book. "What are you going to tell them that will change their minds about some general issue?" It was, I think, a way of warning me not to obsess about the case at hand at the expense of the construction of more general arguments.

I can hardly remember my answer. Yet I do recall that I attempted—unsuccessfully—to quote by memory the paragraph of Italo Calvino's "Whom Do We Write For?" in which he observes, "A writer's work is important to the extent that the ideal bookshelf on which he would like to be placed is still an improbable shelf, containing books that we do not usually put side by side, the juxtaposition of which can produce electric shocks, short circuits" (Calvino 1986, 82). Although my response was not as precise, the idea was there. I would attempt to write a dissertation (and, I hoped, a book) that would transcend the deeply established boundaries—both institutional and mental—between disciplines and subareas, locating it on an "improbable shelf" from the outset. At the same time, every single page of my book would be a struggle against the artificial division between theoretical and empirical work, deeply entrenched in the sociological discipline, even after the persuasive calls against such separation by such authors as C. Wright Mills or Pierre Bourdieu. From the very beginning, then, I would refuse to write the "theoretical framework" chapter, the "literature review" chapter, the "case studies" chapters—a way of proceeding that implicitly reproduces the sterile division between theory and empirical research by ignoring the fact that "the best theory is that which is virtually inseparable from the object it brings to light" (Wacquant 1998, 6).

Is this "network analysis," "cultural analysis," "urban sociology"? Why should we care about Villa Paraíso? Those questions continued to haunt me during the three years of fieldwork, writing, group discussion, and teaching. All the while, I was obsessed with my case and with the way in which (some of) the concepts and theoretical tools that I learned during the years of my graduate studies could be exercised or, better, "put into practice" (Bourdieu 1993, 271). If only I would be able to use those theoretical instruments in an adequate way, I would see the case at hand in a different light, and a reader who is not particularly concerned about Villa Paraíso would begin to gain some interest in my narrative.

In the meantime, I came across different scholarly works that turned out to be decisive influences on my writing, providing me with powerful conceptual tools with which to construct an answer to those hard-to-forget questions. Philippe Bourgois's *In Search of Respect* (1995), Beth Roy's *Some Trouble with Cows* (1994), Nancy Scheper-Hughes's *Death without Weeping* (1992), and Wacquant's (1994b, 1995b) work on boxing deal with subjects and places quite removed from my own. Yet someone who is not particularly interested in El Barrio, Panipur, Alto do Cruzeiro, or the black ghetto can learn many lessons that transcend those places and even their specific subjects. The epistemological issues that these works confront, the validity of the methods that they utilize, the instruments of analysis that they offer, all certainly transcend their contexts of origin. What can we learn from Villa Paraíso? To be blunt, besides the case, what is this book about?

One of the most perceptive observers of the new Latin American democracies acknowledges that political clientelism is still an extremely important "informal, permanent, and pervasive" institution in these new polyarchies (see O'Donnell 1996a, 1996b). Students of democratic consolidation, Guillermo O'Donnell (1996a) suggests, should free themselves from the "illusions" fostered by "a fixation on highly formalized and complex organizations" (p. 40). Implicitly recognizing that normative models may become prime epistemological obstacles to an understanding of the way in which democracy works, he points out that "most students of democratization agree that many of the new polyarchies are at best poorly institutionalized. Few seem to have institutionalized anything but elections, at least in terms of what one would expect from looking at older polyarchies. But appearances can be misleading, since other institutions may exist, even though they may not be the ones that most of us would prefer or easily recognize" (p. 37). Clientelism—understood as the particularized exchange of votes and support for goods, favors, and services between the poor and the elites—endures as an "extremely influential, informal, and sometimes concealed institution" (p. 40) that is not "destined to disappear or even to remain on the margins of society with the establishment of modern regimes—whether democratic or authoritarian—or with economic development" (Roniger and Günes-Ayata 1994, 3).

Long before O'Donnell's disenchanting assertion, sociologists and anthropologists insisted on the resilient character of clientelist arrangements in Latin American polities.[5] Many authors have long recognized that, when analyzing the relations between elites and poor masses, we navigate a "sea of particularism and blurred boundaries" (O'Donnell 1996a, 45). In fact, in much the same way as the trope of disorganization has governed the study of the American "dark ghetto" (Clark 1965; Wacquant 1995a) and "anomy and radicalism" have dominated the study of the Latin American shantytown (Perlman 1976; Portés 1972), political clientelism has been one of the strongest and most recurrent images in the study of the political practices of the poor—urban and rural alike—in Latin America, almost to the point of becoming a sort of "metonymic prison" (Appadurai 1988) for this part of the Americas. According to Appadurai, one of the effects of this (pre)constructed "anthology of images" that links places and cultural themes is that it flattens the cultural complexity of the phenomenon under study, locating it in a general—and generalizable—category, in this case *clientelism*. The notion has been used—and, at times, abused—to explain the reasons why poor and destitute people sometimes follow populist leaders and at other times follow authoritarian or conservative ones (De la Torre 1992; Menendez Carrión 1986; Stein 1980). Clientelism is understood as one of the central elements of the populist appeal, but it is also considered to be a mode of vertical political inclusion quite distinct from populism (Mouzelis 1985).

Political clientelism is recurrently associated with the limitations of Latin America's always fragile democracies (O'Donnell 1996a, 1996b; Fox 1994; Gunther, Diamandouros, and Puhle 1996). According to Gunther, Diamandouros, and Puhle (159), clientelism is "antithetical to the quality of democracy," and, if it is pervasive, it could result in its delegitimation. For these authors, insofar as clientelism entails "systematic and persistent power imbalances within society, polity, and economy," it is "incompatible with the unhindered exercise of suffrage." O'Donnell (1996b, 166) rightly observes that this appraisal is "simply empirically untrue." In emphasizing the power imbalances that clientelism perpetuates, Gunther, Diamandouros, and Puhle are, according to O'Donnell, "implicitly making a radical critique of any democracy." "Can they ignore," he incisively asks, "the pervasive consequences of class, status, bureaucratic power, and so on that everywhere also perpetuate unequal treatment and generate systematic and persistent imbalances?"

Clientelism is seen as one of the pillars of oligarchic domination reinforcing and perpetuating the rule of traditional political elites (Hagopian 1992) and as a set of practices that remains "at the core of party behavior" throughout Latin America (Hoskin 1997). The exchange of votes for favors is seen as one of the possible relations between political parties and organized popular groups and/or community associations. In this case, the analysis usually focuses on the efforts made by popular organized groups to bypass traditional mechanisms of political co-optation (Cardoso 1992; see also Escobar 1994) and on the varying vulnerability of local associations to clientelist penetration. Further, political clientelism is examined as a form of atomization and fragmentation of the electorate and/or the "popular sector" (Rock 1972, 1975; O'Donnell 1992b), as a way of inhibiting collective organization and discouraging real political participation. Scholars focusing on cases of "collective clientelism" (Burgwald 1996) find this last examination inadequate. The widely used antinomy (rarely subjected to empirical scrutiny) between traditional, clientelist politics and modern and/or radical forms of participation has been contested in recent analyses as oversimplified.[6]

This resilient and still pervasive informal institution is recurrently considered an "old societal ill" opposed to the participatory ideology of social movements and their emphasis on political autonomy (see the various essays in Escobar and Alvarez 1992), but it is also understood to be based on trust and solidarity (Roniger and Günes-Ayata 1994). Last, but hardly least, vertical clientelist bonds are conceptualized as the exact opposite of those horizontal networks of civic engagement that foster a truly civic community and that, in turn, "make democracy work" (Putnam 1993).

It is common knowledge that clientelist exchanges concatenate into pyramidal networks. The structure of these "domination networks" (Knoke 1990) and the key actors within them (patrons, brokers, and clients) are well-studied phenomena of popular political life (Lomnitz 1975, 1988). With minor differences, most of the literature emphasizes the *structured* character of the "clientelist system." Clientelist exchanges concatenate into a *structure*, often of pyramidal form, in which patrons, brokers, and clients are located (networks, dyads, sets). The stress is put on the functions and consequences (intended or not) that clientelism has for the political system, on the set of positions in which this particular logic of exchange operates, and on the relation between the clientelist system and the level of economic and/or political development of a particular society. The literature on clientelism also agrees that clientelistic relationships are as far from any kind of Simmelian sociability as from Roman *societas leonina* (a partnership in which all the benefits go to one side). The literature concurs in that patron-broker-client relations are a cocktail — to continue with the Simmelian language — of different forms of social interaction: exchange, conflict, domination, and prostitution. Clientelist relationships are seen as hierarchic arrangements, as bonds of dependence and control based on power differences and inequality. Being highly selective, particularistic, and diffuse, they are "characterized by the simultaneous exchange of two different types of resources and services: instrumental (e.g., economic and political) and 'sociational' or expressive (e.g., promises of loyalty and solidarity)." Clientelist relationships are also characterized by having individuals as their protagonists, as opposed to organized corporate groups. Finally, they are said to be neither "fully contractual nor legal — in fact, they are often illegal — but are based on more informal, though tightly binding, understandings" (Roniger 1990, 3–4). Clientelist relationships, much of the literature agrees, constitute a realm of submission, a cluster of bonds of domination in opposition to a realm of mutual recognition, of equality and cooperation. These relations are seen as the exact opposite of Simmelian sociability, "the purest, most transparent, most engaging kind of interaction — that among equals" (Simmel 1971, 133).

Currently, the uses of the notion are being scrutinized and problematized from different perspectives (Gay 1994, 1995, 1998; Burgwald 1996; Escobar 1994). Yet "political clientelism" remains one of those simplifying images and narratives that obscure more than clarify our understanding of the practices and representations of popular groups. It is still being said — and, particularly in Argentina, is insistently being held in the academic, political, and journalistic discourse — that "the poor," "the marginal," give their support to politicians in exchange for favors, goods, and services that will satisfy their immediate needs. This book joins current efforts on the part of other scholars (Gay 1995, 1994; Burgwald 1996) to problematize and test the potential and limitations of the notion of political clientelism. This work can thus be seen as an attempt to build on the spirit of recent scholarship while providing a more finely grained analysis of the cultural complexity of clientelism in the context of contemporary Argentina. But it is not only about this.

The trope of clientelism is, often, the product of what Bourdieu (1990c) considers a "scholastic point of view," an externalist and remote view, a vision that constructs practices of exchange as if they were a spectacle, thus losing sight of the specificity of the logic of those practices. An indicator of this view from afar can be found in the very terms that govern the analysis—*flows, exchange, rational choice*—terms that are foreign to the logic of problem solving enacted through the "clientelist network." This point of view assumes—wrongly—that, because favors, goods, and services circulate one way and support attendance at rallies, and—ultimately—votes circulate the other way, the former are causing the latter, that is, that votes and support come *because of* goods, services, and particular favors. Confusing the circulation with the generative principles of action, this scholastic point of view makes a serious epistemological mistake. It locates in the consciousness of the actors the model constructed by the analyst to account for the practices, assuming that "the constructions that the scientist must produce to understand practice . . . were the main determinants, the actual cause of practice" (Bourdieu 1990c, 384). It seems to me that this point of view is (pre)constructed far from where the real action lies: this is not in the boisterous—and often pathetic—distribution of food packages before a political rally but in the abiding ties, in the enduring webs of relationships that brokers establish with their clients, and in the—sometimes shared (although seldom cooperatively constructed)—array of cultural representations. It is in relations and representations where social action lies, and it is there that we should focus our attention.[7] A view that takes into account these relations will allow us to construct another point of view, one that takes seriously the representations, the collective and individual identities, and the cultural idioms that play a fundamental role in the construction of these exchanges. Thus, this book is also an exercise in relational thinking.

Much of the understanding of politics in Argentina is governed by this spectatorial point of view. While carrying out my fieldwork, I eagerly explored the most recent bibliography on politics in Argentina in order to find some contrasts and some commonalities with my own findings (e.g., Acuña 1995a; Borón et al. 1995; Sidicaro and Mayer 1995; Palermo and Novaro 1996). The search was vain yet at the same time encouraging. The search was vain because many of the studies are (still) dominated by the "top-down" view that permeated much of the research on "transitions to democracy." As Tilly asserts, many of the theories of democratization accorded little (or only a subsidiary) place to popular collective action and accentuated "instrumental maneuvers and bargains among elites" (1994c, 4). In current studies, the way in which politics affects and engages the real lives of people is (almost completely) absent or represented by the poor substitute of survey opinion polls. The search was also encouraging because the absence would provide an extra reason for those interested in Argentine politics to read my work. Far from being an activity reserved for national or provincial elites, politics, for some, is an everyday practice. Yet political analysts recurrently look at one side (the most visible one) of political dynamics at the expense of their most obscure, intricate, and—for me—interesting aspects. This book is also about how politics intermingles with people's everyday lives, becoming—for some—their "paramount, wide-awake reality," to use the language of Schutz (1962). It is about the microphysics of politics.

*

"If one distinct strain identifies Argentine social sciences," writes Elizabeth Jelin (1997, 302), "it is the analysis and interpretation of Peronism." Peronism is the most studied of Argentine political phenomena, both by native and by foreign social scientists and historians. Understandably so, Peronism has been firmly entrenched in Argentine society "both organizationally and as a political identity" (Levitsky 1998a, 80) for more than fifty years. Having been one of the most influential political forces in modern Latin American history, the Peronist Party is, despite its occasional electoral setbacks, the largest political party in Argentina today. As Jelin herself puts it, "Peronism transformed itself but continued as the single most important political force in the country" (1997, 302). Despite the plethora of studies that were (and still are) dedicated to the many aspects of this resilient sociopolitical phenomenon, the specific role of women within Peronism has never been seriously examined.[8] The absence is striking considering the key role that Eva Perón played as the powerful icon of Peronist ideals—during her lifetime as well as and, perhaps more importantly, in the decades following her death in 1952. Following Eva's inspiration (as I analyze in chap. 4), many women are currently involved in the Peronist Party, and, although no precise figures are available, a cursory look shows that they are overrepresented in those key party and government functions related to social welfare, providing personalized assistance to poor people.

It is by now common knowledge that women's participation in politics has substantially increased in Latin America since the 1980s. Women "were involved in politics to a degree and in a variety of forms without precedent in Latin American history. . . . [W]omen's organizations were beginning to carve out a space for themselves in local and national political life and feminism was slowly making inroads into political and academic institutions" (Chinchilla 1997, 218). Women's growing participation in movements of protest and social change has been the subject of engaging debates in the literature of what came to be known as "new social movements" (Jelin 1985, 1987; Feijoo 1989; Jaquette 1989; Escobar and Alvarez 1992; Chinchilla 1997).[9] Many studies also highlight the key role that women play in crafting poor people's strategies for surviving material scarcity (Lomnitz 1975; Elson 1992).[10] These studies also explore the diverse ways in which women's struggles challenge dominant understandings of gender (Lind 1992).

Women's struggles against unequal power relationships and their courageous use of "traditional" gender identities to challenge repressive political orders and/or to support collective claim making are, by now, well-documented sociocultural phenomena in Latin American politics. Often, however, the power of such images obscures women's active participation in the construction and reproduction of modes of political domination and their use of those same "traditional" gender identities, not to challenge, but to reinforce power inequalities. This book is also about a form of political participation, a modality of doing politics, that most of us would prefer not to (easily) recognize: women's participation in domination networks of political clientelism and the use of their subordinate roles to strengthen forms of subordination.

*

It is hardly a new observation that networks of reciprocal help abound among the urban and rural poor in Argentina and throughout Latin

America (Lomnitz 1975, 1988; Hintze 1989). Although political networks have not received much attention in Argentina, they have been studied in Latin America and all over the world (Hagopian 1992; Burgwald 1996; Knoke 1990). Yet the relation between political networks and informal webs of reciprocal help have been underexplored. This book examines the increasing overlap between both types of networks and the array of cultural representations that emerge from such a process. For someone not particularly interested in Argentine politics (and even less so in Villa Paraíso), a detailed exploration of the way in which some poor people solve their everyday survival needs through *personalized political mediation* (my substitute for *political clientelism*) provides a way of seeing the embeddedness of political culture in problem-solving networks.

Current debates in sociology, political science, and anthropology highlight the relevance of political networks and of political culture (see, among others, Putnam 1993, 1995; Tilly 1998). They matter, everyone seems to agree, in the analysis of social processes. As an incentive to read this book, let me say at the outset that the following chapters are as much about this particular place called Villa Paraíso as they are about the complex relation between political culture and political networks and the way in which both must be understood in a historical and political economic context.

We know from such authors as Raymond Williams and E. P. Thompson that cultural traditions are often resilient. A residual cultural element has been "effectively formed in the past." Yet it is still "active in the cultural process, not only and often not at all as an element of the past, but as an effective element of the present" (Williams 1977, 122). This book examines how, in a particular political economic context, these residual elements — "populist" (heterogeneous) traditions, Peronist (competing) memories — are embedded in networks, embodied in performances, and actualized and (re)processed in concrete practices. Through a serious exploration of the narratives and memories anchored in these networks, performances, and practices, I hope to illustrate how "the dead seize the living," to quote Pierre Bourdieu (1977).

*

"There is really nothing more to say—except *why*. But since *why* is difficult to handle, one must take refuge in *how*," writes Toni Morrison in *The Bluest Eye* (1994, 8). A "good enough ethnography" (Scheper-Hughes 1992, 28) will shed some light on the hows of problem solving through personalized political mediation in contexts of material deprivation. The hows will, in turn, illuminate those so-difficult-to-handle whys. The thread of the argument runs as follows. Under the general conditions of the escalation of unemployment and underemployment and state retrenchment (its social welfare component), leading to further impoverishment of the urban poor, and given a governing party with two mutually reinforcing features (relatively stable support at the mass level/strong organization in urban poor areas; access to state-funded programs of social assistance, a poor substitute for state welfare), organizational desertification in enclaves of urban poverty, and residual populism as a cultural tradition, we should expect the strengthening of survival problem solving through personalized political mediation. This way of solving problems, in turn, reinforces the party organization at the grassroot level and its access to state-funded programs. This leads to further organizational desertification among the poor and to a re-creation/reinvention of "populist" traditions.

My key concern in this book is to uncover the central logic of Peronist problem solving, that is, the set of material practices and symbolic constructions that constitute its organizing principles, and to place this logic in a political economic context of growing marginalization. My way of proceeding brings together relational and experiential sociologies (sociologies that, despite claims to the contrary, rarely meet and mesh in the concrete practice of sociological research). I show that participation, active engagement, in Peronist problem-solving networks provides (reinforces, reconfigures) a political identity as much as it provides food and medicine. Through the "Peronist way" of solving problems, a stomach can be filled, pain relieved, the flu cured, and a political identity revealed and transformed. In conceptual terms, this means that this "informal institution" (O'Donnell 1996a) is not only a network of distribution of material resources, but also a symbolic system, a structure that provides ways of ordering reality, thereby rendering the experience of poverty in a particular time and place meaningful.[11] The informal institution of personalized political mediation also shapes the way in which actors remember, reconstruct, and actualize Peronism. In other words, this book reflects as nearly and as clearly as possible the political culture(s) of the urban poor, one revealing and cutting edge of which is the problem-solving networks and the representations and practices embedded in them.

In one of his finest short stories, Borges (1974, 647) defines an *aleph* as "a point in which all the other points converge." The day of the rally described above works as a sort of *aleph* of both the particular and the general issues that I tackle in this book. Moreover, I hope to demonstrate that the rally and the shantytown are also "strategic research sites" (Merton 1987) for the understanding of some central elements—informal networks, performances, narratives, and identities—in the heterogeneous social universe of the urban poor in contemporary Buenos Aires.

CHAPTER ONE

"They Were Mostly Poor People"

Poverty and Inequality in Contemporary Buenos Aires

Introduction: Two Sides

"In one way or another, they fear us. We also fear them."
—Beatriz Sarlo, *Instantáneas*

In her most recent book, *Instantáneas,* Argentine cultural critic Beatriz Sarlo (1996) clearly captures the process of dualization taking place in Argentine society and in particular in the city of Buenos Aires. *Instantáneas* is divided into three sections: "From This Side," "From the Other Side," and "Everything Is Television." Whether it is intended or not, these titles nicely convey the image of the polarized and fragmented society that has slowly developed in Argentina over the last two decades: two sides and the all-encompassing media.

These two sides make up a "paradoxical mix of splendor and decay" (Mollenkopf and Castells 1991, 8). The luxurious wealth of an allegedly cosmopolitan bourgeoisie gives "this side" of Buenos Aires the appearance of other "global cities" (Sassen 1991). The landscape of "La Reina del Plata" is increasingly ornamented with—to quote Saskia Sassen (1991, 9)—"expensive restaurants, luxury housing, luxury hotels, gourmet shops, boutiques, French hand laundries and special cleaners," and one could add to the list the opulent shopping malls and the sumptuous developments in Puerto Madero. On "the other side," the spectacle is that seen in many Third World countries, one presented in some chapters of Sarlo's book as an obscure and impenetrable drama: death, violence, abandonment, homelessness, hunger, child labor, street predators, danger, and poor shantytowns. These two sides represent the "two nations" that Argentina is becoming, following the trends in other major cities.[1]

This chapter provides a straightforward empirical description of this fragmented and polarized society, locating within it the "territories of urban relegation" in which the outcasts that "we fear" dwell.[2] One of those stigmatized places is where the social relations and cultural representations described in the following chapters take place.

It is hardly a new observation that Argentina's social structure is becoming increasingly polarized and fragmented (Nun 1987; Villareal 1996; Torrado 1992; Minujin 1992). According to Mingione (1991), these two apparently contradictory processes—fragmentation and polarization—can be understood as simultaneous and mutually reinforcing. We should realize, he asserts, that social structures might become more and more diversified "but that the micro-typologies tend to concentrate around two major poles, or macro-typologies, which differ greatly in terms of conditions of existence, life-chances, and the quantity and quality of available social resources" (p. 436). Both extremes—"this side" and "the other side," sumptuous wealth and utter destitution—flourish side by side in contemporary Argentina.

On "the other side," fragmented polarization leads to the constitution of a new regime of urban marginality.[3] Although having certain common traits with the "new poverty" of advanced societies (see McFate, Lawson, and Wilson 1995), this "new marginality" has its distinctive features: the structural character of joblessness (the massive loss of blue-collar jobs, the concentration of unemployment among the least skilled and least educated, and the persistence of long-term unemployment) (Iñiguez and Sanchez 1995; Beccaria and Lopez 1996); the growth of underemployment and the increasing insecurity of labor force attachment (the casualization of wage-labor relations) (Nudler 1996; Cieza and Beyreuther 1996); the functional disconnection of employment from macroeconomic change (Lozano and Feletti 1996; Rofman 1996; Monza 1996); and the retrenchment of the welfare component of the state (CEB 1995; Lo Vuolo and Barbeito 1993).

The first two features dovetail with the deep decline of the manufacturing sector, which includes the worsening position of unionized workers, the deterioration of wages, and the proliferation of sweatshops. And all four features entail a process that—although with different rhythms and structural causes—is analogous to the one taking place in more advanced societies (Sassen 1991, 1998), namely, a reorganization of the capital-labor relation in which two simultaneous processes prevail: the maximization of the use of low-wage labor and the minimization of the effectiveness of the mechanisms that have traditionally empowered labor vis-à-vis capital.

Joblessness and Income Reduction

The unemployment rate among the economically active population in Argentina rose from 5.0 percent in 1974 to 18.6 percent in 1995. Underemployment rose from 5.4 percent in 1974 to 11.3 percent in 1995. Since the launching of the Menem-Cavallo "Convertibility Plan" in 1991, unemployment has increased 200 percent (Iñiguez and Sanchez 1995; Beccaria and Lopez 1996).

The Conurbano Bonaerense,[4] which contains 24.4 percent (8,440,000 inhabitants) of Argentina's total population in 1.2 percent of its territory, is home to the largest industrial park in the country, representing 74.4 percent of the total employment of the state of Buenos Aires and 62.3 percent of its total production. It is the region most affected by the process of deindustrialization and the subsequent hyper-unemployment. According to Cieza and Beyreuther (1996, 3), the passage of thousands of workers from factory work to informal and precarious jobs is the most significant economic phenomenon of the last fifteen years. Numerous plant closings and massive layoffs constitute the paramount experience of thousands of working families.

The situation in the Conurbano Bonaerense is one of dramatic levels of unemployment and the casualization of labor. Between 1991 and 1995, there was a 277 percent increase in the number of unemployed people.[5] Unemployment rates doubled between 1991 and 1994 and doubled again in the period 1994–95.

In 1995, the unemployment rate in the Conurbano was 22.6 percent of the economically active population (or 843,840 people). Unemployment and underemployment together accounted for 33.8 percent of the population. For large segments of the working class, mass joblessness resulted in a straightforward deproletarianization. As Iñiguez and Sanchez (1995, 10; my translation) explain: "If something characterizes the change in the Conurbano Bonaerense's landscape, it is the shutdowns of factories and the subsequent transformation of the industrial workers into unemployed, marginals, or workers in the informal sector. The reduction in the proportion of the population employed in the manufacturing sector in Buenos Aires was very severe."

In the last ten years, the Conurbano Bonaerense lost 5,508 industrial plants, and, between 1991 and 1995, the manufacturing sector eliminated 200,000 jobs. The rise in unemployment has not affected every sector of the economy in the same way, nor has it affected the entire population in a similar manner. Manufacturing was most severely affected. In May 1991, 26.7 percent of the employed population in the Conurbano was working in manufacturing. Four years later, this rate had declined to 23.1 percent. In contrast, the "commerce, hotels, and restaurants" sector of the economy, which accounted for 21.1 percent of the jobs in May 1991, had grown to account for 23.3 percent by May 1995, gaining roughly 70,000 more jobs. The most striking increase, however, takes place among those working in the transportation, storage, and communications industries: taking 1991 as the base, for every 100 jobs in that year there were 162 in May 1995. Yet it is important to note that a third of these new jobs can be attributed to self-employment (CEB 1995; Lozano and Feletti 1996).

In other words, what we have witnessed over the last five years is the radicalization of a process that had its starting point in the mid-1970s: a shift in the economy from the manufacturing to the service sector— what is known as an "early and nonmodern tertiarization" (Lo Vuolo and Barbeito 1993), characterized by a great loss of jobs and a general worsening of working conditions. Although the shift from the manufacturing to the service sector in a developing economy has different causes and effects and takes place at a different rate than it does in advanced economies, some of its effects are similar, including "a much larger share of low-wage jobs than is the case with a strong manufacturing-based economy. The overall result is an increased income polarization" (Sassen 1991, 329).

Who Is Unemployed?

Unemployment in the Conurbano, and in the country as a whole, seems like an "epidemic disease" (Kessler 1996) that poses an equal threat to everyone.[6] Yet, contrary to the national propaganda that emphasizes the "globalized," "general," and "transitory" character of unemployment, in the 1990s unemployment was neither randomly distributed nor short-lived. As in other parts of the world (McFate 1995; Wilson 1997; Mingione 1996), unemployment hits certain groups harder than others: the highest rates of unemployment can be found among the lowest income groups, the least educated, the least skilled, and the young.

Secondary school dropouts have the highest unemployment rates. Whereas the average unemployment rate in the Conurbano was 22.6 percent in May 1995, for secondary school dropouts it was 26.8 percent. Primary school dropouts do not do much better. The average unemployment rate among them is 24.3 percent. For those who hold a university degree, the rate of unemployment is 8.7 percent (CEB 1995; see also Murmis and Feldman 1996).[7]

Lozano and Feletti (1996) also show that unemployment hits the poor harder than it does other groups. While in May 1995 the unemployment rate among the total economically active population in Greater Buenos Aires was 20.2 percent, it was 38.8 percent among the lowest income groups.[8] Poor people, thus, must confront much higher levels of unemployment. Unemployment also weighs disproportionately on unskilled workers, who find entrance into the job market increasingly difficult. As Murmis and Feldman (1996) consistently show, in 1995, unskilled workers represent 27.5 percent of the employed population in general and 39 percent of those unemployed in Greater Buenos Aires. Those in the "informal sector" are strongly affected: 62 percent of the unemployed had been holding casual and precarious jobs. Construction workers and domestic service workers were particularly affected, representing 13.9 percent of the employed population and 29.8 percent of those unemployed. I highlight these two occupations because, as we will see in the next chapter, they are (or, better, they were) the two most important sources of employment for the inhabitants of Villa Paraíso. The younger population is greatly affected by the increase in unemployment: 51.8 percent of those between age fifteen and age nineteen were unemployed in May 1995, according to official figures (INDEC 1996). Thus, unemployment is neither generalized nor transitory. Indeed, there has been a notorious increase in the average duration of unemployment. A large proportion of those unemployed have been without a job for at least six months (25.9 percent in Greater Buenos Aires), becoming what is technically known as *the long-term unemployed* (Murmis and Feldman 1996, 200).

The Structural Character of Unemployment and Its Effects

The concentration of unemployment among the least skilled and least educated and the persistence of unemployment clearly lead to a conclusion that is constantly denied in the official discourse on the subject: the structural character of current unemployment (Rofman 1996).

Almost three decades ago, in what would later become one of Latin America's most original and controversial contributions to the social sciences, a group of sociologists tackled the relation between the structural character of unemployment in the region and the escalation of urban marginality. Working within a structural-historical neo-Marxist perspective, these researchers recovered from the realm of modernization theories (represented by the sociologist Gino Germani and the DESAL school) the notion of marginality, which focused on the lack of integration of certain social groups into society owing to their (deviant) values, perceptions, and behavior patterns.[9] According to this approach, marginal groups lack the psychological and psychosocial attributes deemed necessary to participate in modern society. Emerging in the transition to modern, industrial society, marginality was thought to be the product of the coexistence of beliefs, values, attitudes, and behaviors of a previous, more "traditional" stage. Rural migrants were seen as carriers of a "baggage of traditional norms and values which prevent(ed) their successful adaptation to the urban style of life" (Portés 1972, 272).[10]

In contrast with this approach, the structural-historical perspective on marginality focused on the process of import-substitution industrialization and its intrinsic inability to absorb the growing mass of the labor force. As Mollenkopf and Castells (1991, 409) assert, this intellectual tradition "aimed to understand why and how increased industrialization and GNP growth, concentrated in the largest metropolitan areas, went hand in hand with accrued urban poverty and an ever-growing proportion of people excluded from the formal labor market and formal housing and urban services." At that time, Nun, Marín, and Murmis (1968) understood that the functioning of what they called *the dependent labor market* was generating an excessive amount of unemployment (see also Nun 1969, 1972). This "surplus population" transcended the logic of the Marxist concept of an industrial reserve army and led the authors to coin the term *marginal mass*. The marginal mass was neither superfluous nor useless; it was marginal because it was rejected by the same system that had created it. Thus, the marginal mass was a "permanent structural feature" never to be absorbed by the "hegemonic capitalist sector" of the economy, not even during its cyclic expansionary phases.

As the structural-historical approach anticipated, the structural character of the "mass of the unemployed" has had multiple effects, most of which are present in contemporary Argentina.[11] These effects are the lowering of incomes, the deterioration of working conditions and the worsening of contractual guarantees for the labor force. Thirty years later, in addition to this "industrial" marginality, Argentina is experiencing a novel kind of marginality: one related to the functioning of the globalized *post-Fordist* economy (Harvey 1990), the dynamics of the "early and nonmodern tertiarization" (Lo Vuolo and Barbeito 1993), and the resolute adoption of neoliberal adjustment policies by the state.

The sectorial shift in the economy and the steady process of deindustrialization have led to an increase in the numbers of the unemployed and underemployed, a growth in the casual job market—usually the black market—and an increase in the number of people willing to take any job, even one that requires fewer skills or less experience than they possess. The unstable situation of the labor market ensures that even those who do have jobs are uncertain that they will be able to keep them, which in turn erodes workers' bargaining power and, thus, their incomes (Lo Vuolo and Barbeito 1993; Beccaria and Lopez 1996, 10; Murmis and Feldman 1996, 145).

Since 1975, when formal employment lost its dynamism, there has been a steady decrease in real income (together with growing inequality in earnings). According to Beccaria and Lopez (1996, 24), there has been a 37 percent reduction in the real income of wage earners between 1974 and 1990.

Underemployment escalated to unprecedented levels. Although the total number of employed people did not vary between 1991 and 1995, the number of underemployed (calculated on the basis of hours worked) increased 70 percent (170,000 more people in the Conurbano became underemployed during that period). In accordance with Latin American trends, the 1990s saw a sustained growth in clandestine and casual employment.[12] In 1974, 21.5 percent of wage earners were not registered with social security, and they did not enjoy the basic benefits of labor legislation. Fourteen years later, in 1988, 30 percent of wage earners were in this situation.

In May 1995, 28 percent of those employed in the Conurbano were looking for another job. It is hard to imagine that, under the present conditions, the expectation of finding a better job is the motive behind this constant search.[13] On the contrary, it seems more likely that inadequate income and the fear of being fired are the forces driving this job hunting. It is also an indicator of the growing insecurity of the workforce.

Increasing unemployment has been accompanied by a government-led offensive against traditional labor rights, euphemized as the "flexibilization" of shop-floor labor relations (Nudler 1996). According to Levitsky (1996, 11), the Menem government's neoliberal shift entailed, among other things,

a series of policies that ran counter to the interests of organized labor, including a ban on wage increases not linked to increases in productivity (which amounted to a long-term wage freeze in many sectors), the encouragement of firm-level, rather than industry-wide, collective bargaining (which undermined union solidarity and reduced national unions' capacity to act), a ban on strikes in much of the public sector, and a hardline position on strikes when they occur. The government also introduced legislation to reduce the cost of production and "flexibilize" shop floor labor relations through the easing of restrictions on hiring and firing, the flexibilization of work schedules, reductions in employer contributions to union pension and health insurance funds, ceilings on worker accident claims, limits on paid vacations, and the erosion of other privileges enjoyed by unions since the 1940s.

Until the mid-1970s, stable work, wage homogeneity, and legal protection were part of the everyday life of most workers in Argentina. During the last twenty years, however, there has been increased flexibilization in working conditions: fixed-term contracts, the growing relevance of temporary employment agencies, seasonal or casual employment, and a rise in the percentage of the labor force employed under "flexible" contracts (Nudler 1996). October 1996 can be taken as an indicator: although employment grew 0.8 percent in that month, the increase could be attributed to what are known as "low-quality" jobs (those with fixed-term contracts and a probation period); the number of stable jobs decreased 0.2 percent.

Such flexibilization (a euphemism for sheer exploitation) leads not only to a decrease in the income of wage earners but also to a deterioration of the physical and mental health of those who hold jobs (Cieza and Beyreuther 1996).[14]

The casualization of labor conditions and the increasing insecurity of the labor force also have a structural character. As Nudler (1996) asserts, holding a stable job turns out to be, under present conditions, an anachronistic expectation. Secure and continuous employment is a "distant dream" (McFate 1995) for a growing portion of the labor force.

Poverty, Inequality, and the State

Occupational polarization and income inequality become translated into widespread urban dualism (that is, the simultaneous increase of affluence and misery among significant proportions of the population) only when public policy mirrors the naked logic of the market. — Manuel Castells and John Hull Mollenkopf: "Conclusion: Is New York a Dual City?"

The year 1991 marks a vast change in the functional connection between macroeconomic trends and levels of employment (Lozano and Feletti 1996; Monza 1996). From then on, GDP growth is accompanied by an increase in unemployment. According to the data of the National Central Bank and the Ministry of the Economy, real GDP growth was 8.9 percent in 1991, 8.7 percent in 1992, 6.0 percent in 1993, and 7.4 percent in 1994. In this expansionary phase of the economy, the unemployment rate grew, according to the same sources, from 6.9 to 10.7 percent. The functional disconnection between economic growth and employment can be clearly grasped when it is realized that, among the leading industrial firms, there was a 35 percent increase in GDP between 1991 and 1994 and a 10 percent reduction in personnel.

GDP growth, real wage decrease, and unemployment increase mean, in Argentina as elsewhere, a massive rise in business gains and in income inequality (Lozano and Feletti 1996). Not surprisingly—owing to the strong correlation between unemployment and poverty—poverty (and inequality) has accompanied the growth of unemployment described in the previous section.[15] In Greater Buenos Aires, 11.5 percent of households were below the poverty line in 1980, 20.4 percent in 1994, and 25.8 percent in 1995 (Golbert 1996).[16] In 1995, the officially estimated value of family expenses was $976.19.[17] Thirty-nine percent of households in Greater Buenos Aires earned under $703. Nearly 60 percent of households earned under $1,001.70 (very close to the estimated value of family expenses).

The other side of impoverishment, hyper-unemployment and underemployment, is the growing concentration of wealth among high-income groups. According to Barbeito, "The poorest 40 percent of the families in Greater Buenos Aires received 16.9% of the total income in 1977, 15.7% in 1983, and 11.7% in 1989. The wealthiest 10% of the families, on the other hand, received 31.6% in 1977, 32.5% in 1983, and 41.6% in 1989" (quoted in Acuña 1995b, 61). From May 1995 to May 1996, the household income of the poorest 10 percent decreased 9.2 percent; in the same period, the household income of the wealthiest 10 percent increased 7.1 percent. This process of income concentration can also be illustrated by taking into account income differences (see table 1): in 1995, the income of a person belonging to the wealthiest 10 percent was 19.4 times the income of a person belonging to the poorest 10 percent; this proportion was 22.4 in 1996 (see *Página12,* 15 September 1996, *Suplemento CASH,* no. 333).

The impoverishment of ever larger segments of the population constitutes, as Mingione (1991, 252) notes, "a favourable resource for improving the life-styles and opportunities for enrichment of high-income groups." The "other side" provides "this side" with an army of service workers—domestics, baby-sitters, limo drivers, messenger boys—who,

Table 1 Percentage Distribution of Household Income in Greater Buenos Aires

	1974	1995	Change
Poorest 30 percent	13.2	8.1	−38.6
Middle 60 percent	61.5	55.4	−9.9
Richest 10 percent	25.3	36.5	44.3

Source: Beccaria and Lopez (1996, 29).

reproducing the pattern of casual labor, earn derisory wages and almost always fall outside the protection of labor legislation.

In Argentina, social rights are associated with employment (Kessler 1996), and social policies have traditionally been designed under the assumption of full employment (Lo Vuolo and Barbeito 1993). Today, more people are unprotected, not only because they are unemployed, but because the state—with its indifference, its "averted gaze" (Scheper-Hughes 1992, 272)—is reinforcing the pattern of impoverishment and inequality.

The retrenchment and dismantling of the welfare component of the populist state make the risks involved in situations of material deprivation—and the inequalities—even greater. The last decade has witnessed a constant degradation of the public school system. The public health system is also deteriorating rapidly, and there is little public support for low-income housing (see Lo Vuolo and Barbeito 1993). The chaotic character of the policies meant to fight unemployment and poverty makes things even worse: the poor are increasingly vulnerable and weak (see Cetrángolo and Golbert 1995; Golbert 1996; and Prévot Schapira 1996).[18]

Public support of low-income housing is minimal. In 1992, public authorities estimated the housing deficit at 3 million houses (35 percent of the total number of houses in the country). According to Stillwaggon (1998, 54): "One out of three families in Argentina is ill-housed. Over ten million Argentines live in shanties or tenements, in houses without sanitary facilities, in mud houses, lean-tos, or caves, or crowded three or more to a room. The 1980 census indicated deficiencies in 2.4 million housing units. By 1986, that number had climbed to 2.8 million units, of a total housing stock of 7.1 million units."

During the last decade, the public construction/financing of housing units covered 15 percent of all units built in Argentina. In contrast, in 1980, publicly owned housing represented 46 percent of the housing market in England and 37 percent in France (Lo Vuolo and Barbeito 1993; Wacquant 1994a). According to Lo Vuolo and Barbeito (1993), the current government (Menem) practically dismantled public housing policies. In 1992, public investment in housing was 33 percent less than it was in 1980 and 1987. Keeping in mind "the obvious fact that private developers will not build for the poor" (Wacquant 1994a, 158), this dismantling has the effect of leaving the poor without any other resource than their own labor (e.g., Grillo, Lacarrieu, and Raggio 1995).

The public health system in the Conurbano is also deteriorating so rapidly as to be close to the point of total breakdown. Since the 1970s, it has suffered a structural and technological involution (CEB 1995). It is progressively unequal and regionally uneven. Health policy planning is chaotic and fragmented (CEB 1995). The last decade witnessed an expansion of demand that the public health system in the Conurbano has not been able to meet. This increasing demand is basically due to the rising prices in the private health sector. From 1986 to 1991, there has been a 34 percent increase in outpatient consultations in the public hospitals of the province of Buenos Aires. Between 1991 and 1992, the increase was 52 percent (CEB 1995). Yet, in 1994, as the total resources of the province rose 9.4 percent, the state expenditure on the health sector decreased 15.8 percent. A smaller budget confronted burgeoning demand, resulting in a further deterioration in the quality of service. As Stillwaggon (1998, 153) points out: "The public [health] sector has deteriorated because of limits in operational hours, unsatisfactory quality in the delivery of services, lack of medicine and materials, lack of trained personnel in the provincial hospitals, bad maintenance and obsolete and deteriorated physical plant and equipment, care based on hospitalization, failure to innovate, and the failure of *obras sociales* [union and trade association health plans] to pay public hospitals for services."

The casualization of labor means not only lower incomes but also — owing to its connection with employment — a lack of the protection afforded by social security. Among low socioeconomic status women between the ages of fifteen and forty-nine years, 53.6 percent do not have any health coverage whatsoever. This figure is 20.5 percent for upper-middle-class women and 13.1 percent for upper-class women. Among children under six years of age, 62.5 percent of those in the lowest strata and 4.3 percent of those in the upper strata have no health coverage (Beccaria and Lopez 1996).

The school system has also been adversely affected by such inequalities (see, e.g., Lumi, Golbert, and Fanfani 1992).[19] As recent research shows (Beccaria and Lopez 1996), there are striking differences in access to schooling. Only 42 percent of lower-class children aged four through five attend preschool, compared to 72 percent of upper-class children. One hundred percent of upper-class youngsters between the ages of thirteen and seventeen attend some educational institution, while only 50 percent of lower-class youngsters—half of whom have a job—do so. This means that "there is a significant number of adolescents belonging to the lower strata who begin their day without any activity that implies growth or integration" (Beccaria and Lopez 1996, 104; my translation). The most important inequalities can be seen among those youngsters between the ages of eighteen and twenty-five. In the lower strata, only 15 percent are still in the educational system, half still at the secondary level. In the upper strata, 62 percent are still studying, almost all at the university or tertiary level. Against the background of an increasingly restricted and exclusionary job market, this clear inequality in access to educational opportunities is having devastating consequences on the life chances of a huge part of the population (see Sirvent 1998).

How Do the Poor and the Unemployed Survive?

It is hardly a new observation that Argentina is currently witnessing a situation characterized by three simultaneous—and mutually reinforcing—processes: the escalation of unemployment and underemployment, increasing poverty, and the retrenchment of the populist-welfare state. Although the origins of these processes can be located in the mid-1970s with the radical transformation of the social regime of capital accumulation (see Nun 1987), the late 1980s and early 1990s—especially since the launching of Menem's Convertibility Plan—have witnessed a deepening and a radicalization of such dynamics: more poverty, less employment, less government intervention, and, consequently, more inequality. Today, in Argentina, there are—relatively and absolutely speaking—more poor people, more unemployed and underemployed people, and more unprotected people than there were in the early 1970s. Today, Argentina is a much more unequal society than it used to be: the increasing concentration of wealth among high-income groups puts Argentina closer to the Latin American norm (see Smith 1992).[20]

Although this is sociological common sense, the emphasis of the study of this process has been focused on the process of the "impoverishment" of the former middle classes (Minujin 1992; Minujin and Kessler 1996). The *new poverty* in Argentina refers not—as it does in the United States and Europe—to the economic, social, and spatial segregation and marginalization of ever larger segments of the urban population in "spatial enclaves of extreme poverty," to use Wacquant's (1995a) expression, but to the "downward mobility" of ever larger portions of the middle classes.[21]

Those who, before their "fall," were already poor, living in shantytowns, squatter settlements, or squalid and destitute neighborhoods, are being left in the dust by current research interests. Paraphrasing the title of the book that best deals with the emerging problems and experiences caused by the spread of unemployment (Beccaria and Lopez 1996), What is happening to them in a society *sin trabajo,* "without work"? Or, to paraphrase W. J. Wilson (1997), What happens to them *when work disappears?* One striking absence of Beccaria and Lopez's otherwise excellent compilation is that—except for a few scattered remarks (Kessler 1996)—there is no exploration whatsoever of the practical consequences of being unemployed; that is, how do people without jobs solve their everyday problems? This is the exact same question that the marginality school formulated—without arriving at any concrete answer—three decades ago: How does this marginal mass survive? (Nun, Marín, and Murmis 1968, 45). Three decades have passed, and the question is now much more pressing. In a context of generalized unemployment and extremely low wages, how do those without stable jobs obtain cash to pay for their food? How do they take care of their health problems? How do they get their medicine? How do they build their dwellings? The current social and economic situation in Argentina lends new urgency to these elementary questions.

The processes described above hit the neighborhoods traditionally inhabited by the poor—shantytowns and squatter settlements in the Conurbano—harshly, turning them into veritable dumping grounds for the unemployed and the underemployed. As we will see in the next chapter, those whom the literature on the subject describes as more severely affected by the general process of impoverishment and unemployment—those least skilled, least educated, construction workers and domestics, those not covered by the health care system and expelled by the schools—are overrepresented, not only in the shantytown in which I carried out my research, but in most of the shantytowns and squatter settlements in the Conurbano Bonaerense. Although informed studies on the spatial patterning of the processes described in previous sections are not available, in chapter 2 we will see that, in Villa Paraíso, the withering away of employment, the deterioration of purchasing power, and abandonment by the state take a particular form. An examination of the structural (objective) trends of rising unemployment and underemployment, exclusion from education, and welfare retrenchment gives way to an analysis of their experiential (subjective) correlates, that is, the way in which these structural processes are perceived and translated into concrete emotions, cognitions, and actions by the residents of Paraíso. In that space/place, the process of impoverishment and dissociation from the labor market does not merely represent a new form of material deprivation and inequality; it involves a qualitative change in the social relations and expectations of the poor.

The driving force behind this process of qualitative change is the general shift in the way in which extremely poor people cope with day-to-day survival. Monetary income does not adequately explain the life strategies and living standards prevailing in these places/spaces: we witness new methods of satisfying subsistence needs among the un- and underemployed poor. The accumulation of the under- and unemployed poor in these spaces considerably reduces not only the monetary income available to individuals but also the reciprocal networks that have traditionally been considered the safety net of the poor. Although these networks are still important, they are being increasingly depleted.

New methods of satisfying subsistence needs develop as marginality deepens.[22] Cash consumption abruptly decreases, replaced by informal consumption and domestic and self-provisioning activities. Chapters 2 and 3 explore the forms that these new means of consumption take in a concrete geographic setting: a shantytown on the outskirts of the city of Buenos Aires. Here, the principal subsistence needs are satisfied by several means: extremely low incomes, (decreasing) networks of reciprocity between neighbors and relatives, (increasing) underground activities (drug dealing, shoplifting, and predatory crime), (increasing) church charity and state assistance, and (increasing) problem solving through personalized political mediation. These new means of problem solving—new patterns of reproduction—will be examined through an ethnographically guided exploration of the lived experiences of shanty dwellers and through a historical reconstruction of the varying ways in which they have solved their everyday life problems since the shantytown's inception.

CHAPTER TWO

"Most of Them Were Coming from Villa Paraíso"

History and Lived Experiences of Shantytown Dwellers

Introduction

When I told Coca—a longtime resident of Villa Paraíso—that I was planning to conduct my research there, her son Cacho—knowing that I live in New York—jokingly asked me, "This is very much like the Bronx, isn't it?" On that first day of my research, Cacho's media-inspired image nicely encapsulated the general feeling that permeates Villa Paraíso and many shantytowns, squatter settlements, and other destitute neighborhoods in the Conurbano Bonaerense. These enclaves of urban poverty are becoming "theaters of dread and death" (Wacquant 1994a, 232), or, as the priest Farinello says about the slum where he works, "Nowadays the slum is almost an inferno" (Farinello 1996, 48).

Cacho's comment also pointed at something that was repeatedly confirmed in the many interviews and talks I had with the inhabitants of Villa Paraíso, with politicians who work there, and with officials of the local government. Undoubtedly, Villa Paraíso has "made a name for itself." In Cóspito City and elsewhere in the Conurbano, Paraíso—as many residents call the shantytown—is, for many different reasons, very well known.

Villa Paraíso is located in the city of Cóspito, in the southern part of the Conurbano Bonaerense, bordering the federal capital. It sits on the southern bank of the Riachuelo and is one of the oldest shantytowns in the Conurbano Bonaerense. It is also the largest in terms of population (approximately fifteen thousand inhabitants according to the last census [INDEC 1993b]). Villa Paraíso is the place where one of the first realist Argentine films (*Detrás de un largo muro*) was shot in the mid-1950s and where a very important clandestine cell of the Peronist Resistance was organized. Today, one of the streets there is named after one of the generals who, with the Resistance, "fought for the return of Perón," as one old resident told me. Villa Paraíso is also known in Cóspito City as one of the traditional electoral strongholds of the Peronist Party. It is a "very politicized place," another resident told me, "very Peronist," as the local priest admitted. Paraíso is also—according to officials of the provincial government—home to the largest retail narcotics-distribution ring and the most drug addicts in the whole Conurbano Bonaerense.

This chapter is divided into two main parts. The first part reconstructs the history of Paraíso from its origins as a swampy wasteland until today. This history is the product of a particular interaction between macrostructural forces, state policies, and the active engagement that the residents—individually and sometimes collectively—construct with those external pressures. The shantytown is the historical product of the interrelation of contending actors, and not the action of a particular player or force (hyperurbanization, housing policies, Peronism, etc.), and the constant changes in the political opportunity structure along the lines of authoritarian and democratic regimes. In this sense, I propose to understand Paraíso as a relation between the economy, the state, and the agency of the political actors within and outside it.

The second part of this chapter explores the lived experiences of shantytown dwellers as one of the products of the history of their place and of the process of deepening marginalization described in chapter 1. It pays particular attention to the dominant sociocultural antagonisms that, as a consequence of their being recurrently stigmatized, socially isolated, and abandoned by the state, divide the residents of this destitute neighborhood.

The processes described in chapter 1 have a strong effect on the space of the shantytown. From the outside, *persistent joblessness* and *enduring misery* are the two terms that probably best define the reality of Paraíso. The provisional objectivism of the previous chapter now gives way to an inquiry into the way in which the experiences of unemployment and poverty are constituted socially and historically in the place/space of the shantytown.

The (re)construction of the history of Paraíso and of the lived experiences of its residents depicts the following trajectories: from proletarianization to deproletarianization and from a *place* with high organizational density and high levels of political mobilization that, at some point, was lived in as a "community" and in which most of the residents' problems were solved collectively to a *space* characterized by organizational desertification and low levels of political mobilization, perceived by its inhabitants as a potential void, a possible threat, an area to be secured or feared, and in which an increasing number of survival problems are solved in "individualized" ways.[1] In this chapter, I explore the mutually reinforcing processes of deproletarianization, desertification, and increasing everyday violence in the slum. The pervading relevance of "individualized" forms of solving everyday problems (what I call *problem solving through personalized political mediation*) is further examined in chapter 3.

The key concern of this book, namely, the workings of personalized forms of problem solving and the cultural representations encompassing them, will thereby be placed in the context of the history of this place becoming space, of the lived experiences of its (ex)proletarian residents, and of the sociocultural oppositions that divide them. In order to understand the logic(s) of the networks (chap. 3), the performances (chap. 4), the representations (chap. 5), and the memories (chap. 6), we must set them against this background of enduring unemployment, ubiquitous misery, interpersonal violence, and social atomization.

Making History, Making a Name: Behind the Long Wall

Pompeya y más allá la inundación. — "Sur," Homero Manzi and Aníbal Troilo

Pompeya is one of the boroughs in the southwest part of the federal capital, bordering the province of Buenos Aires.[2] The lyrics of the tango "Sur," written in 1948, refer to the swamplands located "beyond Pompeya"—where Villa Paraíso is now situated. Fifty years ago, this no-man's-land was covered by several lagoons. Villa Paraíso is now located in what used to be swampland surrounding the bends of the Riachuelo, one of the branches of the Río de la Plata.

In one of the highest spots, now the center of Villa Paraíso, the first settlers (European immigrants, mainly Poles, Czechs, and Lithuanians) built their dwellings around the 1930s. It has been suggested that the beauty of the front gardens of those houses was the origin of the name of the shantytown: a paradise. In 1933, one Mr. Sparmentano founded Villa Paraíso—at that time part of the city of Avellaneda—"adopting that beautiful name as a prediction of the aspect that the place will have in the future" (Municipalidad de Lanús, n.d.). Other versions point to a derogatory irony as the source of the name—in the 1940s, many shanty-towns were mockingly labeled *Paradise, Garden, Serene,* etc. By that time, the Riachuelo's channel had been straightened and Villa Paraíso moved to higher ground, although still dotted with some lagoons.

During the first decades of this century, the Buenos Aires metropolitan region grew southward, a development that was favored by the early expansion of the railway (in 1909, the railroad Barracas al Sur-Caruhe was opened). This transportation network, the proximity to the capital city, and the possibility of using the river as a means of communicating with the port of Buenos Aires encouraged the opening of many industrial plants in the area surrounding Villa Paraíso.

In the early 1930s, Argentina embarked on a process of import substi-tution, giving birth to a new manufacturing sector dedicated mostly to consumer goods at the expense of heavy industry. The growth of manu-facturing and the decline of the agricultural sector in the pampas and the rest of the interior fostered a massive internal migration from rural areas into Buenos Aires and the subsequent proletarianization of the new urban industrial working classes. As Rock (1987, 232) synthesizes, "Be-tween the triennial averages of 1927–1929 and 1941–1943, manufacturing grew at an annual rate of 3.4 percent, as against only 1.5 percent in the rural sector and 1.8 in gross domestic product. Imports of manufactured consumer goods, around 40 percent of total imports before 1930, had fallen to less than 25 percent by the late 1940s."

Wartime interruptions in foreign trade caused a general decline in the level of cereal exports beginning in the mid-1930s. While unem-ployment was escalating in the countryside, ever-increasing numbers of industrial workers collected in the outskirts of Buenos Aires. Between 1937 and 1947, near 750,000 internal migrants arrived in Greater Buenos Aires. Economic crisis in the countryside and the lure of employment and much better wages (plus the attraction of life in the city) drew many *provincianos* to the city. Employment was easy to find, yet housing was scarce. As Rock (1987, 235) summarizes, "As industrial growth quickened, annual migration increased from an average of 70,000 between 1937 and 1943 to 117,000 between 1943 and 1947. The population of the city of Buenos Aires grew from some 1.5 million in 1914, to 3.4 million in 1935, to 4.7 million by 1947. Numerous migrants also settled in working-class suburbs of the Capital like Avellaneda [where Villa Paraíso was located], which by 1947 had a population of more than 500,000."

In the years that followed the first massive internal migrations, the annual rate of migration to Greater Buenos Aires from the countryside continued to increase. In 1947, 4.7 million people were living in Greater Buenos Aires. Thirteen years later, almost 7 million people were crowded into new suburban settlements: working-class neighborhoods (*barrios*) and shantytowns (*villas*). As standard housing was scarce and beyond the means of the new migrants, deserted land outside the central city and close to newly installed factories, such as that on which Villa Paraíso was built, became natural squatting grounds for thousands of migrant families. For newcomers to the city, the "bridgeheaders," as Portés calls them, "occupation, and not housing, is the paramount consideration" (Portés 1972, 279).

As Grillo, Lacarrieu, and Raggio (1995) comment, the shantytown was at that time one social form available within the "menu" of alternative forms of settlement for the urban poor. In addition to self-constructed shelters, cheap hotels, and lodges, the shantytown became a spatial configuration linked to the outgrowth of import-substitution industrialization. As in many other cities in Latin America, a "growing stream of migrants produced an overflow of the . . . slums into spontaneous or self-developing settlements at the fringe of the formal urban employment" (Lomnitz 1975, 186; see also Gilbert 1994).

Around the 1940s, shantytowns became a permanent element within the urban landscape. In 1956, a census carried out by the Comisión Nacional de la Vivienda reported that 112,350 people were living in shantytowns in Greater Buenos Aires, 1.9 percent of the total population (Yujnovsky 1984).

The massive occupation of Villa Paraíso began around 1948, when the first migrants from the provinces settled here (the area had not been available for urban use owing to what the official lexicon called its "flooding quality"). Villa Paraíso grew by accretion (not by collective invasion), spreading along the paths that ran along solid ground through the large, swampy field. These paths are the origins of the streets that today run through the shantytown from northwest to southeast. At that time, these streets were called *caminos* (roads); there were five *caminos* by which residents entered Paraíso. These roads were the highest parts of the shantytown, and, although they are now paved and have street names, many residents still use the names of the roads: *First Road, Second Road, Third Road, Fourth Road,* and *Fifth Road.* As we will see later, conditions of existence and urban infrastructure deteriorate drastically from the First to the Fifth Road.

As in many other migration processes, familial networks stemming from the province of origin developed sociocultural enclaves within the shantytown. Ignoring urban zoning regulations, relatives and friends of the first settlers subdivided the larger pieces of land and swamps and began constructing dwellings on the higher ground. They filled the small lagoons with garbage, dirt, and debris, and thus was given birth to what are now the alleyways: narrow passages on the sides of the houses that face the street giving access to the dwellings located in the center of the block.

The film *Detrás de un largo muro,* shot in 1956 in Paraíso, is invaluable in that it allows us to observe almost firsthand the shantytown's landscape at that time. Some of its dialogues synthesize better than most sociological analyses much of the lived experience of these recent immigrants.[3]

In the late 1940s, Perón was at the height of his power, and Rosa and her father—the protagonists of the film—have just arrived in Buenos Aires from one of the interior provinces. Olga and Norma—Rosa's friends in the countryside and by then residents of Villa Paraíso—and the latter's boyfriend pick them up at the train station. They are driving through Buenos Aires, heading for Villa Paraíso. Being in Buenos Aires for the first time, Rosa is amazed at the city's buildings, parks, and streets:

ROSA: This is marvelous!

OLGA: Do you like it that much?

ROSA: More than what I could have imagined. . . .

OLGA: Unfortunately, dear, not everything is like this in Buenos Aires.

NORMA: There are also very disgusting things here, things that one could never even suspect.

ROSA: Which things?

NORMA'S BOYFRIEND: You know that nowadays there are a lot of people who come to work in the factories, but—as there is not much building construction—these people have no place to go. . . .

OLGA: The crowd is so big that emergency neighborhoods are being created.

NORMA: We live in one of those . . . Villa Paraíso.

ROSA: Villa Paraíso? The name is very nice!

NORMA: That is the only nice thing about it. . . .

OLGA: But it will be only for a short time; they are about to build new and big neighborhoods.

OLGA'S BOYFRIEND: Show her the pictures. . . .

NORMA: [*Looking at the pictures of the promised houses and apartments.*] See how marvelous. . . . Yet, for the time being, we are going to be quite badly off. . . .

ROSA: That doesn't matter . . . if it is only for a short time.

As soon as Rosa arrives in Paraíso, she is left alone in one of the rooms of the extremely precarious shacks. Astonished at the misery of Villa Paraíso, she begins to cry. Olga consoles her: "I too cried the first day, but you get used to it. . . ." These dialogues are surprisingly similar to those I had with many older residents who had not seen the movie, such as the following exchange with Victoria:

JAVIER AUYERO: What was the first thing you remember about Villa Paraíso?

VICTORIA: It was horrible, you know? It was dreadful. . . . I used to tell my husband: Is this Buenos Aires? Because when you live in the country, you think Buenos Aires is the best thing, you think that it is beautiful. When he brought me here, I think to myself:

Am I gonna live here? But, you know, [that's] necessity . . . and I had to stay. This street was a garbage dump. . . .

CATALINA: And with such a beautiful name . . . Villa Paraíso. . . .

VICTORIA: I didn't even dare go outside my home because I was very shocked . . . stepping on the mud and seeing all that garbage. . . .

The shantytown is, in part, the product of what some authors call *hyperurbanization* (Perlman 1976, 5): existing institutions are unable to expand rapidly enough to accommodate urban expansion and industrialization.[4] While masses of immigrants were flocking to the city of Buenos Aires and the metropolitan area in unprecedented numbers, the Peronist government tolerated their illegal occupation of public and private land. The area on which Paraíso is located was private property, and it was not available for urban use. As many neighbors told me, "This area was not even suited to raising cattle." They all remember the lagoonlike character of the area, the lack of urban amenities (water, sewers, garbage collection, electricity, etc.), and the difficulty of everyday life:

NORA: My father used to tell me that, when they came to the *villa*, this was like a ditch; it was all dirt. . . . There was a lagoon in the Fifth Road. . . . The shacks were made of metal sheets, very tiny shacks. . . .

PASCUAL: When it rained, we used to have water up to our knees. . . . And then there was the fight for the drinking water. In order to fill a bucket of water, you had to go to what people used to call the *four spigots* in the Fifth Road, and there you had to fight with your neighbors. . . . It was a disaster. . . .

TOTO: Seventy percent of Villa Paraíso was covered with water; a river divided the shantytown in two. This was the highest area, where the church is now. I remembered that my dad was in the train station in Villa Rubi and told my mom: "There, on that hill, we are going to build our *rancho*. . . ."

While life in the shantytown was very hard, residence there was seen as temporary. Either because they believed that new apartments were being constructed for them by the Peronist government or because they perceived themselves as upwardly mobile, residents thought that they were going to "leave the shantytown." As one of the protagonists in the film exclaims, looking at the photograph of the promised houses: "Oh, yes! That's my whole dream. I spend the whole day looking at this photograph." The prospect of new houses is something that many inhabitants remember as imminent in their first years of residence in Paraíso. As is clear in the film and is recounted in countless testimonies, the shantytown was understood as something temporary, as a transient leap from rural despair to urban advancement, as part of a quite generalized process of upward social mobility experienced by the working class during the 1950s and 1960s. As many older residents remember, at the time of the first settlement, shantytown-dwellers thought that they were going to be allotted new apartments such as those recently inaugurated in an adjacent area: Barrio Obrero. Either getting a new house or being evicted was part of everyday life for the first inhabitants, especially when Perón was ousted from power in 1955 and the new military regime introduced a drastically different urban policy.

When Rosa and her father arrive at Villa Paraíso, a long wall blocks the view of the shantytown from the outside. This wall gives the movie its name. Rosita asks: "And what's this long wall?" Her father adds: "It looks like the wall of a cemetery. . . ." A ten-foot-high cement barrier runs along one side of Paraíso, the side facing the capital city. The shantytown is a spectacle of misery to be hidden from the outside world.

Although every older resident acknowledges the existence of the wall, there is little agreement on its origins. The movie implies that the wall was constructed by Perón's government; many residents and the only written history of the place (Lazcano 1987) concur. Yet others—all of whom claim a strong Peronist identity—say that they have no idea who built the wall or, more surprisingly, say that it was built by the military government that ousted Perón. The wall is subject to contrasting interpretations; as we will see in chapter 5, this is not the only source of disagreement among the shantytown dwellers. In a dialogue worth quoting at length, Toto presents his own interpretation of the "long wall." According to him, Eisenhower's visit and policies emanating from the military era were the reasons for the wall's construction (implicated by others are the influential visits of David Rockefeller, the ambassador of Japan, and other international figures):

TOTO: When Perón inaugurated the motorcar racetrack, it was spectacular.[5] . . . A lot of people used to come to this area. Eisenhower came for a grand prix, and the military ordered the construction of the wall so that this whole area couldn't be seen. Aramburu and Rojas built it. . . .

JAVIER AUYERO: So . . . it wasn't built in Perón's time, was it?

TOTO: [*Shouting.*] No, sir! It [the wall] was not done under Peronism! It was not done under Peronism!

JAVIER AUYERO: Because there are versions. . . .

TOTO: [*Shouting.*] No, sir! No, sir! [*Shaking his head vigorously and gesturing with his hands.*]

JAVIER AUYERO: Some people told me it was built by Perón. . . .

TOTO: No, sir! They know nothing! It was not under Perón because before the coup [that ousted Perón from power] the wall was not yet there.

In the same way that almost every older resident remembers the swampy character of the shantytown, the procurement of drinking water is recounted as the major problem faced by its residents. Familial, kinship, and friendship networks are remembered as the sources for solving such shortages. Lines formed very early in the morning around the two places where spigots were located, seven blocks away from the center of Paraíso. Procuring drinking water, building their dwellings, filling the lagoons, constructing precarious bridges to cross the small lagoons: everything is said to have been made possible through the active cooperation of neighbors, friends, and relatives.

Many neighbors stress that, although life in Paraíso was difficult and painful, it was also "so much fun." No single interview or life history with older residents skips the amusing quality of life in Paraíso at its inception. Almost all recall the various dance halls scattered throughout that gave Villa Paraíso its reputation as a "very fun place." El Patio Criollo, El Trigo de Oro, El Nuevo Amanecer, Bonito Carnaval, El Gauchoquero—all the original inhabitants of Villa Paraíso remember these places. Some of them came to Paraíso for the first time as visitors to these clubs, meeting a prospective partner who lived there and then moving there.

Thus, Paraíso is recalled as difficult and transitory but also as fun and affording a sense of community. Innumerable testimonies highlight the sense of community, a feature that is considered lost nowadays. Gone now as well are the jobs that drew people to Paraíso in the first place. It is probably Olga who best summarizes how life in the shantytown used to be: "In those years there was a lot of work . . . plenty of jobs. . . . We didn't have light, we didn't have water . . . we didn't have anything at all. There was only one bus to go to the capital, but you had to cross the *villa*. . . . At that time you were able to cross it. I used to cross it at 4:00 A.M., with my child, and it was as if I felt protected because we were all acquaintances. . . .

Villa Paraíso was literally surrounded by large industrial plants, mainly metallurgic and textile firms (Fabricaciones Militares, Siam, Metalúrgica Oesch, Alba, Frigorífico Wilson, etc.), where—through relatives and friends—Paraíso residents got their first industrial jobs. Many inhabitants could find everything they needed, including a job in a store or a factory, nearby. Nowadays, in a context of generalized un(der)employment, residents remember the ready availability of jobs at any of the plants as something that was taken for granted.

In 1954, the first school was opened in Paraíso in what, according to Lazcano (1987, 42), amounted to a "clear recognition [by the Peronist government] of the existence of the shantytown." Lazcano's comments on the opening of the first public school are extremely important because they highlight the pattern of problem solving that would prevail in Paraíso for the next two decades. According to Lazcano, the construction of the school was the "only case in the history of the consolidation of the shantytown's habitat in which the construction of the infrastructure was the product of a government's initiative, with no claims or pressures whatsoever on the part of the neighbors."

The years that followed the opening of the public school would give birth to a distinctive pattern of problem solving that combines a pattern of claim making to the local and provincial governments (and of changing state policies toward the shantytowns) with the collective efforts of Paraíso residents to improve their dwellings and habitat. This pattern of problem solving and claim making refutes any imputation of "culture of dependency" that the shantytown residents might have brought with them from the countryside (and that had supposedly found fertile soil in Paraíso) and confirms what other works (e.g., Castells 1983) found in other low-income urban settings: that grassroots movements played a central role in the acquisition of public services ("collective consumption").

The year 1955 marks a turning point in state policies toward the shantytown. Once Perón was ousted, the Revolución Libertadora began considering the shantytown as a problem: not only a housing problem but also a social one.[6] The "Emergency Plan" crafted by the Comisión Nacional de la Vivienda had as its major aim the removal of the "emergency slums" (Yujnovsky 1984, 98). As threats of eviction began to escalate within Paraíso, the Unión Vecinal de Villa Paraíso—the first neighborhood council—was created. It was the first neighborhood organization designed to deal with land-tenure issues. A detailed analysis of the effect of these and other programs is beyond the scope of this book. Suffice it to say that, not only were the inhabitants of Villa Paraíso not forced out of their dwellings, but, for the first time, a neighborhood organization began to crystallize.

The years after Perón's fall also witnessed the organization within Paraíso of "cells" that formed part of the clandestine Peronist Resistance.[7] The Resistencia, as it was popularly known, had strong union support as well as a presence in many shantytowns and working-class neighborhoods. The Centro de Organizaciones para la Resistencia (COR) based its operations in Villa Paraíso. From Paraíso it organized clandestine gatherings, manufactured homemade bombs and other explosives, took part in strikes, and propagandized for the return of Perón. Don Mario was, according to many versions, the "mailman" of the Resistencia. He is now very old, and, although still reluctant to talk about that period, he succinctly describes some of the activities of the Resistance: "You know, *teníamos máquinas, teníamos herramientas* [guns]." As another of the peripheral participants in the movement within Paraíso describes: "We did a lot of propaganda work. We clandestinely painted political graffiti on the walls. To speak about Perón was something incredible. . . . It was a very difficult time. . . . They [two military men] brought us information; we had to keep working for the return of Perón. "Perón comes back [*Perón vuelve*]," "Perón comes back," "Perón comes back." . . . We organized rallies. We secretly listened to Perón's speeches. . . . [8]

As James (1988, 77) explains, the Peronist Resistance in the factories was "inextricably bound up with resistance on other terrains. This involved a heterogeneous mixture of different types of activity; the Resistance included in popular Peronist consciousness a diverse set of responses ranging from individual protest on the mundane level, through individual sabotage to clandestine activity and beyond to attempted military uprisings." A wide range of activities—from hanging portraits of Perón and Evita in homes when doing so was strictly prohibited, fabricating busts of Perón in the only blacksmith's shop in Paraíso, and going to the soccer stadiums and playing the traditional Peronist drum (*bombo peronista*), to participating in the attempted military uprisings— is recounted by some as taking place in Paraíso.

The democratic interregnum of 1958–62 meant further change in the policies toward the shantytowns in the federal capital and Greater Buenos Aires. Evictions were rescinded, and, in consonance with Frondizi's developmentalist attempts to harmonize all social classes and subordinate them to the interests of the nation-state, specific policies regarding the shantytown population (known as *asistencialismo*) were put in place.

These changes at the state level had a direct effect on Villa Paraíso: the provincial government sanctioned Law 6526 (1962), which put a halt to the attempt by the owners of the land on which Paraíso was located to have it razed. The law was a turning point in the history of the neighborhood. Residence there ceased to be transitory, and conditions improved rapidly. The lagoons were filled, the first roads were paved, and the installation of the first waterworks and public lighting began. At the same time, the passage of the law strengthened the image of the local organization—the Junta Vecinal—that claimed credit for it.

Owing to the support of the local and provincial governments (under Mayor Monserrat and Governor Alende), Paraíso changed drastically. The 1960s witnessed the pavement of the first two streets (the most important event in the shantytown), the lagoons were almost completely drained, and the shantytown's ground level was significantly elevated. A first—precarious—health center was built, and the waterworks were considerably extended.

Law 6526 declared the plot of land on which Paraíso is located "subject to expropriation," which meant—in practice—that the shantytown dwellers were not going to be evicted. Since then, not only did Paraíso improve its habitat, but dozens of citizens' groups were formed. In retrospect, the number of organizations that sprung up in those years is impressive. Residents organized around specific issues (paving or lighting an alleyway, installing part of the waterworks, digging the sewer, etc.), and more broadly focused groups—like the Junta Vecinal or the Sociedad de Fomento—became the links between Paraíso and the local and provincial governments.

Although they might sound idyllic from today's perspective, memories of a warm and supporting community abound among the older residents. Even though those memories are bound to be highly idealized, the longing for a sense of community now lost offers an interesting critique of present conditions: social isolation, marginalization, and little social activism.

In the 1960s, people were building their *place,* and the collective effort included neighborhood organizations, interactions with the state, and individual efforts of residents. Of course, the increasing organizational density meant that growth and development were far from harmonious; conflicts between the "owners" and the "intruders" and between those living in the alleyways and those living in the front were part of everyday life. Yet what prevails in the narratives of older residents is the sense of belonging to a place that they themselves were making. When older residents say that "we used to know each other," that "the neighborhood council of the time was working very well," and that "we made this and that, all together, struggling hard," their voices stand in sharp contrast to present living conditions. Against the background of today's extreme material deprivation and of the loss of control over the way in which society represents—stereotypes, actually—them, the *sense of living in a self-constructed place* that residents recount gains its full significance.

The military takeover in 1966 marked yet another change in government policy toward the shantytowns. At the same time, unprecedented flooding struck southern Greater Buenos Aires. In October 1967, "the month that Che Guevara was killed," as a neighbor told me, taking me by surprise, Villa Paraíso was literally covered with water. Photographs of a devastated Villa Paraíso covered the front pages of the popular press. *A nightmare* and *horrid* are the terms used by residents when they recall the experience, the flooding leaving them "without the few things that we used to have." The floods sparked two movements: a government-led offensive to eradicate the shantytowns and a generalized mobilization of Paraíso residents and the birth of several community organizations. The military government crafted the Plan de Erradicación de las Villas de Emergencia de la Capital Federal y del Gran Buenos Aires (PEVE), whose aim was the removal of the more than 70,000 families inhabiting the shantytowns of the capital and Greater Buenos Aires, a population of approximately 280,000. Defining itself as a "totalizing and coherent" policy (Yujnovsky 1984, 163), the removal program was aimed not only at the relocation of these people, but also at their "reintegration" into society.[9]

In a direct response to the flooding and to the renewed attempt at removal, in 1967 the Junta Coordinadora de Entidades de Bien Público was created. The Junta served as an umbrella organization covering eleven neighborhood associations, four from Villa Paraíso (Junta Vecinal de Villa Paraíso, Club Unión y Progreso de Villa Paraíso, Centro Comunitario de Villa Paraíso, and Sociedad de Fomento). The late 1960s were characterized by political upheaval in Argentina. This was reflected in Paraíso by the mushrooming of small activist groups (the Group of the Fifth Road, the Association of the Fourth Road, etc.). The Junta Coordinadora and these other groups worked not only to halt the evictions but also to accelerate public works projects: for example, road building and school construction.

According to one resident, the 1970s were "the most active period in the neighborhood. The cardboard houses disappeared; the alleyways were improved; light and water were installed" (Lazcano 1987, 117). Evictions were, once again, suspended, and, in the general context of the mass upheaval and the political radicalization of the early 1970s, different groups (Peronist Youth, Third World Priests, and Communist activists) worked in Villa Paraíso—as in many other shantytowns and poor neighborhoods—supporting local organizations. Collective action in pursuit of common ends was at its peak. The involvement of individuals and organizations from outside Paraíso was crucial. During the Peronist government, the most important common end of neighborhood organizations was the health center, which was finally inaugurated under the military regime after 1976. As one resident recollects: "The experts showed up because they were very sensitive people. I guess some of them were activists. Besides, we did have acquaintances at the municipality: architects, physicians, sociologists. For example, an architect drew the plans for the health center" (cited in Lazcano 1987, 112; my translation).

The Siege

"People don't want to talk much about that. *They* created panic, terror. *They* took many *compañeros* from the neighborhood: Rene, Liliana, Estanislao, and Porfi Araujo. People said that they were *gente solidaria*. . . . Every day, between 1:30 and 3:00 A.M., there were executions in the garbage dump. . . . Homeless people [*cirujas*] found two or three dead bodies every single day. [They were] young people, sometimes [placed] in nylon bags. A worker from [the nearby factory] Fabricaciones Militares told me that *they* used to bring big containers with dead bodies and *they* put those containers in the *fundicion. They* brought them in trucks, at dawn. The stench was nauseating [*vomitivo*] . . ." (quoted in Lazcano 1987, 120; my translation). Anyone with the slightest familiarity with recent Argentine history will recognize this account. It is one of the hundreds of testimonies that, coming to light after democracy returned to Argentina, recounted the horrors perpetrated by the military and the police (the *they* in this account) during the military dictatorship (1976–83). This particular tale of terror and death comes from a resident of Paraíso. The shantytown was not a casual military target. Given its high levels of social organization and political mobilization during the early 1970s, Villa Paraíso was a target well chosen by a military in search of "subversive activity." Juan, the former secretary of the Sociedad de Fomento and now president of a UB, describes for me the grassroots political activity: "We were working for the asphalt and for the health center. There were block delegates and delegates for each alley, and then there was the executive council of the neighborhood association. It was a real mess." He then recounts what happened after 1976: "They did not look only for those who were involved. When they took me [*me levantan*], they took my mother, my sister, the whole block. . . . That generated dread among the neighbors, panic. . . . Many children were never seen again. . . . They captured us at dawn, they took us out from our houses . . . I don't know where they brought us. . . . There is one thing I remembered, though. When I lived in the province, rainy days were really sad. But when it was raining while I was in jail . . . it was my only connection to life. . . . Now, when it rains, it makes me really happy." Juan was lucky enough; the military released him after months of captivity in a secret jail: "They forbade me to engage in any kind of political activity: 'Don't get yourself involved in the neighborhood association because we will blow up your family.' . . . It was not easy to come back."

After the military coup of 1976, "the cities and countryside were divided up into zones that were searched in operatives known as *rastrillos* ('to rake'). Entire neighborhoods were blocked off, one by one, as military forces searched homes asking for identification of all those present and the whereabouts of those absent" (Taylor 1997, 97). Although there are no precise accounts, twelve people who, at that time, were politically active in the shantytown are now counted among the *desaparecidos*. Even though no further attempts to eradicate the shantytowns were made (in sharp contrast to the "cleansing" policy carried out in the federal capital), on 17 May 1978 the military began a twelve-day siege of Paraíso:[10] "They showed up at 4:30 in the morning, they surrounded everything. . . . They cleaned a lot . . . because you have to admit it: they took a lot of people, I don't know what class of people they were, but they filled trucks with people. In order to enter and to leave [Paraíso], we had to show our IDs. It was like a concentration camp." After the siege, all community organizations were banned except the Sociedad de Fomento, whose work was extremely limited and sharply controlled: "Every member of the executive council [of the Sociedad] had to report his activities to the *comando militar* and fill out a form detailing our activities. They asked what we've done, who had shown up at the meetings. . . . We couldn't do anything" (quoted in Lazcano 1987, 121, 122; my translation). Such traumatic experiences have resulted in a collective silence. Fifteen years after the return of democracy to Argentina, "I don't want to talk about it" is still the most common response among those shantytown dwellers who were politically engaged during the "glorious 1970s." In refusing to allow me to tape his reminiscences about his participation in the Peronist Resistance, an old activist of the Peronist Party exemplifies this still-present fear: "A ver si me vienen a buscar" (They might come and look for me). The military repression had, in Paraíso as elsewhere (Villarreal 1985), a lasting effect on subsequent attempts at organization. Part of the current absence of strong community associations and leaders can be traced back to the "dirty war."

Changing Problems, Changing Solutions

Fifty years after their emergence in the urban landscape as transitory phenomena typical of a "stage of development," shantytowns are still a part of the geography of Buenos Aires and, indeed, most Latin American cities. During these fifty years, the shantytowns have captured the imagination of Argentine filmmakers (Lucas Demare), novelists (Bernardo Verbistky), political activists (Grupo Praxis, the Montoneros, the People's Revolutionary Army, and the Peronists during the 1960s and 1970s, the Christian Democrats, the Intransigentes, the Communists, and the Peronists during the 1980s and 1990s), priests (José De Luca), and social scientists (Hugo Ratier). In fact, one can hardly think of an urban form that was (and still is) the repository of so many (mis)representations, of so many hopes in the past and so many fears in the present. Shantytowns were portrayed as the best example of the failure of Peronist populism during the 1950s, as project sites for the modernizing dreams of the 1960s, as the places where revolution was germinating during the 1970s, as either obstacles to progress or subversive territories during the 1980s, and as places of immorality, crime, and lawlessness in the 1990s. Today, hardly a conversation about public (in)security passes without mention of the *villa* or the *villeros* (a label that is equally applied to people living in poor areas regardless of whether they in fact live in shantytowns) as the symbolic (but no less real) threat to be avoided. In today's fragmented and polarized Argentina, shantytowns are no-go areas, patches of crime to be feared and avoided. Media accounts periodically refer to the fear that shantytown dwellers incite unrest, focusing on the reactions of non–shantytown dwellers toward these "refuges [*aguantaderos*] of criminal activities." Unfortunately, very little empirical research focuses on the everyday lives of the stigmatized shantytown dwellers and, specifically, on the effect that the combined withdrawal of the state and the market has on these enclaves. This lack is striking given the skyrocketing Argentine shantytown population. Since 1991, there has been a 65 percent increase in the shantytown population in the city of Buenos Aires, from 52,472 to 86,666 inhabitants (*Clarín,* 24 January 1999). Since 1983, the shantytown population has been growing in the province as well (Stillwaggon 1998).

Between 1956 and 1970, the shantytown population in metropolitan

Buenos Aires grew at an annual rate of 8.4 percent. In 1956, 78,430 people were living in shantytowns; ten years later, 500,000 were shantytown dwellers. In 1980, almost 300,000 were still living in shantytowns. In Cóspito City, where Paraíso is located, 8.2 percent of the population was living in shantytowns in 1956, 13.8 percent in 1970, and 9.7 percent in 1980 (Yujnovsky 1984, 353–60; see also Stillwaggon 1998). Residence in the shantytown is no longer seen as temporary; now it is permanent. And, having survived state repression and macroeconomic transformation, its residents live their lives differently. Gone are the high-visibility neighborhood organizations, replaced with unofficial problem-solving networks. Whereas, formerly, essential city services were obtained through collective action and subsistence needs met through paid employment, workers now find themselves under- or unemployed, and the resources on which the unofficial networks rely are increasingly strained. Shantytown dwellers today face more pressing problems than public works projects; they are fighting for sheer survival.[11]

Coping with Poverty behind the "Invisible Wall"

The following four vignettes offer a summary of what, following Clark's (1965) seminal analysis, I term *the cry of the shantytown,* a cry that comes from behind the invisible wall that now separates the inhabitants of the shantytown from society at large:[12]

> *Deprivation.*—Roberto is thirty-five years old and has been living in Paraíso for almost ten years. He works in a textile factory half an hour from home, where he earns one peso, twenty cents per hour (one peso is equivalent to one U.S. dollar). The round-trip bus ticket costs one peso: "Almost an hour of my work is spent on the ticket." He used to go to work on his bicycle, "but now the bike is broken, and I don't have the money to fix it."
>
> *Shame.*—Juan, a longtime resident of Paraíso, is in his late forties. He was a carpenter until the factory where he worked for over ten years shut down. He is now a garbage collector. He heads for work every day early in the morning, at 3:30 A.M. That time of day is "kind of dangerous here. I already changed my bus stop three times because the kids on the corner . . . are always doing drugs . . . and they began

to 'charge me a toll,' you know, a coin or a cigarette. . . . If I didn't have it, they wouldn't let me pass. . . . The other day they robbed me of the two pesos I had for the bus, and they even got angry with me because that was all the money I had." Half jokingly, but with an expression of grief on his face, he recounts what the robbers told him: "Come on, man. . . . You are a grown-up. . . . Aren't you ashamed of having only two pesos?"

Violence.—Cachún is a high school dropout who has been unemployed for the last eight months. Last week, he was coming back from a bar in the city (Buenos Aires) with some friends. They were high on cocaine, and the police stopped them near Paraíso. The cops pushed them against the wall and made them stand spread-eagle to be searched for drugs. "The cops took my coke," Cachún tells me, "cut a line on the hood of their car, and snorted it. . . . Can you believe it, man?" The cops, a friend of Cachún's adds, are "all crazy. . . . They become cops so that they can smoke pot and sniff coke for free!"

Stigma.—Catalina is a high school dropout who has been unemployed for the past six months. She will soon turn twenty-six. She says that she does not like living in Paraíso at all: "I would like to cross Rosario Street and live on the other side." Rosario is the street that divides Paraíso from an adjacent working-class neighborhood, Villa Rubi. I ask her if she has ever faced any sort of discrimination because she lives in Villa Paraíso. "I never say that I live here. When they ask me, I say that I live in Cóspito City. On my ID it doesn't say anything about Villa Paraíso. . . ." She adds: "When you go to work, or when you have friends, it is like a conflict, you know? Because people badmouth the shantytown, and I used to be embarrassed, you know? I didn't want to tell anybody that I lived in the shantytown because I knew that most of the things that were said about it were true; there are good people and bad people. I had friends who came to visit me and were robbed, with guns . . . and what can you do against that? Your own friend tells you that she is not coming to your house. . . . That is the conflict."

The floundering wage-labor economy, the casualization of blue-collar jobs, and the neglect provoked by the state's structural adjustment policies (described in chap. 1) cause widespread material deprivation, persistent joblessness and misery, and the merciless pressure of economic necessity in Villa Paraíso. The "real" wall constructed forty years ago to hide Paraíso from the eyes of respectable citizens has disappeared (some of its pieces have been incorporated in shantytown houses), but another wall has taken its place: the invisible wall of economic redundancy, educational exclusion, state abandonment, and sustained stigmatization. Those four voices synthesize the paramount reality of shantytown dweller's lives: continual violence and humiliation, state corruption, educational failure, joblessness or extreme job uncertainty, and increasing drug consumption and trafficking, fostering pervasive social and physical insecurity.

Drawing on data from the census (1991) and my own survey conducted in Paraíso from September to October 1996 (see chap. 3, n. 10), the next section analyzes the employment, education, housing, and health situation of the population of Villa Paraíso. Such an analysis is a necessary prerequisite to an exploration of the meanings and living experiences of poverty/exclusion/marginality/downward mobility as they take shape in this space, where multiple material deprivations accumulate and reinforce each other. The section after that draws on my in-depth interviews and observations of the daily routines of shantytown dwellers carried out during 1995–96.

Fragmented Polarization Seen from the Shantytown

Here, in the shantytown, you meet heroic people, really . . . men and women in the daily struggle to get ahead with their families . . . heroic, heroic. —Mariano, priest of Villa Paraíso

The history of Villa Paraíso, briefly summarized in previous sections, is nothing but a *particular specification* of the collective history of the working classes and the urban poor of the Conurbano Bonaerense since the 1940s. The last decade has witnessed major improvements in city services (almost all the streets are now paved, many houses have private telephones and electric lighting, and the alleyways and the sewer systems have been considerably improved). Comparing Paraíso today with the shantytown shown in the movie *Detrás de un largo muro* and with the image conveyed in the testimonies of older residents, it is almost unrecognizable: it is now in much better shape than it was in the 1960s, 1970s, and early 1980s. Many residents perceive that their living arrangements are better now than they were twenty or thirty years ago; that is, their conditions of existence have improved.

However, once we shift our empirical focus from conditions to connections, another image emerges, one that casts doubt on the future of the shantytown. On the one hand, significant structural deficiencies still exist, putting the lie to the picture of general and sustained improvement painted by the state. On the other hand, many of the residents' ties to the larger society—for example, participation in the labor market and in the school system—have been seriously weakened and, in some cases, severed. In short, the residents of Paraíso (as are residents of most enclaves of poverty in Argentina) are beset by problems both old and new. Since the slum's inception in the 1930s, its residents have known little but concentrated, chronic poverty. The neoliberal policies of the 1980s and 1990s produced a new marginality. Since the early 1980s, the residents of Villa Paraíso have been increasingly confined in what Mingione (1996, 9) describes as "highly malign circuits of social marginalization."

Overcrowding, unhealthy living conditions, higher than average rates of un- and underemployment, rampant and stigmatized misery— none of these things are the product of a mere two decades of neoliberalism. Present since the Paraíso's inception, these problems were just beginning to be overcome during the 1960s and 1970s. But the 1980s and 1990s changed all that, intensifying the already-present marginality of the shantytown dwellers to the point at which social exclusion becomes the defining characteristic of their existence.

To employ a not very accurate analogy, attempting to improve living conditions in the shantytown is akin to redecorating the passenger cabins on the *Titanic*. Life might be better for the moment, the cabins might be more comfortable, but. . . ."[13] In other words, despite the general improvement in the physical geography of the shantytown, Paraíso has ceased to be a place where the lower segments of the labor market reproduce themselves, a transitory place in the process of upward mobility of the working classes (Rubinich 1991). Paraíso is now a space of survival for those excluded from the rest of society.

Housing, Health, Education, and Employment in the Shantytown

More than half the people living in Paraíso have what studies of poverty call *unmet basic needs.*"[14] Overcrowding in extremely precarious and unsanitary housing is, fifty years after the first residents began to populate the area, the dominant and defining feature of the shantytown. More than a third of its residents live in houses with more than three persons per room. In 12.7 percent of the households in Paraíso, there are more than three persons per room; in the center of Cóspito City, this figure is 0.4 percent. Overcrowding is characteristic not just of specific dwellings but of the shantytown as a whole. In some blocks, more than two hundred families live in close proximity, navigating passageways sometimes no wider than a meter.

Twenty-five percent of the dwellings do not have running water, and only a tiny portion (2.7 percent) of the houses obtain their gas from a public network. Almost all the houses get their gas for cooking and heating from pressurized containers that must be purchased periodically. Almost 70 percent of the dwellings have roofs made of metal sheets. Houses are cold in winter, damp and insufficiently ventilated year-round, and—because of inadequate ventilation and metal roofs—extremely hot during the summer.

Contrary to a general tendency in Cóspito and in the nineteen districts of Greater Buenos Aires (INDEC 1993b), 71 percent of the population of Paraíso does not own the land on which their precarious homes are built. There are also striking differences in the types of housing in which the population lives. More than half the population of Paraíso live in substandard housing. A third live in what INDEC defines as *rancho/ casilla* and 19.8 percent in type B houses.[15] In contrast, 14 percent of the population of Cóspito City lives in what is considered inadequate housing.[16]

The environment that shantytown dwellers confront daily outside their houses is not much better. Household waste water and rainwater run in open ditches through many areas of the shantytown, producing a stench that can, at times, be nauseating, even for residents. Located in a flood zone adjacent to a stream (the Riachuelo) killed by industrial waste and sewage and close to a huge garbage dump, the shantytown is damp and extremely unhealthy.

In this environment, shantytown dwellers suffer high rates of respiratory illnesses (such as asthma), gastrointestinal and parasitic diseases, and epidemic skin diseases (scabies, lice infestation). On the basis of her research in shantytowns in Argentina, Stillwaggon (1998, 74–75) also points out that infantile tuberculosis and measles predominantly affect shantytown children (80 percent of such cases are found among shantytown children). As she reports: "In an investigation of the 1984 measles outbreak, in which there were 32,000 reported cases, it was found that among children under five years old there were three times as many cases of measles in poor areas than in nonpoor areas. The study found that 45 percent of the difference could be attributed to socioeconomic causes. In the 1991 outbreak, there were more than 95,000 cases. Argentina has the same rate of measles infection as the United States did in 1924, many years before the vaccine was invented."

In the interviews that I conducted in the municipality, public officials pointed out the few improvements in living conditions without acknowledging the fact that a municipal truck must bring water on a daily basis to many areas of the shantytown. Those lucky enough to have running water have it only because of an unauthorized connection to the city water supply. And, since the majority of the pipes used in this unauthorized connection are plastic, the defects in the joints and the countless breaks mean that the water is contaminated by the time it reaches people's homes. As a result, diarrhea is, according to the physicians at the local health center, the most common disease among children and adults during the summer. During the winter, bronchitis, angina, and pneumonia plague the shantytown dwellers. In their daily struggle for survival, the prescribed cure—rest—is a luxury that they cannot afford. Obviously, these diseases are not restricted to the shantytown population. Yet, according to physicians at the local health center—who also work in private clinics in downtown Cóspito—they are overrepresented among the shantytown population. "There are the same germs, yet the conditions are different," one of the physicians asserts. "People who do not eat well are prone to any kind of sickness," she summarizes.

More than half (54% according to the 1991 census, nowadays probably more) the population of Villa Paraíso have no health insurance at all. This makes them dependent on the crumbling public health sector. And, without health insurance, prescribed medicine must be obtained from private sources: family networks, local charities, or political brokers.

A comparison with the center of Cóspito City clearly illustrates the obstacles that the inhabitants of Villa Paraíso face in their attempts to gain an education. Eighty-one percent of school-age children attend deteriorating public institutions. In the center of Cóspito, this figure is only 55 percent. Almost 6 percent of the population over three years of age has never attended school at all (only 1 percent in the city center). Of the total number of people who have at one point attended school but are not currently doing so, only 5.9 percent finished high school (22.9 percent in the city center). Clearly, the most likely future awaiting the young people of Villa Paraíso and many other such areas of Greater Buenos Aires is school failure and un- and underemployment.

Widespread unemployment is the single, most significant characteristic defining Villa Paraíso. My own survey shows that 62 percent of the population between the ages of eighteen and sixty is currently unemployed or underemployed. Unemployment affects women more than men, and long-term unemployment is rampant: more than half of those who are unemployed have not held a steady job in the last year.

Among those living in Paraíso who were lucky enough to have jobs, most women worked in domestic service (according to the most recent [1991] census),[17] most men in construction (according to my own survey). About 14 percent of the employed population is currently working in, and almost 30 percent of the unemployed population had been working in, construction or domestic service (Murmis and Feldman 1996). Most unemployed individuals rely on casual, temporary odd jobs for what little money they do manage to earn.

Informal work at home and "off the books" is another source of income, but the pay received for such work has been steadily and dramatically declining in recent years. Pedro, Coco, and Rosa make Pierre Cardin purses in their home. "Pierre Cardin made in Paraíso," they jokingly tell me. They work for a large firm that gives them the purse's model and the materials. They work for more than fourteen hours a day, with no insurance or health coverage. Two years ago they made $700 every two weeks; now they are making $800 every month, an amount that places their household (five adults and three children) well below the official poverty line. The purses that they make for $10 are being sold in the most expensive stores in the city (under the label *Pierre Cardin–Paris*) for more than $100. At least they have their revenge: they are the only ones who know that the purses are not authentic Pierre Cardin. They are as fake as the U.S. $100 bill they once received from the owner of the factory in payment for their work. "You have to watch out; everybody is trying to screw you," Pedro told me.

Down and Out: The Experience of Living in the Shantytown

The surrounding landscape of the shantytown and the internal makeup of the alleyways are probably the best indicators of the fate of this space. In the northwest part of the shantytown, the huge building of the Fabricaciones Militares factory is now an abandoned skeleton; in the southeast, the home-appliance factory where many inhabitants of Paraíso used to work is now no more than a storage facility; in the northeast, the metallurgic factory has been significantly downsized. These empty, underutilized buildings serve as a symbol of sorts for the state of the shantytown and its inhabitants and for the way in which the withering away of the wage-labor economy is being inscribed on the urban landscape: abandoned buildings and desolate gates. Once the place of the newborn working class, Villa Paraíso is now the space where the *un*-population (the unemployed and uneducated) clings to survival.

The alleyways also serve as an unconventional sociological indicator of the changes the shantytown has seen in the last fifteen years: the height of the walls of the houses facing the alleyways has been substantially increased. Once, the alleyways were roads from which the interiors of the houses could be seen, and neighbors could talk across them. Now, the alleyways look like veritable tunnels: the high walls serve as a defense against the predators that prowl the shantytown.

As I mentioned earlier, Villa Paraíso is a very heterogeneous place. From east to west, from the First Road to the Fifth, conditions significantly deteriorate. The nearer one comes to the northwest border of Paraíso, the more marked the deterioration. Yet all the inhabitants feel that conditions in Paraíso have changed dramatically in the last ten years. That the streets are now paved with asphalt is a major achievement, one that they feel marks a turning point in the history of Paraíso.[18] Before, it was considered a shantytown (*una villa*); now, it is seen as a neighborhood (*un barrio*). Such changes have affected all the residents of Paraíso. For most of them, the shantytown is "much better," so much so that it is not a shantytown any more:

> There was a lot of poverty, of misery . . . nothing like how it is now. One tries to be better, to improve the house. . . . The truth is that many things have changed in the neighborhood. (Jose)

> Now, it is as if you were walking in Corrientes Avenue.[19] Some time ago, you couldn't even walk in the alleyways; it was all dirt, infection, everything was mud. (Susana)

> The neighborhood was a disaster; it was not as it is now. Now I see it as a neighborhood [*barrio*]; I don't see it as a shantytown. . . . Sometimes I get offended when people say that this is a shantytown because this is not a shantytown. There are alleyways as there are in the shantytowns, that's right. . . . But, before, it was awful because the streets were muddy, in the alleyways you couldn't even walk into them, the houses were a disaster. Now, you enter a house and you say, "This is a nice house." (Mimi)

> When I was a kid [in the mid-1960s], the houses were very precarious . . . a world of difference to how they are now. The streets were muddy; we were surrounded by mud. (Estela)

Although some of the residents (especially those living in the area adjacent to the Fifth Road) consider Paraíso a shantytown, most agree that the asphalt, the lighting, the water network (although still not completely dependable), the telephones, all are indicators that prove that this is not a *villa* anymore but a *barrio* or even "a city," as Rodolfo cordially told me: "When you get married, you can come and live in Ciudad Paraíso."

Yet two qualifications should be noted: all the inhabitants are aware that there are still improvements to be made, and almost all of them are aware that, while things have improved, the living conditions in Paraíso are still not good. Mario wonderfully synthesizes this feeling: "Yes . . . we are much better now; there is light, pavement, phones. . . . But you know what, brother? . . . We live very bad."

The Fifth Road: Dealers, "Little Pirates," and Shoplifters

Almost twenty years after the military coup, I am sitting in the main hall of the neighborhood association waiting for the beginning of the elder club's monthly meeting. "See those guys over there?" Eloisa, an old-time resident of Paraíso asks me. "They always steal cars." They were parking a new car in front of the neighborhood association. Eloisa looks at them with resignation and expresses the feeling of separation from the institutions and services that (a decreasing part of) the rest of society still takes for granted: "I don't know. . . . Here, as times goes by, we are more and more isolated. . . . cabdrivers don't want to come here. . . . They say that they don't want to be robbed." The repressive state violence of the 1970s has been replaced by a pernicious kind of interpersonal violence (no doubt causally related to the state's current indifference to the plight of its poorer citizens) and by the structural violence of unemployment. State violence has not completely withdrawn from the shantytown; it now takes the form of sporadic and fiercely brutal raids that target (mostly) young people. However, the violence that dominates the daily experience and routines of the residents of Paraíso is that inflicted on them by other residents.

Paraíso is a locality bad-mouthed by everyone, a blemished place. The mere fact of residence there degrades its inhabitants; they are the *villeros,* objects of public scorn. The stigmatizing gaze is yet another part of the reality of exclusion that the shantytown dwellers experience. Their demoralization, their resignation, their lack of hope, all are consequences of their (symbolic) rejection and material deprivation.

The stigma of residence in Paraíso affects virtually all social interaction:[20] from friendships (Nilda's son, e.g., keeps asking her when they can leave the alleyways because he is ashamed to bring his friends there; recall also Catalina's testimony) to young people's everyday dealings with the police. Embodied in its dilapidation (the crumbling infrastructure, the unreliable public services), the shantytown's bad reputation is reaffirmed by the everyday attitudes of outsiders: drivers are afraid to make deliveries to local stores; cabdrivers refuse to cross the bridge leading to Paraíso; relatives and friends rarely venture there.

As Hugo says, "The men who sell milk, soda, and bread do not enter this area any more because they get robbed. . . . They stole my bicycle

. . . the ones who come to buy drugs stole my bicycle." Or Mario, "No . . . my daughters don't come here; it's dangerous."

As in many other poor neighborhoods, the territorial stigmatization, the sense of the indignity of living in a "cursed place," is, many times, deflected by thrusting the stigma onto others. A specific "forbidden zone" within the area (in this case, the Fifth Road), a specific social group (the "streetcorner guys who are drinking beer all day long, and God knows what is inside the bottle"), or a specific ethnic group that has gained visibility in the last years (the Koreans, or the Bolivians "who steal our jobs," or the Paraguayans who are said to be profiting from the distribution of food carried out by the municipality) is singled out as responsible for the overall situation of the shantytown:

> When you tell a Paraguayan that they are distributing food in the municipality, he will go with all his family, his daughters, his sons-in-law . . . and he will get food for the whole month. (Hugo)

> Here, foreigners have access to everything. Bolivians and Chileans come to this country to have their surgery. . . . Why do they get priority? If an Argentine goes to Paraguay, they won't even look at him. (Marta)

What from the outside appears to be a "monolithic ensemble is seen by its members as a finely differentiated congeries of 'micro-locales'" (Wacquant 1994a, 238). The prevalence of unemployment and underemployment and the inadequacy of public assistance foster a wide range of illegal activities in the shantytown, like drug dealing, petty crime, and the selling of stolen merchandise (obtained by shoplifters, popularly known as *mecheras*), activities that find fertile ground in the intricate alleyways of the Fifth Road, the most deteriorated sector of Paraíso. With its narrow—and, for the outsider, almost impenetrable—passages, the Fifth Road is the place where the petty entrepreneurialism of drug dealing and predatory crime takes root.

The Little Pirates were a gang of adolescents who used to rob private cars, buses, and trucks by lying in the streets, waiting for vehicles to slow down, and assaulting them like pirates commandeering an enemy ship. They would later hide in the alleyways from the (always late arriving) police. As many residents acknowledge, the Pirates are the ones who know the passages best. They would also hide in the abandoned factory that borders the Fifth Road.

Along with the drug dealers, the Little Pirates terrorize the neighborhood and feed the dominant antagonism that runs through Paraíso: the youngsters versus everyone else. The older residents consistently point to the youngsters as the major source of crime and insecurity. Holding them publicly responsible for everything bad that happens, and signaling out the Fifth Road as the place where they hide themselves, seems to be the most important strategy of stigma displacement in which residents engage.

Youngsters are, thus, the ultimate targets of stigmatization within the shantytown: they are "the usual suspects." They are seen as dangerous and unpredictable, perceived as the ultimate cause of a process that some authors detect in other social settings: the decreasing level of trust among neighbors (Bourgois 1995) or the "depacification of everyday life" (Wacquant 1993, 1996b) in the shantytown. The everyday socioeconomic and symbolic violence of which the youngsters are victims (their harassment by the police, the constant rejection that they face in the labor market, worthlessness of whatever education they have managed to obtain) fosters the defiant attitude that the other residents of Paraíso fear and condemn.

There is, however, another strand of antagonism that runs through Paraíso, one related to the experience of unemployment: Argentines versus immigrants. Succumbing to the classic divide-and-conquer logic (Bourgois 1995, 166), many residents—and especially the youngsters—channel their discontent over their structural vulnerability (chap. 1) in the labor market and within capital-labor relations into antagonism toward recent immigrants, mainly Bolivians and Paraguayans. Although underemployment and unemployment are believed to be affecting "everybody everywhere," immigrants are increasingly becoming the scapegoats on whom is vented the shantytown dwellers' frustration over the poverty and exclusion with which they are faced. As a group of youngsters who hang out in Matilde's UB told me:

> Foreigners screwed us up, the Bolivians really fucked us. . . . They are cheap labor. . . . They earn the money here . . . and they send it to Bolivia.

There are a lot of Peruvians and Bolivians who earn very little, but they do not claim anything else. . . . People will hire them because they won't demand anything. . . . They won't hire me because I will claim the payment I deserve.

I used to work in a shoe factory, and the Paraguayans have taken over the place. . . . We used to get eighty cents for a pair of shoes. I was sick for a week, and when I came back there were two Paraguayans working for forty cents a pair. And the guy at the factory told me: "The job is yours, but for forty cents a pair." Fuck you, I said. What can I do? Burn the factory?

According to the latest census, 14 percent of Paraíso's population was born in a country bordering Argentina (Bolivia, Brazil, Chile, Uruguay, or Paraguay). Immigrants have been part of the reality of the shantytown for a long time, as indicated in the fact that 20.3 percent of residents between the ages of fifty and sixty-four were born in a bordering country. Yet, given the widespread unemployment and the (material and symbolic) disappearance of the state within the shantytown, immigrants have become more visible there. Even though labor market experts publish evidence to the contrary, Bolivians, Paraguayans, and Peruvians are accused of "stealing our jobs" (because they are more "exploitable"), of "sending the money back" to their countries, and of profiting from social assistance programs for which they should not be eligible "because they are not from here."

"Youngsters versus everyone else," "Argentines versus foreigners," "law-abiding citizens versus drug dealers"—these antagonisms sometimes overlap: "Here, on the corner, there's a young Bolivian couple who sell drugs. . . . They are making a lot of money." These antagonisms increase the level of distrust and divide the residents. In a generalized absence of employment and cash income, the escalation of the drug economy and the increased presence of drug dealers cast doubts on previously taken-for-granted moral judgments. "You know, sometimes I feel like all of us should be selling drugs. . . . We would be making a lot of money," Tota told me after explaining that she has bought her jeans from one of the *mecheras* (shoplifters) of the shantytown.

The destructive consequences of the drug economy that have been analyzed in other "neighborhoods of relegation" (see Wacquant 1996a,

1996d; Bourgois 1995; Williams 1989; and Kotlowitz 1991) strongly affect Paraíso,[21] which, according to official sources, has the highest incidence of drug trafficking and addiction in Greater Buenos Aires. Especially in the area adjacent to the Fifth Road, insecurity is pervasive among the inhabitants. Drugs are contaminating the space of the neighborhood, terrifying and humiliating residents, and casting their own future into doubt.

Drug dealers and addicts constitute a tiny minority of the population, but they have managed to degrade the tone of public life in the shantytown. As the residents put it:

> The problem here is drugs. . . . This has to be combatted . . . because dealers are killing the children. (Lucho)

> This is terrible. . . . On the corner, many children get together, and they smoke . . . weird things. . . . You can't take your children to the sidewalk because of the smell. And at night it is terrible; they fire their guns at the police. (Adela)

> There are a lot of drugs, insecurity. . . . Sometimes you laugh at the things that happen here. The other day I saw a guy running with a pig on his shoulders. They were trying to catch him. . . . It was tragi-comic. (Juan)

> You can't allow your children to play on the sidewalk because everyone is smoking marijuana, doing drugs. (Victoria)

> There are a lot of children who have been stealing since they were five or six. . . . They act as lookouts, who tell the others if the police come. (Josefina)

Drug trafficking and various addictions (mainly alcohol, marijuana, and cocaine) are devastating the lives of the shantytown dwellers. Their feelings about dealers and buyers point up not only the insecurity they feel, their fear of being mugged or assaulted, but also the abandonment and the impotence they experience. Violence is becoming, to quote Elias, an "unavoidable and everyday event," pervading "the whole atmosphere of this unpredictable and insecure life" (1994, 448–49). The state is viewed as unable to solve the problem; it is also viewed as conspiring with the dealers:

You can't trust the police. (Juan)

No one cares if you denounce people selling drugs. . . . I cannot say that it is true, but I heard that the councilwoman knows about the drug problem and doesn't do anything about it. A neighbor of mine sells drugs, and he is with the famous Matilde's Band. (Adela)

Most people are afraid to complain about the drug deals going down or see no point in denouncing dealers because the police *and* state officials "are with them." Others, like the president of the local council of the nearby neighborhood, are ready to launch their own private war against them: "I've been telling people about this idea I have. . . . If we burn the house of one of the dealers, you will see that nobody else will dare to do it." But the generalized feeling is one of fatality, a mix of anger toward and pity for streetcorner youngsters:

Everybody knows where it [drugs] is sold, but no one dares to come between that. . . . One thinks about the punishment. . . . They have killed [*reventado*] a lot of people because of drugs. (Susy)

I don't denounce them because if they find out that I am the one who is accusing them . . . you know . . . I have children, I don't want to risk my family. . . . You can't do anything about drugs because you are afraid for your children's lives. . . . No one wants to risk their own children. (Victoria)

Here in the alleyway, there is a woman who was badly hurt, and she doesn't want to denounce them because she is afraid. . . . She has two daughters. . . . And the guy who hurt her walked in and out of the alleyway. (Alejandra)

We are not going to have any future if we don't lend a hand to the children. . . . They do drugs as if they were eating a candy. When you are cleaning the alleyway, you find lots of [hypodermic] needles. . . . They do drugs everywhere, there is no respect. . . . Sometimes you feel anger because you are helpless, you can't do anything. Because if their parents don't do anything, maybe we go to help them, and they kick our ass. (Monica)

Most of those living close to the Fifth Road know that there are at least five locales for retail narcotics distribution on the block near the local school. Occasionally, I would step on hypodermic needles near that area. Hugo and Alejandra, both living on the Fifth Road, provide the best summary of the generalized feeling that pervades much of Paraíso: that of being socially isolated, abandoned by the state, and at the mercy of the drug addicts and dealers who terrorize residents:

> During the weekend this is like the Wild West, there are a lot of shots. . . . At night you can't sleep.

> The guy next door sells drugs. You can't denounce him anywhere because he might rob you or, even worse, hurt you. Every night they are smoking pot or shooting right behind my window. . . . We are cursed.

With the increasing marginalization, the challenge for the (ex-)proletarian families living in Villa Paraíso is not, as it used to be twenty or thirty years ago, to improve their homes and their environment but to survive. As a result, their lives are permeated by a feeling of fatality, pessimism, gloom. The future—once seen as ever brighter as one more street was paved, one more alleyway lit—is now dim, obscure; it is limited to tomorrow or, even worse, as Chango (a young dweller from a nearby shantytown) puts it, quoting the lyrics of a popular rock song, "The future is already here." First just a transitory residence, then a place where improvements were possible—a "shantytown of hope," to paraphrase Eckstein (1990b)—Paraíso is now desolate, a space of despair, of social immobility, and of pervasive physical and social insecurity. In this context, the images of the Bronx (referred at the opening of this chapter) and the Wild West (global bywords for destitution, violence, and isolation) are the residents' ways of expressing the fact that "paradise" is becoming hell.

Future Tasks: Other Place, Other Problems

In this chapter, I have reconstructed the history of the shantytown in terms of the changing ways in which its dwellers have solved their major problems, stressing the continuous interplay between the various levels of government and the residents (individually or through their organizations). Only someone deaf to the hundreds of stories and anecdotes recounting how difficult life was in the early days of the shantytown, someone blind to the images of the debris-ridden swamp portrayed in the film *Detrás de un largo muro,* can fail to see that the shantytown is now in much better shape than it was in the past. Although there are still structural problems to be solved (the most important ones being overcrowding and the lack of an adequate waterworks and sewage system), there is no doubt whatsoever that Paraíso has changed radically.

In the past, life was hard, but people had jobs and were able to feed their families, send their children to school, improve their living conditions.[22] Certainly, delinquents hid out in Paraíso, but they did not terrorize it; in fact, they are remembered as "protecting" the residents against outsiders, "criminals." And, when faced with a problem, the residents organized to get something done about it—successfully, as evinced by the paved roads, the health center, and the lit streets.

But times have changed and, with them, the problems. The fully employed worker is the exception rather than the rule. And unemployed and underemployed people have incomes inadequate to meet the challenges of survival. Networks of reciprocal help—the safety net of the unemployed—are still important, but their resources are depleted. Social security—traditionally tied to employment—is of little help. In short, people are finding it increasingly difficult to obtain the food and medicine that they need.

How are the residents of Villa Paraíso dealing with these problems?[23] There is no one answer to this question. The next chapter will explore some of the most significant ways in which the shantytown dwellers obtain the necessities of life in the absence of a reliable source of cash income. In it, I pay special attention to the functioning of an emerging network, one that puts those with problems in direct contact with problem solvers on the grassroots committees (the UBS) of the Peronist Party.

CHAPTER THREE

"They Knew Matilde"

The Problem-Solving Network

The task consists in grasping a hidden reality which veils itself by unveiling itself, which offers itself to observers only in the anecdotal form of the interaction that conceals it. —Pierre Bourdieu, *Language and Symbolic Power*

Children's Day, a traditional holiday in Argentina, is celebrated every year on the first Sunday in August. This year, Councilwoman Matilde and her followers are organizing three different public gatherings in different areas of Villa Paraíso to celebrate the Día del Niño. It is 10:00 A.M. when Matilde, Adolfo, Pedro, Paco, and Luis, and Mimi, Brigitte, and Marcela—the big woman and her entourage—arrive at Cholo's Fifth Road UB.

Adolfo came in the municipal station wagon together with Oreja—a member of Matilde's Band—and Patón. Patón is a public employee who works for the undersecretary of public works. He usually drives the truck that brings drinking water to the Fifth Road on a daily basis. As soon as they arrive, Patón and Oreja unload milk bottles, bags full of toys, and two brand-new bicycles. The milk comes from Plan Vida. It is not supposed to be used for political purposes; at least, that is what "Chiche" Duhalde—the governor's wife and director of the program—repeatedly asserts. Yet preparing hot chocolate for the children of Paraíso on "their day" is a "good cause"—as Matilde tells me—noble enough to divert public resources for political use.

The same private utilization of public resources applies to the use of the station wagon. On the back of the vehicle a legend reads: "This unit was bought with money that you have paid. In the service of the people." A local newspaper recently denounced the use of this same station wagon by a group of youngsters involved in campaigning against a councilman of the Radical Party (the main opposition party in Cóspito). After describing what it called the "dubious activities" of this group of youngsters, the report ended with a rhetorical question: "At the service of which people?" (*La Defensa,* 9 October 1996, 2). The group is well known in Villa Paraíso as Matilde's Band—a group of nearly seventy adolescents and youngsters who accompany Matilde to every political rally, playing their drums and carrying banners with Matilde's and Rolo's names on them. The group is also in charge of political propaganda for Matilde: members paint political graffiti and hang banners. Pedro—one of Matilde's sons—is the one who "directs and pays them." As one of the members of the band told me: "He is in charge of the dirty work." The day before Children's Day, I heard Matilde telling Pedro: "On that wall, where the name of Pedele is painted . . . I want my name there." That same night, Pedro drove members of the band to that spot in that municipal truck, where they inscribed on the wall: "Forever with Rolo. Matilde's Band."

Pedro is also in charge of the distribution of wine, cigarettes, and marijuana to band members; he prepares the barbecue (the traditional *asado*) after every public rally that the band attends and also after one of their "propaganda raids."[1]

Every month, Cholo receives powdered milk from Plan Materno-Infantil to be distributed among pregnant women and children aged one through five living in what he calls "his area."[2] He also obtains packages of food (noodles, rice, *yerba mate,* polenta, etc.) and medicine (pain relievers, aspirins, antibiotics, etc.) from Matilde once a month. He receives extra food packages every time there is a political rally. The two bicycles that Matilde brought with her are the prizes in a raffle that Cholo and Matilde will organize later that day among the participants in "their Children's Day." Matilde has given Cholo the bicycles and other toys (soccer balls, dolls, etc.) to be raffled off among the children of the Fifth Road.

In front of Cholo's UB, clowns brought by Matilde perform on a very precarious stage. The stage is ornamented with colorful balloons, balloons that have the face of the mayor stamped on them and two phrases, one attributed to Juan Perón ("The only privileged people are the children"), the other to Rolo Fontana ("Everything for the happiness of a child"). Children's Day is a good occasion on which to overlook these "insignificant" confusions between party politics and state activities. Everything can be done for the happiness of a child: stamping your face on the balloons with which they play, diverting resources from state-funded programs, mixing party politics with official responsibilities.

Later, on that same stage, Matilde offers a brief but very significant speech. She starts by saying that the mayor could not come to celebrate with them, "but you see him every day, so it's not a big problem." In order to celebrate Children's Day, she says that "people should get together with their families": "We have a custom: we work as a family, for the family, and with the family. . . . As I always tell you: the people, the government, and the intermediate organizations . . . together . . . we will make big things happen."

Later that day, at the southwestern border of Villa Paraíso, Matilde and her whole family meet the mayor at another Children's Day celebration, this one organized by Juana Medina, a Peronist activist of the UB Chacho Peñaloza. This time, Pedele (a Peronist councilman from a nearby district) is funding the gathering (paying for the bicycles to be raffled off and for the band that plays after the mayor gives his speech). Right in front of the portraits of Juan and Eva Perón, the mayor acknowledges Pedele as the moving spirit behind the gathering and says, "This party is organized for the happiness of the children. We are repeating what that great Argentine woman, Eva Perón, did in the past. We carry that great woman in our hearts. . . . The Peronist government is here, working to give more aid to the people, especially now that the situation is quite difficult. . . . We simply have to do what Eva Perón and Juan Perón have done."

It is 2:00 P.M. when we return to Matilde's house after an exhausting day. I am just about to leave when she tells me: "You see? After what you just saw . . . votes will come. I don't have to go and look for them . . . votes will come anyway." She became a councilwoman in the last general election (1995), in which the Peronist Party obtained almost 60 percent of the votes in Villa Paraíso, a striking percentage considering that the party obtained 50.62 percent of the votes in the Cóspito City mayoral elections.

Matilde is what the literature on political clientelism terms a *broker,* a mediator between the political patron—the mayor—and his supporters, known as *clients.* Whether called *capitulero* (in Peru in the 1930s and 1940s [Stein 1980]), *cabo eleitoral* (in Brazil from the 1930s on [Conniff 1981; Mouzelis 1985; Roniger 1990; see also Gay 1994]), *gestor, padrino político,* or *cacique* (in Mexico at various points in its history [Ugalde 1973; Cornelius 1973; Roniger 1990]), *precinct captain* (in the Chicago political machine and elsewhere in the United States [Kornblum 1974; Guterbock 1980; Katznelson 1981; see also Knoke 1990]), *caudillo barrial* (in the Radical and the Conservative Parties in Argentina in the 1920s [Rock 1975, 1972; Walter 1985; Bitran and Schneider 1991]), or *referente* or *puntero peronista* (in Argentina in the 1990s), brokers the world over function in essentially the same way, as go-betweens.[3] They mediate between their *caudillos, chefes políticos, ward bosses,* and clients. Enjoying the power that comes with their mediating function, brokers are expert manipulators of information and of people, channeling resources from their patron to their clients and votes and support from their clients to the person in control of the (material and symbolic) resources.[4]

In Villa Paraíso, there are five UBS, each controlled by a broker: Medina's UB Chacho Peñaloza, Pisutti's UB The Leader, Andrea's UB Fernando Fontana, Cholo's UB 27 de Abril, and Matilde's UB Three Generations. The UBS are dispersed throughout Paraíso (although Matilde's is located outside the administrative limits of the shantytown, its political/social work targets the shantytown population). Their work extends beyond politics and election times.[5] Many serve as centers from which food and medicine are distributed, and brokers can be approached for small favors all year round. During recent years, these UBS have become the most important sites of survival problem solving.

*

This chapter provides an empirical description of the relevance of the Peronist problem-solving network in the shantytown, of its form, functions, tensions, resources, and effects. It is divided into four main parts. First, I describe the process by which informal networks of survival and political networks become overlapping and locate the notion of brokerage within what I label the *Peronist problem-solving network* in Villa Paraíso (i.e., the web of relations that some residents establish with local political brokers). I argue that, although it is not the only such network, the Peronist problem-solving network has acquired an increasing importance during recent years.

Then I examine the form, functions, and major actors in the Peronist problem-solving network. Matilde's and Pisutti's cliques are significant starting points from which to explore the two basic functions of Peronist problem-solving networks: *resource control* and *information hoarding*. By focusing on "anecdotal interactions" that occurred during my fieldwork, I illustrate these two functions.

Although brokers control similar types of networks and perform similar types of functions, they can be distinguished in terms of their differential access to resources (their source of power) and the cooperation/competition that exists among them. An examination of these distinguishing features will allow us to grasp the dynamism of the world of personalized political mediation.

Next, I consider the workings and the rhetoric of Plan Vida, which embody what I term *the Peronist way* of solving problems among the poor. An examination of the way in which Plan Vida functions reveals the source of brokers' resources. An examination of the discourse surrounding it reveals that, while officially eschewing party politics, Plan Vida and similar state-sponsored assistance programs are profoundly political and personal in nature. Of particular interest is the way in which the women who participate in the program as *manzaneras* (block delegates) evaluate it.[6]

Finally, I propose a hypothesis—that as poor people utilize these problem-solving networks they participate in and reproduce (for the most part unknowingly) a powerful web of political domination. Chapters 4–6 go on to explore the perceptual and behavioral consequences that such networks have for those involved with them.

Surviving in the Shantytown

In contexts of extreme material deprivation and deproletarianization, how do people with little or no income, with no pension or other benefits, manage to obtain the means of subsistence? Is there any institution or person within the shantytown to whom they can resort to obtain help? What contacts do they establish? Who has contacts with whom? What is the content of this relationship? How do the form and the content of the relationship affect the behavior of those involved?

It is hardly a new observation that networks of reciprocal help abound in poor neighborhoods both in Argentina and throughout Latin America. Enzo Mingione (1991) has coined the term *popular economy* to designate the "combination of activities undertaken for direct subsistence and for low monetary income" (p. 87). In Villa Paraíso, these activities include raising animals, selling food in public stalls, the exchange of labor for building and repairs, and subcontracting for industrial work to be done in the home. Family and neighborhood networks "have always made it possible for these various activities to coagulate into a poor but socially protected way of life" (p. 87).[7] In her study of Cerrada del Cóndor, a shantytown in Mexico City, Lomnitz (1975, 1988) also observes that social networks based on residence and kinship function as a surrogate social security system among shantytown dwellers. "Proximate networks of reciprocity with neighbors and kin" (Friedman and Salguero 1988, 11) are thus well-studied elements in our understanding of how people confront the challenge of survival and of what types of relationships they establish in the process.

Informal networks of reciprocity have been thoroughly examined in Latin America, many times as the source of the "survival strategies" developed by the urban and rural poor. Political networks have also been studied in Latin America and all over the world (Conniff 1981; Burgwald 1996; Kornblum 1974; Guterbock 1980; Katznelson 1981; Knoke 1990). Yet the relations between informal networks of reciprocal help and political networks have not been so well explored.[8]

In Villa Paraíso, and in many other poor neighborhoods in the Conurbano Bonaerense, we witness an overlapping of informal networks of survival and political networks: the UBS, political brokers, and state-funded programs have become the sources of resources that circulate within the informal networks of survival. With the withering away of paid work and the subsequent draining of the shantytown economy, informal reciprocal networks are being increasingly relied on. Those who once were able to support temporarily unemployed relatives and friends because they had jobs are now themselves unemployed. With nowhere else to turn, desperate shantytown dwellers resort to the most readily available state agency or Peronist committee or broker. In other words, Villa Paraíso survival strategies are increasingly embedded in political networks.[9]

The expanding relevance of political networks does not mean that networks of reciprocal help have disappeared. In Villa Paraíso, these networks are still central to the survival strategies of the shantytown dwellers. More than 20 percent of those surveyed mention their relatives as sources of help when they need medicine.[10] Many of those interviewed rely on kin and friends whenever they run short of food. Even a superficial observation will attest to the fact that reciprocal favors abound in the shantytown economy. Yet, with the escalation of un- and underemployment, and with the generalization of income reduction, these networks are being progressively drained of resources. With unemployment running rampant (as high as 60 percent in the shantytown), and with those sectors of the economy to which the unskilled population of Villa Paraíso has access plagued by declining wage rates, the lifeline of money income entering the shantytown from the outside world has been severely restricted, and the social economy of the shantytown is no longer able to function as it traditionally has. No longer is the popular economy able to cushion the effects of economic hard times. As in other areas of relegation harboring those living on the margins, "individuals durably excluded from paid employment in neighborhoods of relegation cannot readily rely on collective informal support while they wait for later work which, moreover, may never come" (Wacquant 1996d, 127).

Almost 40 percent of the shantytown population receive food for themselves or for their children from one or more state assistance programs serving Villa Paraíso. These programs (among them Plan Vida, Plan Materno Infantil, Plan Asoma, and Plan Pro-Bienestar) distribute milk, eggs, noodles, cereals, corn oil, polenta, *yerba mate,* lentils, cheese, vegetables, and several other products. Some people also go to the annex of the main municipal building, where, twice a month, the local social welfare secretariat distributes nine food products per person (sugar, rice, flour, noodles, polenta, lentils, corn oil, and *yerba mate*). According to my own survey, nearly half the population of Villa Paraíso knows that food is distributed in the annex of the main municipal building, and 30 percent of those who do know this have gone to obtain the "nine kilos" at least once during the last year.

The *manzaneras,* in charge of the distribution of milk and eggs for Plan Vida, have become well known in Villa Paraíso since the launching of the program in December 1995. Almost 60 percent of the shantytown population surveyed mention the *manzaneras* of Plan Vida as the major distributors of food in Paraíso. The *manzaneras* are also regarded as persons who make an important contribution to the improvement of the living conditions of residents. The Peronist grassroots committees or those in charge of them are also considered "helpful" by a significant portion of the population (16 percent). Some think that the local Catholic church is the most helpful institution (10 percent).

When it comes to obtaining medicine, 21 percent of Paraíso residents rely on relatives, and 20 percent (those who are employed) rely on their *obra social* (work-related benefits). Others have recourse to the local health center (18 percent) or to a grassroots Peronist committee or broker (6 percent).

Attesting to the dramatic deterioration of living conditions in the shantytown, the Catholic church has recently opened a soup kitchen. Nearly ninety children and women eat their lunch every weekday in the church soup kitchen. It is important to note, however, that, as Nora, the person in charge of the soup kitchen and of Caritas, the local Catholic charity, points out, "90 percent of the soup kitchen is funded by the municipality." She also acknowledges that the Welfare Department does not send dairy products, fruit, or vegetables. "If I want to make spaghetti with butter, I have to buy the butter." As we will see later, local brokers attempt to take advantage of these needs to enhance their power.

Caritas is also expanding its activities. Every month, it distributes food and clothing to roughly one hundred families, and it also sells cheap clothing that has been donated. Mariano, the local priest, has received a donation from the Red Cross, and Caritas is now distributing free medicine. Both he and Nora agree that, during the last year, the demand for food and medicine has increased substantially. As Mariano comments, "In Caritas, we use to help some families for limited periods of time, let's say, for three months, until they were able to solve the difficult situation in which they were involved, for example, when they were laid off. But now we simply cannot stop helping them, and there are more people coming, and we are overwhelmed."[11]

Although Caritas does not fully acknowledge its increasing dependence on state resources, it does admit that its own resources are dwindling day by day. As Nora points out, "Here, we are alone because we are not receiving the aid that we use to receive from other nearby parishes. The assistance that we use to obtain from them [other parishes with more resources] is less and less every day."

Both Mariano and Nora concede that the church is not able to keep pace with the increasing demand for aid and point at the local Peronist grassroots committees (UBS) as the source of possible solutions for the extreme scarcity endured by the shantytown dwellers. Both, in turn, also criticize the UBS for the "price" that they say people must pay for their assistance. In the next chapter, I examine the way in which Nora explicitly dissociates herself from the aid that she gives, in sharp contrast to the performances of some Peronist brokers who implicitly associate themselves with the aid given and the favors granted. Here, I examine the distinction that Nora makes between the ways in which the distributive practices of the local Catholic church and those of the Peronist Party are carried out. What she points out also indicates the common conflation between the Peronist Party and the local government, which I analyze further below:

> The difference between us [Caritas] and a UB that hands out food is that we do not ask anybody if that person comes to pray, if he is Catholic; we have to help him because he is a human being. It seems that the municipality pushes a little bit to do politics, to attend rallies, to become a member of the party . . . and if you don't want to, they won't give you anything. "If you come to the rallies, if you are always available to do politics, then we will help you." That's the difference with us. We have a lot of mothers who are evangelical, but we do not question that; we have no reason whatsoever to do it.

"What is your relationship with local Peronist brokers?" I asked Mariano. "It's the same as the one I have with the International Red Cross. I ask [for things, *yo pido*]. If they give me [things] for the people, I accept them. But everybody knows I am not into politics. The church cannot get involved in politics."

Despite the facts that both the Peronist Party and the Catholic church are the main problem-solving institutions in the shantytown and that the latter is increasingly dependent on the Peronist state for its resources, the two are not in competition with each other in the strict sense of the term. On the one hand, the Peronists and the church are seeking out different types of loyalty and competing against other institutions for that loyalty: political parties in the case of the Peronists (especially the centrist Alianza, which is trying to make inroads in the shantytown), the evangelical churches that have been burgeoning in Paraíso as elsewhere during the past decade in the case of the church. On the other hand, from the perspective of the shantytown dwellers, both networks are alternative (but not mutually exclusive) means for making ends meet. As Mariano acknowledges, "I am conscious of the fact that the families that get aid from Caritas also obtain goods at the UB."

In the end, it is the Peronist Party that has the most direct access at all levels—local, provincial, and national—to the resources of the state. In poverty-stricken neighborhoods, squatter settlements, and shantytowns, the UBS constitute one of the most important places in which basic needs can be satisfied, through which basic problems can be solved. The UBS lend incredible organizational strength to the Peronist Party and ensure the party high (and unmatched) levels of territorial penetration. The UBS are the sites in which Peronist brokers are located. As Levitsky points out, the Peronist Party "is deeply entrenched at the base level. . . . Peronism is linked to its mass base through trade unions, neighborhood associations, and soccer clubs. The party is also linked to working and lower class society by means of clientelistic ties to local and neighborhood bosses, who serve as brokers between the municipal and provincial Peronist governments and the mass base" (Levitsky 1996, 20). It is to these UBS and their Peronist brokers that I now turn my attention.

Brokers and Their Network

Goods are used for establishing social relations.
—Mary Douglas, *Purity and Danger*

Quite some time ago, Eric Wolf introduced the idea of the *cultural broker*. Brokers are actors or group of actors "who mediate between community oriented groups and nation oriented groups which operate through national institutions." Brokers "stand guard over the critical junctures and synapses of relationships which connect the local system to the larger whole. Their basic function is to relate community-oriented individuals who want to stabilize or improve their life chances, but who lack economic security and political connections, with nation-oriented individuals who operate primarily in terms of complex cultural forms standardized as national institutions, but whose success in these operations depends on the size and strength of their personal following" (Wolf quoted in Powell 1977, 148).

Although designed and conceived of in relation to peasant societies and very strongly influenced by the idea of separate systems, the notion of brokerage may still be used to highlight the role that brokers fulfill within political parties in urban settings, namely, channeling resources, goods, and services from the party or a particular state structure to a neighborhood through a particular party organization. However, brokerage tends to be less stable in urban than in rural settings.[12]

Brokers, hinge groups, mediators, buffers, all are terms that have emerged from anthropology's and sociology's study of the contact between and interpenetration of peasant and national cultures (Powell 1977). Although the distinction between inside and outside, local and national, now seems problematic, these descriptions of the role of the mediators have the merit of leading us to a central issue concerning the position of the brokers. What is distinctive about them is the amount of *social capital* they have. Social capital (i.e., connections and group memberships) is a central means of distinguishing brokers from their clients.[13]

Brokers (known as *referentes* or *punteros*) usually own or rent a UB. Matilde, Pisutti, Juana Medina, and Rafael Bianco (Cholo) are the legal owners of the places in which their UBs function. Andrea Andrade rents hers. All of them (except Juana) are employed by the municipality and have constructed a network (*una red*) of followers that often dovetails with their UB's geographic catchment area. Like ward bosses in Chicago (Guterbock 1980) and street gangs in major North American cities (Sanchez Jankowski 1991), the *referentes Peronistas* construct and defend a territory over which they claim to be the rulers. "Their people" are in "their territory." Yet, in contrast with gangs and ward bosses, criminal behavior is not the major feature of the *referentes'* rule, at least as far as I am aware.[14]

Certainly, brokers do "favors" for their clients, but they do not work alone. They almost always have an inner circle of followers. These followers are the brokers' "personal satellites," to use Sahlins's (1977, 222) apt expression. The problem-solving network consists of a series of wheels of irregular shape, pivoting around the different brokers. The broker is related to the members of his or her inner circle through *strong ties:* friendship, kinship, or "fictive kinship" (*comadrazgo/compadrazgo*).[15] Both Matilde and Juancito—the two most important and powerful local leaders—have this "effective network" (Epstein 1969) around them, people with whom interactions are more intense and more regular.

Besides her family and her band, Matilde has a circle of men and women who visit her almost weekly. They, like Lucina, who used to be Matilde's cleaning lady, receive medicine from her. Lucina had a stroke and got a pension of $110 from Matilde, who at that time was the secretary of social welfare of the municipality of Cóspito. She suffers from high blood pressure and receives her daily medication from Matilde. Adolfo (Matilde's husband) got Lucina's husband a job at the office of the undersecretariat of public works. Lucina spends almost every afternoon at the Jauretche Cultural Center (of which Matilde's son, Paco, is the president), manufacturing puppets that they either sell or distribute at special occasions at the center (e.g., Children's Day). Lucina and her *comadre,* Antonia, make the puppets with a sewing machine belonging to Plan País.[16] Lucina considers herself a friend of Matilde's. "She always lends you a hand," she told me. She has known Matilde since 1984 and is a *manzanera* of Plan Vida. Matilde also helps her with food.

Brigitte occupies Lucina's place as Matilde's cleaning lady. She is in charge of opening and closing the cultural center and of distributing the medicine and food packages that Matilde brings from the municipality. She also participates in the organization of the rallies together with two of Matilde's sons (Pedro and Paco), distributing T-shirts, cigarettes, and drinks before the rallies. Briggite is also a *manzanera* of Plan Vida. Her grandmother has recently suffered a heart attack. Matilde provides some of the extremely expensive and vital medicine.[17]

Brigitte's mother told me that she hoped that Matilde would soon get a job at the municipality for her daughter. The expectation of a job works as a very important cohesive element within the inner circle. Although not everyone is employed by the municipality, the fact that someone gets a fixed-term contract or a part-time job has an important demonstration effect. If one is patient, sooner or later he or she will be rewarded with a post, too.

Mario got his job at the local health center after participating (for free) in Matilde's band as a drum player. After six months, Matilde offered him the vacant job. He now attends every single rally in which Matilde participates. Mario's wife, Victoria, also participates in Plan Vida as one of the twenty-three *manzaneras* of Villa Paraíso.

Matilde's circle has other circles within it, like Cholo's network. In his words, Cholo "works for Matilde. . . . She coordinates what I have to do." As we saw in the introduction, Matilde provides Cholo's UB with food packages and medicines to be distributed among "his people" in the area adjacent to the Fifth Road. He is what in the local political jargon is called a *puntero*. He is "Matilde's *puntero*," as some neighbors told me. He is also what in Argentina is known as a *ñoqui*, a party activist who collects a paycheck as a ghost employee of the municipality of Cóspito. He holds a fixed-term contract job that must be renewed every three months with the approval of Matilde. She also provided him with the pipes to build the sewage system in his area and promised to send the machines to level the piece of land in front of Cholo's UB. He wants to build a soccer field there so that he can earn $150 a month renting it out.

Cholo notes, "When I started working with Matilde, she told me that the UB should be open every day of the year." To that end, she gave him a key resource: the first public pay phone in the area. People would go to Cholo's UB to use the phone, to look for powdered milk from Plan Materno-Infantil, or to ask for some antibiotics. Now that the newly privatized public telephone company has installed private phones in many dwellings in Paraíso, the public phone is not such an important resource. Yet those who still do not have a phone and those who find their service canceled because they cannot pay the extremely expensive bills resort to "Cholo's phone."[18] Cholo still distributes milk, food, and medicine and opens his UB almost every day of the year. Many residents identify this UB with the municipality. Asking people whether they knew Cholo,

I would often receive the same answer: "Yes, there in the corner, at the municipality."

Cholo is, in Matilde's words, a "key component of the group." He is relatively well known in "his area" and—as we will see in chapter 5—praised by some dwellers as the one who has done the most for the improvement of the shantytown. Cholo also works for Plan Vida. Every morning (except Sundays), Cholo accompanies the Plan Vida truck on its route through Villa Paraíso and the different shantytowns and poor neighborhoods adjacent to it. He and two other men distribute the milk, cereal, and eggs to the block delegates (*manzaneras*) of Plan Vida. He distributes the program's newspaper as well as news concerning the plan (a forthcoming rally at which the governor or the governor's wife will be present) and news related to the Peronist Party (the time at which to meet for a rally, invitations for a barbecue, etc.). He reports any problem a *manzanera* might have (a new member of the program, a dropout, a complaint about shortage of food) to Mimi—Matilde's daughter-in-law—who is the area's program coordinator. For this he earns $50 a week.

In terms of its structure, Pisutti's inner circle is identical to Matilde's. Yet fewer people have close, personal relationships with him; his inner circle is narrower. His family does not participate in his activities as Matilde's family does in hers. Alfonsina got her job at a public school through the intervention of Pisutti, Rosa gets the medicine for her hemoplegy from him, and Marta also obtains her father's medicine from him. As in the case of Matilde's inner circle, these "problem holders" provide problem solvers, like Juancito Pisutti, with services. This inner circle helps the broker solve shantytown dwellers' everyday problems: they are the ones who run the soup kitchens at the broker's UB; they are normally in charge of opening, cleaning, and maintaining the building; they usually announce when the broker is available and spread the news that food is being distributed at the UB or the municipal building. Unlike Matilde, Juancito does not have another UB working for him. His area of influence is much more limited than Matilde's, covering only the four blocks that surround his UB. Spallina, an old friend of Juancito's and a longtime resident of Paraíso, is the one in charge of spreading the news beyond the inner circle. He is a kind of itinerant ambassador of Pisutti's UB.

The potential beneficiaries of the broker's distributive capacities are related to the broker through *weak ties*. They contact the broker when problems arise or when a special favor is needed (a food package, some medicine, a driver's license, the water truck, getting a friend out of jail, etc.), but they do not develop ties of friendship or fictive kinship with brokers. Although they may attend rallies or gatherings organized by the broker or even vote for him or her, an everyday, close, intimate relationship does not develop. In other words, brokers' ties to their inner circles are dense and intense; their ties to others are more sparse and intermittently activated.

The bases for this strong or hot relationship are many. Those who are part of the broker's inner circle have known him or her for quite a long time (usually more than four or five years), and the broker has "lent a hand" — as I was repeatedly told — in times of extreme hardship. In the life stories and interviews that I recorded, most of the members of the inner circle highlighted a foundational favor that inaugurated this long-lasting and "very useful" relationship. Brokers are portrayed as "coming to the rescue" without ulterior motive. With that foundational favor, a relationship of "mutual help" is established. Paraphrasing Durkheim (1984, 173), we may say that the members of the inner circle are linked to the brokers "by ties that extend well beyond the very brief moment when the act of exchange is being accomplished." The foundational transactions develop into ties, which will in turn concatenate into networks.[19]

Controlling Resources and Information

Problem-solving networks are neither frozen, timeless structures nor the intended outcome of a politician's calculated, planned — and often cynical — action. They are the long-term product of regular interactions that, although usually inaugurated by a foundational favor, must be continuously cultivated. It might be the case that, given his current position in the local political game, Juancito does not have much access to resources distributed by the municipality. But he must be available to listen to and support the members of his circle. He does this in his biweekly meetings at his UB.

Like a North American university professor, Juancito has his "office hours" at the UB. He spends most of Wednesday afternoons and Saturday mornings helping the stream of people who show up at his UB. His inner circle is usually there, preparing *mate,* distributing powdered milk, catching up on the news. Juancito will take time to listen to everyone who comes to his UB. Although most of the people come to ask him for something that is out of his reach (jobs), he does tell them when food will be distributed at the annex of the municipal building and the way they should proceed to obtain their "nine kilos." Juancito also uses his contacts at the Hospital Evita or his own *obra social* to obtain medicine in case of emergency.

In one of my first journal entries (December 1995), I was extremely surprised at the resemblance between a UB and a physician's waiting room:

> Today was my first day at Pisutti's UB. At the municipal building, he had told me to go and see him at the UB because the third floor of the municipal building was a "crazy place to talk." After asking some neighbors whether they knew where his UB was located (most of them knew about him), I entered the UB realizing that this was my first time at a UB. I was extremely anxious.
>
> As I entered the UB, I saw approximately ten people sitting and talking in a lively manner to each other. The place was full of portraits of Perón and Evita, Duhalde and Rolo Fontana. Right in front of the entrance Oscar was writing down the names of each new visitor. Mabel was preparing *mate* and offering cookies to everyone. Alejandra and Alfonsina were distributing powdered milk (Plan Materno Infantil). They were in front of a desk that separated the locale in two. Behind them, there was a huge curtain. The space behind the curtain is Pisutti's "office." He was "taking care of" some other people (*atendiendo* was the verb that Alejandra and Alfonsina used when I asked them where Juan was). "He told me to come today," I told them (after giving my name to Oscar). "He is now helping someone else, there are five more persons before you." At that time, Don Mario came out from behind the curtain (from Pisutti's "office"), and I heard Juancito telling him: "Congratulations . . . I heard your granddaughter got married." . . . Alfonsina also greeted Don Mario and said: "Next!" A young woman with her daughter entered into P's office.

Now I realize that I was stupidly nervous about my first encounter with Juancito at the UB (I had already met him very briefly at the municipal building, but today I was supposed to give him a detailed explanation of my work). . . . Much like those who were waiting for Juancito, I also had "a problem to be solved": my doctoral dissertation. Will Juancito (or Matilde) allow me to carry out my fieldwork? Will they "help" me?

Within the Peronist problem-solving network, Peronist brokers function as *gatekeepers,* as go-betweens directing the goods and services coming from the executive branch of the municipal government (the mayor) to the individuals (the clients) who are to receive them. Resources come from the municipality to the UBs, where the brokers have discretionary power over them. The information concerning food distribution at the annex of the municipal building also circulates through the UBs. As Juana from the UB Chacho Peñaloza told me: "Every month, at the party meetings, the mayor informs us [the 140 UBs that usually attend the meeting] of the date when they are going to give out food. . . . We tell our neighbors."

Being employed by the municipality, and being members of the Peronist Party, brokers have the connections that enable them to gain access to knowledge about resource distribution. They enjoy what network analysts call *positional centrality;* their location gives them "access to resources that could be converted to influence over the outcome of political controversies" (Knoke 1990, 130).

Spallina and Cholo (members of Juancito's and Matilde's inner circles) are the agents who spread the word about who has help (and who needs it). Although, in general, neighbors know about the food distribution at the municipality, they are not aware of the precise date on which the distribution will be carried out. Furthermore, they are not always familiar with the ever-changing procedures to obtain the "nine kilos." Brokers do know the dates and have the specially designed cards without which people cannot obtain the food. These cards are small tickets that have numbers on them indicating the date on which food will be distributed. Whether the general population's ignorance is "deliberately created" or "just happens" (Erickson 1996), I do not know. Yet, as the following episode (again from my journal) illustrates, there are some occasions on which brokers intentionally confuse people in order to establish themselves as channels of information between Paraíso and the municipality:

> At the beginning of August 1996, Pisutti gets in touch with the coordinator (Nora) of the soup kitchen that functions in the local Catholic church. He introduces himself as a municipal official who is able to obtain dairy products and vegetables for the better functioning of the soup kitchen. The secretariat of social welfare does not provide the soup kitchen with milk, cheese, or vegetables. Nora tells him that she usually asks Graciela (the social worker at the secretariat of social welfare) if and when the soup kitchen needs anything. Whatever problems they have at the soup kitchen, Nora tells Pisutti, "we get in touch with Graciela." Pisutti tells Nora, "It's exactly the same thing; you can contact me or Graciela." The social worker was indignant about this episode. She believes that "there is a lot of confusion" concerning the place each one [she and Pisutti] should occupy.

This episode depicts the typical movement of Peronist *punteros* or *referentes* pursuing the true nature of brokerage: erecting themselves as *the* channels through which resources flow, *the* facilitators of transactions. It also illustrates the obstacles with which they are confronted. Social workers, nongovernment-organization agents, and other community activists are usually the Peronist brokers' most outspoken opponents.

In any event, the truth is that the "ignorance" is structurally induced. In a context of organizational desertification (where few—if any—neighborhood organizations function properly, and where residents are increasingly isolated from each other), people have few networks through which to get information. In contrast, brokers and their inner circles *do* have access to that helpful and, more often than not, vital information.[20] To the extent that many shantytown dwellers depend on brokers for information and material resources, we can assert that brokers enjoy "positional power" (Knoke 1990, 10).[21] In other words, brokers' power derives from their position within the network and from the position of the network itself within the larger social structure of the shantytown. As I mentioned earlier, the problem-solving network is gaining increasing relevance, spreading within the territory of the shantytown like an oil slick that gradually covers the water.

These functions of gatekeeping and information hoarding are shared

Table 2 Types of Brokers and Ideal Type of a Broker's Trajectory

	Potential (Mimi)	Beginner (Cholo, Andrea, Juana)	Consolidated (Matilde)	Declining (Juancito)
Resources from above	↑	↗	↑	↓
Resources from below	↗	→	↑	↙

Note: → = stable; ↓ = sharply declining; ↗ = moderately increasing; ↙ = moderately decreasing; and ↑ = rapidly increasing.

by many of the different types of brokers in diverse historical and geographic settings. Precinct captains, *capituleros, cabos eleitorales, caudillos,* and *punteros* all partake of the same structural location and function: "A political broker can either obstruct or facilitate the flow of demands, favors, goods and services to or from some constituency" (Carlos and Anderson 1991, 172–73).[22] Yet, although the function of brokers is the same, their power varies. Their control of resources from above (goods and services) determines the amount of resources from below (people) that they control. The next section identifies the four types of Peronist brokers operating in Villa Paraíso. These four types also offer a wonderful illustration of the ideal type of a broker's possible trajectory (see table 2). He or she can be a potential broker or a beginner, a consolidated broker or a declining one

Becoming a Broker

The bigger the faction the greater the renown. . . . Any ambitious man who can gather a following can launch a societal career. —Marshall Sahlins, "Poor Man, Rich Man, Big-Man, Chief"

The fact that, in Villa Paraíso, the five existing brokers are all Peronists and that they all belong to the internal faction of the mayor, Rolo Fontana, does not mean that they do not compete among one another. It is hard to dissect the real source of the rivalries, but we can explore the effect that those rivalries have on the problem-solving network.

Brokers may compete among each other (Pissuti vs. Matilde), work for each other (Cholo for Matilde), or simply collaborate with each other (Andrea and Matilde). Attendance at rallies gives a good illustration of these three possibilities. Followers of Pissuti would never attend a rally with Matilde (and vice versa). Cholo's circle will meet Matilde's followers before a rally and attend together (as we saw in the introduction). The followers of those brokers who collaborate are "free" to choose among the brokers with whom they want to attend rallies.

In this sense, attendance at rallies provides information about individuals' commitments to brokers (and brokers' commitments to their followers). As such, the rally is a *ritual,* in Paige and Paige's sense of the term: an opportunity to declare one's own intentions and evaluate those of others. It is also an opportunity to influence the other players in the field of local politics. The axiom seems to be: "Tell me how many people you move, and I (the mayor) will tell who you are." Thereby, as rituals, and as dramatizations, rallies are "attempts to persuade others, assess others' intentions, gauge public opinion, and manipulate perceptions" (Paige and Paige 1981, 261).

In terms of problem solving, the concentric circles of those brokers who collaborate (or, at least, do not compete) partially overlap one with another. Silvia, part of Andrea's circle, may go to Matilde's UB to ask for medicine or a package of food. And, of course, Cholo's circle of followers is located within Matilde's larger circle.

On the contrary, when the focal points of the network compete on the local political field—as is the case of relations between Matilde and Juancito—there is no overlapping between each circle of followers. As Coca (herself part of Juancito's inner circle) succinctly and wonderfully summarizes: "If you go and ask a favor from Matilde, you cannot go and ask Juancito."

Thus, the relations that brokers maintain with their followers—relations that must be continuously cultivated—are always mediated and, somehow, determined by the relations that brokers sustain with their competitors. They can help their followers "in so far (and only in so far) as they *also* serve themselves while serving others" (Bourdieu 1991, 183). This leads us into a heretofore underexplored dimension of political brokerage, namely, the different types of existing brokers. As we will see in chapter 4, women Peronist brokers carry out their practice with a specific cultural repertoire attached to it: that of *performance.* Yet this is not the only difference that we will find among brokers. Although their structural position is similar, there is a recognizable broker's trajectory that is the source of variation among brokers' capacities. It is worth (re)constructing this trajectory in order not to lose sight of the internal differences among brokers that are extremely important in a world that appears homogeneous only from a distance.

Brokers' capacity to serve their inner circles is contingent on the stage their careers have reached or, what amounts to the same thing, their position in the local political structure. The closer to the center of power (the mayor), the better the access to resources, and the better their followers will be served. In turn, "the better the service," the bigger the faction.[23] Differences among brokers are, thus, a matter not only of the relations between them but also of power. Their power is proportional to the stage their careers have reached and the size of their circle.

Pisutti used to be Paraíso's big man. Formerly secretary of the neighborhood association, he climbed the municipal hierarchy until he reached higher positions in local politics. He was the secretary of neighborhood relations: a key position at the municipal level. Owing to causes that neither he nor his closest followers would disclose, the mayor removed him from this position and appointed him to a new—and politically irrelevant—position: adviser in the social welfare area. This practice seems to be a usual tactic of the "last *caudillo*"—as his closest followers know the mayor. Rolo Fontana would "play chess" with his appointments, and, as soon as someone amassed too much personal power, he would "cut off his head."[24]

Pisutti still has his UB, where he distributes resources from Plan Materno Infantil and hands out food packages from the social welfare secretariat. But his access to state resources has been severely curtailed. In his own words, "You know, those things that politics have. . . . Now we are doing what we can do, we are trying to *preserve our family.*"

In the next chapter, I elaborate on the construction of the broker's inner circle as a "family," a "community." Here, I focus on what Juancito says about the preservation of his own group. As he has limited access to resources from above, his resources from below are diminishing as well. In order to continue to function as a broker, he must maintain some access to both. As the last rally we attended together attests, his attempt is not particularly successful: he was surrounded by no more than ten people (against the four hundred that Matilde mobilized). In the survey that I conducted, his name was hardly mentioned among the "most helpful persons or institutions in the shantytown." Those who did mention him were those living no more than a block away from his UB.

Juana Medina has recently opened her UB in the front part of her house.[25] She named it Chacho Peñaloza after the famous nineteenth-century northwestern *caudillo*. Pedele (a councilman from a nearby city) is becoming another big man in the southern part of the Conurbano Bonaerense. He is trying to make inroads into Cóspito with the intention of becoming either the next mayor or a provincial deputy. Pedele is opening UBs in many poor neighborhoods and shantytowns, and Juana tells me that she has "got in touch with him in the inaugural rally of Menem's presidential campaign."

At that time, Juana had lost her job as a cleaning woman and her husband his as a construction worker. They had recently opened a grocery store in the front part of their house. "But, you know, I had just opened the grocery, and things were not working very well, so I decided to open a UB and see what happened." What happened was that her decision coincided with the ascending career of Pedele. He is now paying Juana's utilities and provides her family with small amounts of cash. Juana is now Pedele's *puntera*.

Juana's resources from above are limited. She distributes powdered milk from Programa Materno Infantil, but she does not have direct access to the food distributed by the secretariat of social welfare (although she knows the exact date of distribution through her participation in party meetings). Although her access to material resources is restricted, "I compensate with other things," she told me. These "other things" involve the organization of short trips for Paraíso residents. Pedele provides her with one or two buses from the nearby municipality of El Mirador, and she gets rolls and sausage at the annex of the municipal building of Cóspito. Once a month, she takes forty to fifty children to a nearby beach resort or to a park. "They are really happy," she told me. "They surely are," I replied, "but isn't it a lot of work, to get the buses and the food and to take care of the children?" In responding, she described — most likely unwittingly — one of the key secrets of the broker's practice:

"It is not so difficult to obtain goods. You have to know how to pull the right strings, knock at the right door. The most important thing is to know the right person."

For the time being, Juana knows the right person (Pedele), and, if he advances in local politics, she will surely have access to more resources. If she is able to mobilize people for her own patron, she will predictably have access to even more goods and more information. What recently happened to her would not occur again: "You know . . . I missed Plan Vida, but I have Plan Materno."

"I missed Plan Vida, but I have Plan Materno"; "I had just opened the grocery, and things were not working very well, so I decided to open a UB"—these anecdotes condense two central aspects of political brokerage: it depends, in a very significant way, on state resources, and it offers an attractive means of social mobility.

Social assistance programs are the booty that brokers attempt to obtain in order to further their careers. Those programs represent the resources from above that they need to solve problems and, in turn, to do politics. *Politics* means "to have your own people," your own faction. The bigger the faction, the greater the renown, as with the Melanesian big man analyzed by Sahlins (1977). The greater the renown, the greater the access to resources. The greater the access to resources, the greater the brokers' capacity to solve problems, and the better their chances of getting a public post (whether elected or appointed). Again, Juana illustrates the point. I asked her if she was expecting a job at the municipality now that she was associated with Pedele (significantly enough, she is the only *puntera* without a public job): "No, not yet. Maybe in [the] 1999 [elections]."

Andrea offers another anecdotal interaction through which we can grasp the broker's particular way of doing politics. We were at her house, and she was waiting for a young man who had asked her for a letter from the mayor. This man had a friend who had recently died of AIDS, and he had no money for the funeral. He was asking Andrea for some help, and she got a letter from the mayor in which he asked the neighborhood's funeral company not to charge him. Another day, she mentioned this example as "her way of doing things." We were at her UB, located in the center of Villa Paraíso, and she was showing me a survey of the shantytown that a nongovernment organization had carried out a year ago:

"They wanted to improve conditions . . . but to do that they want to mobilize a lot of people. . . . That's not the way I do things. . . . I solve better small problems, like the funeral, instead of mobilizing a lot of people and creating false expectations. . . . I prefer to do smaller works, like being able to hand out medicine in the middle of the night." In other words, for the poor, small (and poor) solutions; for their problems, small but personal responses. That seems to be "her own way."

Mimi and Matilde offer further insight into the types and trajectories of political brokers. They incarnate, in an almost ideal-typical form, the potential for becoming a broker (Mimi) and what a neighborhood political broker looks like when she is at the top of her career (Matilde).

In the next section, I explore what makes Mimi a potential broker, namely, being the coordinator of Plan Vida in Villa Paraíso. I examine this recently inaugurated social assistance program, paying particular attention to the government rhetoric surrounding Plan Vida, the way in which the *manzaneras* evaluate the program, and the way in which the plan's network overlaps with the Peronist problem-solving network. As I show, the program turns out to be a wonderful resource base from which Mimi can launch her career as a political broker. Owing to the cultural richness of the performance of Mimi's mother-in-law, I leave the analysis of the consolidated broker to the next chapter.

Plan Vida

For Plan Vida, we organized a meeting at the Catholic church, and we called people from the community, people who were working for the church, neighbors who were interested in the new social program. The manzaneras *emerged from that meeting.* —Mimi

The first meeting of Plan Vida was organized here in the church. It was full of people linked to Matilde and Cholo; they wanted to control the thing. I'm not stupid. . . . I've been ten years in a UB, *and I know that Plan Vida is all about the manipulation of the people.* —Toni

Inspired by the Chilean Plan de Alimentación Complementaria and by the functioning of the Cuban Comités de Defensa de la Revolución, Plan Vida (lit., Life Program; hereafter PV) is the largest food-distribution program currently carried out by the government of the province of

Buenos Aires. A pet project of "Chiche" Duhalde, the governor's wife, it was launched in one of the poorest districts of the Conurbano Bonaerense over two years ago. According to official figures (November 1996), PV reaches thirty-eight districts in Buenos Aires, covering 644 neighborhoods. It is funded by state resources from the Consejo Provincial de la Familia y Desarrollo Humano, which is presided over by Chiche Duhalde. She is also the president of the women's branch of the Peronist Party.

PV distributes milk, cereals, and eggs to almost 500,000 children aged one through six and to pregnant women. These children and women live in neighborhoods that the official poverty map (INDEC 1985) considers areas with "unmet basic needs." The daily distribution of milk and the weekly distribution of cereals and eggs are carried out by block delegates, *manzaneras*. These *manzaneras* receive no monetary remuneration for their work, except a half liter of milk per day and the weekly allowance of eggs and cereal that all the beneficiaries of PV receive. As with many other supplementary feeding programs in Latin America, the plan exemplifies the unequal burden that women are forced to bear in the unpaid maintenance and reproduction of human resources.[26]

In the words of one of the few journalists who has paid attention to this large-scale social program, the *manzaneras* represent "an army of ten thousand women working for free in the largest social program in Argentina" (*Página12*, 30 August 1996, 8). In November 1996, the *manzaneras* already numbered thirteen thousand.

PV has a district coordinator who is employed by the *secretaria de acción social* of their respective municipality. Each district coordinator, in turn, is in charge of a variable number of area coordinators. Mimi coordinates the daily work of twenty-three *manzaneras* in Villa Paraíso.

Chiche Duhalde also directs the soup-kitchen program. This program was designed to equip community soup kitchens and to supply them with food. These soup kitchens are also funded by the Consejo Provincial de la Familia y Desarrollo Humano and coordinated at the district level by an official of the secretariat of social welfare. In Cóspito, the soup kitchens are coordinated by Susana Gutierrez, the mayor's adviser in the secretariat of social welfare. Susana is a consolidated broker in another poor *barrio* of Cóspito (see the next chapter).

In this section, I concentrate on the discursive framework of PV and of the soup-kitchen program, paying particular attention to the words of their director, Chiche Duhalde, and of the officials who ceaselessly propagandize these programs. The key element in this rhetoric is the alleged apolitical nature of these food programs. I then contrast this claim with reality, with the day-to-day operations of both programs.

The official point of view must be taken seriously insofar as it constitutes a distinctive feature of the state as the entity holding the monopoly on symbolic violence. Yet the state-elite's discursive repertoire is a dialogic construction produced in a (sometimes more, sometimes less) contentious historical process. In the last part of this section, I analyze the other side of the official point of view. I examine the evaluations of the *manzaneras* of PV and of some of the beneficiaries in Villa Paraíso. The major claim of these programs (the absolute lack of party favoritism) will thus be contrasted with my own view of the working of the programs and with the (different) views of the *manzaneras*. Although no blatant and direct political manipulation is apparent, I show that the effect of the official rhetoric is much more subtle: the programs are personalized in the figure of the governor and the governor's wife. In the words of one of the PV beneficiaries: "Neither Menem nor the government are involved in the program. This is not a political party thing. . . . This belongs to Chiche" (*Página12,* 30 August 1996, 8).

This section is based on a year-round (1996) reading of the major local newspaper of the southern part of the Conurbano Bonaerense, *La Unión.* The newspaper's political bias in favor of Duhalde's government is obvious, offering an unmatched source for the analysis of the official point of view. Since June 1996, the governor's wife appeared in the pages of *La Unión* at least once every two weeks. Either in interviews or when opening a PV branch in any of the districts of Buenos Aires, Chiche's words were almost always the same. As she repeated time and again the same catchphrases and insisted on exactly the same points, a detailed, week-by-week exposition is not necessary. Instead, I concentrate on her speeches' major points. I also make reference to some published interviews with her and articles about her. The last part of this section draws on in-depth interviews that I carried out with the twenty-three PV *manzaneras* in Villa Paraíso. It also relies on my daily observations of the working of both programs and on my own participation in some rallies inaugurating the PV and the soup-kitchen programs.

"This Has Nothing to Do with Politics": The Official Point of View

Always accompanied with great fanfare, the rallies inaugurating PV branches constitute occasions on which Chiche Duhalde personally meets with the *manzaneras*. In her speeches, Chiche continuously insists on two major issues: that the program should be understood as an expression of the *manzaneras'* effort, solidarity, and love for their disadvantaged and poor neighbors and that the program should not be contaminated by politics.

Chiche constantly remarks on the "sacrifices" made by the *manzaneras* "in their daily struggle for the success of the program." According to her, PV is almost a unique experience in Latin America: there are few precedents for such a strong women's organization carrying out state-funded social programs. The program relies mostly on mothers "who, as they feel so much love for their children, are capable of carrying out the program in a disinterested way" (*La Unión,* 19 October 1996, 16). Chiche regularly highlights the "mysticism" with which the *manzaneras* manifest their solidarity with their neighbors.

Social assistance for the poor is invariably gendered female: women, according to Chiche, are much more creative than men, which enables them to carry out "social work" (*La Unión,* 22 September 1996, 12). Chiche usually urges the *manzaneras* not to "give up." Solidarity, love, affection, and true vocation are presented by Chiche and by the officials in charge of PV as the (feminine) driving forces of the program.

A typical day of a *manzanera* in Villa Paraíso and elsewhere starts around 5:00 A.M., when the PV truck unloads the milk and eggs. Each block delegate will later hand out (usually from 8:00 to 12:00 A.M.) the daily allowance to a variable number of children and pregnant women (in Villa Paraíso, the number of beneficiaries for which each *manzanera* is responsible ranges from 39 to 170). This fatiguing work is "worth the sacrifice," Chiche and government officials repeatedly assert. It is worth the sacrifice because Chiche and the *manzaneras* do "everything for love."[27]

As if to mark the truly arduous (and unpaid) work of the *manzaneras* with poetic symbolism, Peronists associate it with that of Eva Perón. In an article worth quoting at length, a Peronist councilman engages in a supreme act of condescension:[28] "They [the *manzaneras*] are not on the covers of the magazines, but they are beautiful women who have given a new impulse to social work. . . . They are the authentic inheritors of

Evita: they carry Eva's voice in each of their words and Eva's eyes in each of their glances. They know that the road to social justice is conquered by generosity, a generosity typical of those who are ready to give up their soul for a more dignified life" (*La Unión,* 8 September 1996, 7).

The populist celebration of the efforts of these "humble women" and the personalization of the program in the figure of the governor are clearly demonstrated in the words of the minister of public health. Without specifying whom he is accusing, he says, "They want us to believe that successful women are the ones with perfect figures; they want us to believe that we have to imitate them. But the real successful women are our dark, plump, and short women who work for the others so that they can have their daily food. . . . You are Duhalde's women. . . . You, the Martas, the Juanas, the Marias, and Josefas, will become the women of Duhalde who take Plan Vida to the *barrios*" (*La Unión,* 20 November 1996, 11).

Although perplexing because of their condescension, racism, and sexism, these words are hardly uncommon. They are repeated over and over again in the almost weekly rallies, in the donations that Chiche makes to the soup kitchens (ovens, refrigerators, etc.), in the celebrations inaugurating other social programs (Plan Barrios Bonaerenses, Plan Documentario "Eva Perón").

The official point of view on the social assistance programs insists on the lack of party favoritism or political manipulation. As if to drive the evil spirit of politics away from the social programs that she conducts, Chiche will publicly exhort the *manzaneras* to stay away from politics: "Do not allow anybody from our party [the Peronists] or from any other party to politicize the program because, if that happens, the profound meaning of Plan Vida will be lost. . . . No one should use you" (*La Unión,* 3 December 1996, 11). In a rally in Cóspito City, she warned the *manzaneras:* "We should not allow anyone to politicize the program. . . . No one should think that we do this to obtain votes." Politics should never "infect" the program; politics is an activity alien to the *manzaneras.* They should do social work; we, the politicians, do politics. Politics, in turn, is defined as an action that is foreign to everyday life. By way of defending the plan from charges of political contamination, everyday life should be insulated from politics. As Chiche puts it, "We don't ask you to think in political terms as we do but to think about the children of the neighborhood in which you live and to think that your actions can save many lives."

Although Chiche Duhalde ceaseless criticizes those who "deny food to those who do not share their political ideology," she never names names. "We cannot do politics with this [program] because at stake are those whom we love the most." This obviously implies that there are people who allow politics to affect their work. Yet she will never make explicit reference to those who, in her words, "take advantage of the *manzaneras*." Her constant public admonitions ("I beg you: do not exchange a bag of food for an affiliation to the party, and denounce those who do that. . . . Do not allow this to continue") are more than mere window dressing. On the one hand, they contain an element of truth: as we will see, the Peronist party uses these as well as many other programs for political purposes. On the other hand, in presenting herself as an impartial juror, Chiche erects herself as the only guarantor of the original "social" (i.e., pure, uncontaminated) intentions of these programs.

There is probably no better way to analyze the claims of political impartiality than to examine the statements made by Chiche and the area coordinators of the program on the occasion of the launching of the program in a new neighborhood. To me, the most obvious question is how *manzaneras* are recruited. The official version highlights the disinterested participation of the community in the selection of the *manzaneras*. Mimi told me that, "for Plan Vida [in Paraíso], we organized a meeting at the Catholic church, and we called people from the community, people who were working for the church, residents interested in the new social program. The *manzaneras* emerged from that meeting." On a more general level, Chiche will invariably tell the same story: "In order to avoid politicizing Plan Vida, we rely on community institutions like the church, the schools, the neighborhood councils, the health centers. We do so in order to choose a specific type of solidary social worker. This type of woman is going to defend the program without being subject to political fluctuations" (*La Unión*, 22 September 1996, 12). In another interview, she asserts, "Whenever we start to organize social work in a new neighborhood, we look for the support of the community and its organizations. I try to get people involved; I resort to the church, the school, the neighborhood council." She straightforwardly rejects the conflation of party politics and social assistance programs. Explicitly using the term *punteros* (but, again, without naming names), she says that state resources should be channeled through the municipalities and the recognized intermediate organizations (*Revista Semanal–El Día,* 25 August 1996, 4).

Although it is constantly denied in official discourse, in fact PV and the soup-kitchen program *are* "politically contaminated." Like many other community-development programs throughout Latin America, they allow governments to function as political mediators and to exercise control (see, e.g., Graham 1991). The political manipulation is not as blatant as in other contexts, but it is clear that party interests abound in these and other programs.[29]

In November 1996, Chiche came to Cóspito City to donate ovens, refrigerators, and cookware to the forty state-funded soup kitchens. While approximately five hundred people were nervously waiting for *la señora,* I met Rosa. She is in charge of the soup kitchen Unión y Lealtad, and she is the secretary of the UB of the same name. I innocently asked her whether she is the secretary of the soup kitchen or of the UB. "Same thing," she replied. She added that the neighborhood association also operates out of the same place. Although the coordinator of the soup kitchens at the municipal level, Susana Gutierrez, constantly emphasizes that the kitchens are located in private homes or in the offices of the neighborhood council, thirty-three of forty soup kitchens operate out of UBs (Peronist Party offices) or in the private homes of party brokers in the city of Cóspito. Although the area coordinator of PV, Mimi, points out that the *manzaneras* "naturally" emerged from the community, twenty of twenty-three *manzaneras* in Villa Paraíso were recruited by a Peronist Party broker. Almost two-thirds of them are *manzaneras* because Matilde or—what almost amounts to the same thing—Cholo has—in their words—"invited" them to become part of PV.

Most of the meetings between Mimi and the *manzaneras* of Villa Paraíso were held at Matilde's UB. That simple fact should be enough to explode the facade of political impartiality erected by the state. Yet I want to focus on the "truth effects" (Bourdieu 1991) that the official rhetoric has. In stressing the love that inspires the *manzaneras* and the incessant activity of Chiche, and in claiming political impartiality, the official point of view constructs an image of the governor and his wife as the sole guarantors of the programs' success. In other words, the official discourse presents the programs as personal endeavors of the Duhaldes'. In terms of day-to-day operations, it is the area coordinators who actually do all the work for which the Duhaldes claim credit. Given the fact that the area coordinators are in daily contact with the *manzaneras,* PV is potentially a major source of political power. What Juana told me—"I missed Plan Vida, but I have Plan Materno"—thus gains its full significance: PV is a source of resources from above, something extremely useful to someone launching a career as a political broker.

I now turn my attention to the *manzaneras* in order to examine the way in which the official discourse is understood by them. What do they say about the way officials view them? Does the personalization of PV in the figures of the governor and his wife have any effect? Is there open resistance to or hidden agendas behind support for the equation of the Duhaldes with these programs?

Views "from the Middle" and "from Below"

At the time of writing, PV has been distributing milk, eggs, and cereals for more than a year in Villa Paraíso, reaching almost three thousand children and pregnant women.

What immediately catches one's attention in almost every interview is that the *manzaneras* remark how well PV functions. In the risky, degraded, and violent social world of the Paraíso, PV introduces certitude: invariably, the PV truck comes every day. Almost every *manzanera* set PV against the background of the current economic situation: "At least, we know that we will get milk every day" (Marta). "It's not a lot, but it's a relief" (Adela). "It's a real help" (Rosita). "PV is not a means of subsistence, but it's something. It's an aid" (Manuela). Beneficiaries of PV agree: "PV is very good because you save money. Now you know that you don't have to buy rice."

The "help," the "relief," is "sent by Chiche." She is not like politicians who make promises and never make things happen. On the contrary, "she really delivers." Adela and Manuela best summarize the feeling that most *manzaneras* have toward Chiche: "I am very grateful because she really helps people." "I like her humbleness. She treats people very well; she is very simple. You can trust her because she is so humble."

In December 1995, PV was introduced in Villa Paraíso and nearby areas, with an inaugural meeting at the social club of Villa Tamara. Most of the *manzaneras* recall that meeting as a moving experience, furthering the personalization of PV in the figure of the governor's wife. Their answers to my question, What do you remember most about that meeting? are worth quoting at length:

> I remember that Duhalde's wife talked to us, that she was really tender and affectionate. She explained to us what we had to do, and she told us that we were doing this for our neighbors. It was very nice. . . . I really liked what she said. She is a woman who expresses tenderness whenever she speaks, the way in which she talks. (Victoria)

> It was very nice; it was very moving. Just to think that this woman [Chiche] was coming here, that she has so many good ideas. It is so good. Because she did come here. . . . I mean, Duhalde's wife, you know? Her work is really important because no one could have imagined something like this. I really liked what she said. She addressed people like me [and told us] that we have to work hard, without surrendering. (Marta)

> It was really moving to meet Chiche because I had only seen her on TV or in the newspapers, but I hadn't had her so close. It seems to me that she is a person full of tenderness. . . . She is very accessible to people. She doesn't say, "I am at the top, and I look down at everybody." (Aurelia)

> I almost cried when I listened to Duhalde's wife at the launching rally. I saw a lot of love in her persona. She really loves people; it was really touching. (Mabel)

Amalia also remembers the launching rally as a "nice experience." She, Aurelia, and some others recall receiving the badges that identify them as *manzaneras* as something that made them proud. As Aurelia explains, "I don't know if this is tacky or outmoded, but for me carrying the ID of a *manzanera* was really moving; it was a kind of distinction." Others recall the rose that officials gave them as a form of congratulations.

Only a misguided perspective can understand these evaluations to be the result of the "traditional values of dependence" that supposedly pervade popular life and that the *manzaneras* allegedly reproduce. On the contrary, they should be examined within the historical, political, and economic contexts delineated in chapters 1 and 2. These evaluations should be contextualized in the sense of abandonment, social isolation, and fear that pervades Paraíso. In this context, the daily delivery of milk, cereals, and eggs, a caring word, an ID badge, a flower, all make a huge difference. They show that someone cares for them *personally,* that they are not forsaken.

PV constitutes an emerging problem-solving network. Many *manzaneras* remark on the fact that, now, the residents of Paraíso are becoming more "connected." For Adela, PV has formed a sort of "chain, and that chain is growing. When we notice something going on, we pass on the word." In this network, all routes lead to Mimi, the PV coordinator in Villa Paraíso:

> JAVIER AUYERO: What do you do when people come to you with a problem?
>
> MARTA: I urgently look for Mimi. She always says that I make her crazy because I am always trying to find out who is the right person I should contact to solve this or that problem. There are a lot of people who don't know how to manage themselves.

Despite official claims to the contrary, the PV problem-solving network is increasingly overlapping with the Peronist problem-solving network. Not only were most of the *manzaneras* recruited through the party and most of the meetings held at a UB, but PV is being utilized by the local brokers. There is no need to be a network analyst to realize the obvious fact that the big woman in Villa Paraíso and the coordinator of PV in Villa Paraíso are "connected": Matilde is Mimi's mother-in-law. Every single *manzanera* knows this and realizes the potential for problem solving that it represents. It is probably Cristina who best synthesizes the situation. She was telling me that Matilde sometimes distributes food at her UB:

> JAVIER AUYERO: Does Matilde ask you for something in exchange for the food she gives you?
>
> CRISTINA: No, when there are rallies, Matilde invites us. Now that we are in PV she invites us. If it is far away, she gives us a bus. . . . We

are in charge of inviting the people who are in PV, and we bring as many people as we are able.

In all their frankness, Adela and her daughter also acknowledge this overlapping of networks and the way in which the "exchange" is implicit.[30] I was asking them about their involvement with PV:

JAVIER AUYERO: How did you get involved in the program because it seems like a lot of work?

ADELA: Matilde! [*Giggling.*] Mimi told my other daughter [the one who got the job through Matilde]: "Luisa, you and your sister are the *manzaneras.*"

JAVIER AUYERO: Did you know Mimi beforehand?

ADELA'S DAUGHTER: Yes, because we have a good relationship with Matilde, with Mimi, with everybody.

ADELA: [*Laughing.*] She didn't ask us. . . . She just said: "You are gonna do this."

ADELA'S DAUGHTER: We couldn't say no.

ADELA: And so we became *manzaneras.*

JAVIER AUYERO: Why weren't you able to say no?

ADELA: Because it is a good friendship that we have.

ADELA'S DAUGHTER: After a while, I started to like it [being a *manzanera*].

Despite the fact that they were recruited for PV through political brokers and that the meetings are, more often than not, held at a UB, most of the *manzaneras* emphatically deny that the program has anything to do with politics. And, as Victoria, the *manzanera* quoted at the beginning of this section, admits, they all give the credit for PV to Chiche and her husband. Yet there are some dissident voices worth exploring.

After recounting that she almost cried at the inaugural meeting, Mabel added, "Chiche might have a lot of love to give; the problem is that she has to delegate responsibilities." She continues: "Let's be sincere. . . . There's politics in PV. Although Duhalde's wife says there is no politics in PV . . . the program is controlled through politics. There are people from the UBs; the majority of the *manzaneras* are in the program because they have some acquaintance in politics." Toni, the porter of the local church, agrees with her: "The first PV meeting was organized here in the church. It was full of people linked to Matilde and Cholo; they wanted to control the thing. I'm not stupid. . . . I've been ten years in a UB, and I know that PV is all about manipulating the people." Alicia, another *manzanera,* also acknowledges the political aspects of PV: "The one who really benefits from PV is the one who is at the top and who says: 'I arranged for this many *manzaneras.*' They never say, 'These are the people who work for PV.' Instead, they say, 'X has so many *manzaneras,*' and X appears as the first figure. . . . It's a pity, but it's like that . . . politics is always like that. If it were not like that, we would be much better off." For Alicia, the flowers, the diplomas, and the badges that officials give them at the inaugural rallies are not enough: "I can't cook with them." These dissident voices, however, are a minority and, coincidentally, come from those *manzaneras* (three of twenty-three) who are not part of any broker's inner circle.

The political implications of PV can be approached from yet another perspective. Thirty-eight percent of the population of Villa Paraíso say that they would vote for Duhalde if elections were held today. Of the twenty-three *manzaneras,* twenty-one would vote for Duhalde. Most would agree with Silvia, who "really likes Duhalde . . . as a person and as a governor. We haven't had anyone like him. No one has done what he does. We have never seen things like this program [PV]. We receive milk every day, and they are never late. . . . I really trust them." Being a beneficiary of PV also makes a difference in voting patterns: among those who are currently receiving food from PV (38.5 percent of those surveyed between eighteen and sixty years old), 54 percent would vote for a Peronist candidate.

Thus, PV is not only an effective food-distribution program. It is also a problem-solving network that reinforces the political position of the governor and his wife on a daily basis, through an extreme personalization of the material and symbolic benefits conferred. As one journalist put it: "An army of 10,000 women . . . that constitutes an enviable political network for [Duhalde's] presidential ambitions" (*Página12,* 30 August 1996, 8). In addition, it is a network that, contrary to the official discourse, strengthens rather than weakens Peronist political networks. By entrusting the coordination of the program in the area to the big woman's daughter-in-law, PV reinforces an already-present tendency within the problem-solving opportunity structure in Villa Paraíso:

increasingly, all avenues to the solution of survival problems lead to Matilde.

Reconsidering Problem Solving:
Domination through Constellations of Interests

Network *(English): 1.* red, *malla, retículo.*
Red *(Spanish): 1. Net, particularly for fishing and fowling. . . . 5. Snare.* — *The New Revised Velázquez Spanish and English Dictionary*

In order to conclude, I return to two statements (quoted earlier) that Matilde made: "We have a custom: we work as a family, for the family, and with the family." "You see? After what you just saw . . . votes will come. I don't have to go and look for them . . . votes will come anyway." Together, they encapsulate brokers' particular way of doing politics by negating politics.

A Family

Surely without intending it, Matilde directs our attention to the central characteristic of her problem-solving network and others. As feminists have repeatedly noted, families are economic systems, sites of "labor, exchange, calculation, distribution, and exploitation" (Fraser 1989, 120). As far as problem solving is concerned, the "family" is a site of power relations, and brokers' networks are undoubtedly "domination networks" (Knoke 1990).

Weber's (1968) notion of "domination by virtue of a constellation of interests" best captures the nature of problem-solving networks. In particular, his notion of domination "by virtue of a position of monopoly" seems almost purposely designed to understand the effect of problem-solving networks and the significance of brokers' practices within them. According to Weber, this type of domination is "based upon influence derived exclusively from the possession of goods or marketable skills guaranteed in some way and acting upon the conduct of those dominated, who remain, however, formally free and are motivated simply by the pursuit of their own interests." Owing to its monopolistic position in the capital market, any large banking or credit institution can impose its own terms, to its own advantage, for the granting of credit, exercising, in this way, a "dominating influence" on the capital market. "The potential debtors, if they really need the credit, must in their own interest submit to these conditions and must even guarantee this submission by supplying collateral security. The credit banks . . . simply pursue their own interests and realize them best when the dominated persons, acting with formal freedom, rationally pursue their own interests as they are *forced upon them* by *objective circumstances*" (p. 943; emphasis added). Under this type of domination, the dominant party does not directly control the actions of a dominated group; in pursuing its own interests, the dominant party (in this case, the monopoly bankers) has the capacity to constrain or narrow the possibilities open to those it dominates (in this case, the people who need money).[31]

The Peronist Party in Villa Paraíso holds a position similar to that of a large banking institution. Brokers pursue their own political careers, try to accumulate as much political power as they can, and improve their positions in the local political arena. In order to do so, they gather resources and hoard information vital to solving problems: they become problem solvers. Surely, they do not directly command the actions of the poor people with pressing survival needs (what Weber would call "domination by virtue of authority, i.e., power to command and duty to obey").[32] Yet only an approach that focuses on individuals rather than relations can fail to see the structural effects of domination that the position of the Peronist brokers entails. In pursuing their own interests, some brokers gain quasi monopolies over problem solving. In so doing, they increase their capacity to constrain the possibilities of problem holders.

An examination of the relationships that brokers establish with their inner circles reveals an interesting viewpoint on the way in which dominance is established and maintained. By supplying information and goods that appeal to their close followers' self-interest, voluntary compliance is secured at low cost. Power is, in this sense, economical. Yet the expectation of a benefit (say, a public post) is also present in the relationship. The velvet glove of "sweet reason" (Knoke 1990) always covers the iron fist of the brokers' authority. In this sense, Peronist problem-solving networks resemble (in a way that I could not quite fathom at the beginning of my fieldwork) the classic urban party machines. Both are "systems of domination, relying on both rewards and punishments to keep their entourages in line" (Knoke 1990, 4). In the act of getting help, problem holders become increasingly ensnared within the Peronist web.

Expecting Votes

As Matilde implies, brokers do favors for and stay in constant touch with shantytown residents in order to generate political support. Much like the members of the Chicago ward club studied by Guterbock (1980), Peronist brokers believe in the exchange models of political support. Most of their actions—doing favors, transmitting information, "trying to preserve the family"—are guided by that belief. As Guterbock asserts, the "material exchange model" explains the support that the political machine receives in the following terms: party agents generate a network of obligations through their service activities; people are said to repay these obligations by voting as they are told. In this model, the voter-broker relationship is face-to-face but mainly utilitarian and limited in its functional scope. According to the material exchange model, the machine supporter is "materially motivated and responds to material incentives." On the contrary, according to the "affectual exchange model," the relationship between voter and broker is "face-to-face, personal, affective, and functionally diffuse." Political brokers do offer incentives in exchange for votes, but these incentives are of a different kind. As Guterbock explains, "The specific incentives that the party's agents offer in exchange for votes are 'solidary' rather than material and the distribution of favors is but a mechanism by which personal attachments can be developed and maintained" (Guterbock 1980, 7, 8).

Yet brokers do not explicitly announce that their favors, goods, and information are offered on a quid pro quo basis. On the contrary, as we saw, they constantly deny the political content of their actions. As we will see in the next chapter, this negation comes together with a presentation of the broker's self: a public performance. Matilde's and Pisutti's familistic rhetoric and Andrea's rejection of "grand solutions" (and her firm defense of "small answers" to problems) lead us in a heretofore unexplored dimension of political problem solving. Not only do brokers exercise domination by virtue of their structural position, increasingly monopolizing access to resources and information (solutions); they also propose (and attempt to inculcate) a cultural definition of the way in which to handle problems.

Throughout this chapter, I have explored the social context and the ongoing series of transactions and ties in and through which some poor shantytown dwellers solve their everyday life problems. I have paid particular attention to the form and functions common to the Peronist problem-solving cliques; I have also explored the different types of existing brokers in terms of their access to resources (i.e., power) and their interactions. I chose to examine Plan Vida, not simply because it synthesizes the personalized Peronist way of solving problems among the poor, but also because it clearly illustrates the source of the broker's resources and the increasing overlapping of party and state networks.

The structure of relations among brokers, "clients," inner circles, and state officials and the location of individual actors in the network form the basis for an exploration of their behaviors, perceptions, and attitudes. Through a serious examination of the brokers' public performances, chapter 4 explores the sociocultural definitions of problem solving that brokers propose. Through a detailed (re)construction of problem-holders' points of view, chapter 5 examines the ways in which these cultural definitions are either accepted or challenged. Chapter 6, in turn, explores the consequences that relations between brokers and problem holders have for the memory of Peronism that the latter hold.

CHAPTER FOUR

"We Will Fight Forever, We Are Peronists"

Eva Perón as a Public Performance

Introduction

Everything I did, I did out of love for this people. I am not anything because I did something, I am not anything because I renounced anything; I am not anything because I am somebody or have something. All that I have, I have in my heart, it hurts my soul, it hurts my flesh and it burns my nerves, and that is my love for this people and for Perón. And I thank you, my General, for having taught me to know that love and value it. Were the people to ask me for my life, I would give it to them singing, for the happiness of one descamisado *is worth more than my own life.* —Eva Perón, public speech, 17 October 1951

"I gave birth to forty-seven children, and I want to raise them." The "children" to whom Susana Gutierrez is referring are the soup kitchens for children (*comedores infantiles*) that have been feeding the children and adolescents of poverty-stricken neighborhoods in the city of Cóspito for the last four years. Susana was appointed by the mayor as his adviser in the social welfare area of the municipality of Cóspito. She has been in charge of the soup kitchens and other social policy tasks for the last five years. In March 1996, she was to assume the presidency of the women's branch of the Peronist Party of Cóspito.

"I was born with Peronism"—on 24 February 1946, the same day Perón won his first general election—she told me, and she has been active in politics since 1983, always within the faction of the mayor of

Cóspito, Rodolfo Fontana, or "Rolo," the nickname by which every inhabitant of Cóspito knows him. Rolo was mayor from 1973 to 1976, and, after the military dictatorship, he took office again. He has been mayor since 1983; in December 1995, the citizens of Cóspito—some of them at least—were celebrating Rolo's fifth consecutive term in office. "Come and Celebrate with Rolo, Master of Mayors!" the banner trailing the airplane flying over Cóspito and nearby cities announced.

"My passion is the people," Matilde told me on a hot afternoon in Villa Herrera as we were walking toward her UB. "I take care of them as if they were my own children." "They" are the youngsters who spend the afternoon at her UB. They are part of "Matilde's Band," the band that accompanies every public political function she attends. With their drums, the roughly seventy musicians announce Matilde's presence at each public meeting. Together with the "other three hundred that I usually mobilize," the band allows Matilde to make numbers visible at each *acto peronista,* one of the most pure, the most elementary forms of political objectification.

As I mentioned in the previous chapter, Matilde was the press secretary of the Peronist Party of Cóspito in the 1980s and is now the women's secretary of the Peronist Party there. She was also director of the "social action" division of the municipality of Cóspito and is now an elected councilwoman. Her father was an active member of the Peronist Party. She too was born in 1946, "Peronist from the crib . . . born in the house of a [Peronist] activist."

Insignificant as it might appear at this point, both Matilde and Susana have bleached blonde hair and have been involved in social work since they were young. Both were precocious children: early in their lives, they were extirpating "lice from the hair of the poor." Both have been Peronist since birth. Both have known the mayor since birth. Both wear a wristwatch adorned with the image of Eva Perón.

Matilde and Susana are consolidated brokers. They are *referentes peronistas* whose resources from above and from below are rapidly increasing. They are at the peak of their power, becoming the big women of their respective neighborhoods.

The structural location of the brokers within the network, analyzed in the previous chapter, is a necessary starting point for examining their role. Nevertheless, their structural position does not tell us much about the way in which they carry out their practices. In the first part of this chapter, I stress the need to explore the brokers' public presentation in order to examine the way in which the place of the giver and the act of giving interanimate each other in practice.

The second part of the chapter closely examines two women Peronist brokers' performances. Drawing on Goffman and Bourdieu, I explore the way in which brokers foster impressions in their audiences and construct a particular sociodicy of their social place. Being at the peak of their power, consolidated brokers offer an almost ideal-typical incarnation of the Peronist public performance and a vantage point from which to analyze the "lessons" that they attempt to teach about the solution of survival problems.

In the third part, I propose a hypothesis about the meaning of these consolidated brokers' performances. Drawing on Schechner's (1985) idea of performance as "restored behavior," I examine the brokers' presentations of themselves as a restoration of the speeches and acts of one of the founding figures of Peronism: Eva Perón.

Votes for Favors?

Matilde and Susana are mediators between the mayor and his "clients," that is, people who—so part of the literature on political clientelism asserts—support and vote for patrons and brokers *presumably* in exchange for favors, services, and other nonmaterial goods (Roniger 1990). I emphasize the word *presumably* because the presumption is just that: a presumption that votes and loyalty come *because of* goods and services.[1] In the context of Peronism—a social and political movement that has been in and out of state power for the last fifty years and that has been one of the major political actors in Argentina—the question is more problematic still. What guarantees that voters will vote for a given "patron" (read politician) because of the favors performed by him or his inner circle of brokers and not because they support the Peronist Party itself?

A half century of voting studies shows us that this question requires a complex response.[2] In order to take a multidimensional approach to the question and problematize the presumption of clientelist studies,

I focus on the types of relationships established between brokers and voters/supporters/clients. In this chapter, I do so from the standpoint of the broker. In chapter 5, I explore the client's point of view.

As much of the literature on political clientelism suggests (although the subject is inadequately explored), the distribution of goods and services is a necessary, but not the only, condition for the operation of the clientelist world (see Roniger and Günes-Ayata 1994; Eisenstadt 1995; Schmidt et al. 1977; Gellner and Waterbury 1977; and Eisenstadt and Roniger 1984). Because exchanges are, to use E. P. Thompson's phrase, *lived human experiences,* the cluster of beliefs, assumptions, styles, skills, repertoires, and habits encompassing them—explaining and clarifying them, justifying and legitimizing them—is as important as the exchanges themselves. Because things must be distributed in a certain way—with a certain representation attached to them—as both Lévi-Strauss (1963) and Mauss (1967) have taught us—what is being given and how it is being given are facets of political clientelism that, in the case of Peronism, acquire a special relevance.

Although understanding the location of brokers within the relevant networks is central to understanding the structure of the clientelist network, such an understanding does not tell us much about the way in which brokers act, about their practices and their relationships with their clients. My contention is that, through a particular and historically specific type of performance, brokers function as gatekeepers but present themselves to the public—the beneficiaries of their favors and third parties alike—as if they are merely their representatives or disinterested coordinators. This chapter explores a way in which three of the ideal-typical brokerage relations (gatekeeping, representation, and coordination) become articulated in a single practice: the brokers' political performance or, to borrow Goffman's (1959) expression, the presentation of the broker's self in everyday political life.[3]

It is almost impossible empirically to detect the exchange of favors for votes that much of the literature on political clientelism takes for granted, but we can explore a process that might tell us something about how to solve the riddle: the process by which the actors who grant favors and distribute the goods present themselves, justify their function and place, and, last but not least, attempt to teach something to "their" beneficiaries. Peronist brokers strive hard to teach one essential lesson to their public: that no matter how terrible the social situation is, they (the brokers) are the only ones who can guarantee the flow of goods in the form of social assistance programs. In order not to lose sight of the effect that brokers have on their clients, it is important to view their interactions with their clients in this light. With each problem that they solve for a client, brokers are continually better positioning themselves so that, at election time, they will essentially be able to blackmail their clients, the implied threat being that, if the broker and his or her patron are forced from office, the broker's clients will no longer receive the benefits of the social programs established by the patron and run by the broker. This "blackmail," however, is embedded in a system of representations that masks its true nature, a system that must be explored if the interaction between broker and client is not to be reduced to mere reflex action, the client acting (voting, supporting, demonstrating) automatically in response to a preprogrammed stimulus (the receipt of goods and favors).

Patrons and brokers do not explicitly exchange votes for favors. Rather, they position themselves in such a way that they become synonymous with the goods received, the favors granted. For such "blackmail" to work, however, benefits must be conferred in a certain way; a performance must be enacted that publicly represents the thing given or the favor granted, not as a bribe, but as a gift bestowed because of a great love for the people, because of one's duty as a good *referente,* because it is what Evita would have done, because it is what a good Peronist does. Thus, clientelist practices must be understood, not simply as the exchange of goods and services for votes, but also as performance.

Drawing inspiration from Erving Goffman and Diana Taylor, I understand performance to be the set of practices through which actors present themselves and their activity in public interactions that serve to influence any of the other participants in the interaction. Although, in my definition, a performance need not have artistic aspirations, it must have an origin in order to distinguish it from other sorts of patterned actions taking place in public space. A performance seeks a reinvention/restoration of a past that is recognized—by the observer—as the source of the performance. Thus, through this broad concept of performance, we are able to "explore numerous manifestations of 'dramatic' behavior in the public sphere which tend to drop out of more traditional approaches to theater" (Taylor and Villegas 1994, 13) and to examine the perpetuation and/or reinvention of cultural traditions.[4] Performance is here understood neither as being in opposition to "reality" nor as implying artificiality: "More in keeping with its etymological origins, performance suggests a *carrying through*, actualizing, making something happen" (Taylor and Villegas 1994, 276). What is the reality that Peronist brokers bring about each time they grant a favor, each time they hand out a food package or medicine? Which tradition are they reinventing?

In the Theater

Matilde and Susana are the presidents of two UBs. Matilde owns a UB in Villa Herrera, but her area of influence extends to Villa Paraíso, Villa Edace, and Barrio Pomo. Susana is the president of the UB Cuca Gutierrez in Villa Edace. As has been mentioned, both work for the municipality of Cóspito—Susana in the welfare section, and Matilde in the Consejo Deliberante. Susana is in charge of the special program of soup kitchens for children, kitchens located in poverty-stricken neighborhoods that every weekday of the year prepare lunch for a variable number of children (ranging from twenty to fifty per soup kitchen).

Susana is responsible for securing the food and fuel for cooking, for supervising the kitchens and making sure that they are safe to cook in, and for deciding whether to close a kitchen if problems arise there. It is to her that the coordinators of the kitchens (all women) come when problems occur, from personal problems between the women coordinating the activities, to a shortage of provisions, to demands to feed more people. Susana has a team of female social workers assisting her in her work.

People come to see her not just because of the kitchens. People drop by—there is no secretary to control access to her—to ask for various types of things: to obtain a scholarship to summer camp for their children, to have a ticket fixed, to ask for a job, and, most often, to ask for food and medicine. And she always seems to be available.

Some mornings, Susana is occupied with another task. She moves to the annex of the municipal building, where, twice a month, food is distributed directly to anyone who asks for it; all that is required is that petitioners show identification attesting to the fact that they live in the city of Cóspito. Bags in hand, people wait for hours in a line that is two blocks long to receive nine items (sugar, rice, flour, *yerba mate,* noodles, polenta, lentils, corn oil). In front of the distribution center is a gate at which Susana stands. She is the first municipal official with whom people are confronted. While she is not in charge of the distribution of food, she is the one who checks IDs and thereby controls access. Some of the people in line do not have enough money to get back home; Susana will give them money: "See, they don't even have the money to go back," she tells me, her hands opened showing the change she carries with her for such occasions.

How do these people know when food is being distributed? The various Peronist *referentes* know. Susana and Matilde know, and they send people here, where Susana functions literally as the gatekeeper. But, as we will see, she is not the impersonal bureaucrat who specializes in the "production of indifference" typical of Western bureaucracies (Herzfeld 1992). She gives reasons why she is refusing entry.

Every weekday, Susana leaves her office at 2:00 P.M. She returns home to Villa Edace and has lunch. After a short nap, she goes to her UB, where she oversees weaving, food distribution, and one of the forty-seven soup kitchens for which she is responsible. There, once a month, poor children will have their hair cut, and every afternoon Susana will be available to assist people with whatever problems they present.

Although as a councilwoman Matilde is not at this time in charge of any special program at the municipal level, she was the director of the "social action area" for the municipality and was also in charge of a food-distribution program not very different from that with which Susana works.

The residents of Villa Paraíso or Villa Herrera may knock on her door at any time of the day. One of her sons, her husband, or she herself opens the door and listens to this or that demand: a medicine that is too expensive, the lack of drinkable water in the block and hence the need to bring in the municipal water truck. People also ask her for such things as a plot of land on which to build their *casilla* (shack) or a job with the municipality. She listens to them, takes note of their requests, and, if possible, promises to get in touch with them as soon as she finds a solution to the problem. Plots of land or jobs are almost impossible demands for her to fulfill, but food and medicine are things that she can obtain, problems that she can solve.

The (Social) Elimination of Bureaucratic Indifference

Power of any kind must be clothed in effective means of displaying it, and will have different effects depending upon how it is dramatized. —Erving Goffman, *The Presentation of Self in Everyday Life*

As is any other social position or status, brokerage "is not a material thing, to be possessed and then displayed; it is a pattern of appropriate conduct, coherent, embellished, and well articulated. Performed with ease or clumsiness, awareness or not, guile or good faith, it is nonetheless something that must be enacted and portrayed, something that must be realized" (Goffman 1959, 75). When appearing in public, brokers have many motives for trying to control the impression the audience receives of the situation. Here, I explore some of the common techniques of impression management utilized by brokers appearing before an audience (whether their regular clients or me). My interest dovetails with Goffman's central concern when exploring the presentation of the self, namely, "the participant's dramaturgical problems of presenting the activity before others" (p. 15).

"How beautiful you are today, darling!" Susana tells a lady in her fifties who has been waiting for four hours to receive her "nine kilos." Glancing at the picture on his ID, she tells a man in his late seventies, "How young you are in this picture, *abuelo!*" "Oh, look who's here! You finally showed up!" she tells another woman. She seems to know every one of the more than five hundred people who are waiting in line under the hot summer sun. She orders the two men at her back to open the gate: "They can pass; I know them all." She also says no when someone shows up without ID: "The one who sent you should know about this."

The UBS, the third floor of the municipal building, or the annex where food is distributed are the theaters in which Matilde and Susana perform their parts, the places in which their everyday work is conducted and they present themselves and their activities to others, trying to control the impression formed of them.

Those seeking food or favors, the women coordinating the soup kitchens, stray sociologists—all these and many others constitute the audience in front of which the municipal officials and the brokers perform. And, when my presence in the audience went unremarked, the broker's presentation of his or her public self remained remarkably consistent. Only when my presence was recognized, and especially during personal interviews, were certain aspects of the presentation amplified.[5]

What is the "routine"—the predetermined script—followed by brokers when they are granting favors or distributing goods? Six elements central to the presentations of women brokers can be identified: Their work is more to them than just a job; it is a vocation, a mission fueled by a compassion for the poor that was recognized early in life. Their birth coincided with that of Peronism, and their political careers are closely tied to that of the mayor. They have a special relationship with the poor—in terms of mutual obligations, in terms of the love they feel for them—that keeps at bay bureaucratic indifference. Their work is motivated by a "passion for the people." They are willing to sacrifice all and work themselves to exhaustion on behalf of the poor. And, while they claim to be just "one among many," they are at the same time special: because they have a special relationship with the poor, because their work is not a job but something that comes naturally to them, because they are self-sacrificing and hardworking, they are the mothers of the poor.[6]

That the brokers position themselves as the mothers of the poor almost always has the effect of personalizing the favor performed, the good bestowed.[7] But it also has another consequence: the construction of a gendered view of politics and the reproduction of gendered relations within the political arena. The division of political labor is thus gendered. While the actual decision making involved in governing, its formal aspect, is the domain of men, the informal implementation of policies and some of the actual operations of government—solving problems, granting favors, distributing food—are the domain of women.

The Brokers' Sociodicy

Bourdieu and Passeron (1977, 208) assert that school "succeeds, with the ideology of natural 'gifts' and innate 'tastes,' in legitimating the circular reproduction of social hierarchies and educational hierarchies." Constructing an analogy with Weber's (1968, 518–14) notion of theodicy, they term this process *sociodicy,* meaning "the justification of society as it is."

Susana and Matilde claim to bear "natural gifts" and "innate tastes" that justify their position. As do some of the performers analyzed by Goffman, Susana and Matilde foster the impression that they have the ideal motives for doing what they are doing—they were born to do it—and the ideal qualifications. Because these ideal motives and qualifications were instilled at birth, it follows that they present their jobs and their roles as brokers as something that they do "naturally": "I think that people are born to be priests, to be nuns, to be doctors. . . . It seems to me that I was born with a gift, the gift of being able to help the one who is in need, so, if I can do it, I am happy, and I thank God when I go to sleep and when I wake up for being able to help someone" (Susana).

Early in life, they were socially concerned children. "I think that so-cial activity starts when one is a child, when one does a good deed for an old man, or when someone asks you for something and you try to get it," Susana tells me. Matilde comments, "When I first came to Villa Paraíso, I was so blonde, so delicate . . . I didn't match with the environment. I used to sit in my doorway and clean children's noses."

The cleaning motif is always present when they discuss the origins of their work. Cleaning lice from heads, cleaning noses full of mucus, bathing poor children, cleaning the sidewalks full of dust—they were born to clean, born to put things back in their place (to paraphrase Mary Douglas). They were born to clean with passion, as frantic house-wives: "Politics for me is a passion; one has been living in that passion. . . . It is a very great passion, the great fondness I have always had for children. Since I was a teenager, I have always brought [these two pas-sions] together. When I was sixteen years old, in the hairdressing salon, I cleaned and washed them [children]. Hidden from the clients, I even removed lice from their hair because children were my passion. When I came to the neighborhood, I realized that there was a need" (Matilde).

These precocious children were born Peronists and asserted their Peronist identity early in childhood. "I am a Peronist from the crib," Matilde asserts. "I was born on 24 February 1946, so you can imagine":

> I was nine years old when the revolution came [the coup that expelled Perón from power in 1955], and I remember a teacher saying from her

pulpit: "Those delinquents, those *negroes*. . . ." And I remember I was looking at her, and one day I stood up, with my bright eyes, and with my hair, which was as blonde as it is now because it [the blonde color of her hair] is mine [*touching her hair*]; now, as it is gray, I dye it, but it is *mine*. So I stared at the teacher and asked her: "And where were you born? Because, if you work as a teacher, I am sure you are not rich." Then I told my classmates, "Let's sing the Peronist march!" and we sang the Peronist march. From that day on, I told myself that I was going to be a Peronist militant.

Oral histories do not necessarily reveal behavior patterns (Passerini 1987). I am not concerned here with whether this anecdote is true (whatever that might mean). When we are confronted with a narrative, it is the tension between forms of behavior and mental patterns that should draw our attention. What Matilde is saying is that she was born a Peronist, that she was born to lead, in one way or another, and that she was born to defend the poor (personified in the *delinquents* and *negroes*). Hers is an anecdote that matters, not because of what it tells us about the precociousness of her political attitude, but because of what it tells us about the way in which she presents herself to the public: a "born Peronist," a "born leader." Paradoxical as it might seem, what we confront in this anecdote is the performance of an essentialism that serves the purpose of encoding a particular sociodicy. Thus, it is the sociodicy inherent to the anecdote that should draw our attention.

"Gradually, I began to love this place [Villa Paraíso and Villa Herrera], with those children who broke my heart," Matilde tells me when referring to the moment she arrived in Villa Paraíso. "I used to clean their noses, play marbles with them. . . . This is how I am, my persona, not my post." The love for children is the basis — the founding feeling — of both Matilde's and Susana's political careers. In loving the children of their neighborhoods, they started to become what they are now: the mothers of the poor.

Not only were they "born Peronists" and "born activists," but they have also known Rolo Fontana, the mayor, the leader of the Peronist Party of Cóspito City, and — as Susana openly says — the "last *caudillo*," since they were born: "I am related to Rolo . . . my sister is married to his nephew. She started to date him when she was thirteen. She is now fifty-one, and I am fifty . . . so you can see how long [Rolo and I have] known each other. We are even part of the same family." Matilde has known Rolo "since I was born . . . he is younger than my father." Later in the interview, Matilde identifies herself with both Rolo and Peronism:

[Rolo] walks throughout the neighborhoods, from neighbor to neighbor, he goes alone, only with his chauffeur. Saturdays, Sundays . . . the residents got used to that . . . because they have Rolo at hand, as they have Matilde. People stop him in the street, and he gives them a card. Maybe he cannot solve their problems, but he listens to them. He is *from our school, the Peronist school, the school of Perón and Evita,* and that is what many politicians lack, it doesn't matter the political party to which they belong. The people need the people; there lies the secret. (my emphasis)

It is part of the broker's public presentation to display the closeness that she has with the "last *caudillo.*" She was there, near him, from the beginning, collaborating with Rolo, the leader, the man.

Like Matilde, Susana associates her practice with love, and, in the same move, she links her activity with that of Eva Perón:

When the *compañeras* ask me when I will take office in the women's secretary of the [Peronist] Party, I feel really happy because I receive so much affection, so much love from them, but I also tell them: Evita was not only Argentine, Evita was worldly, a woman who represented all women, mostly because of the way she carried out "social aid." And not everybody loved her; some people hated her. I do not claim that everybody loves me . . . but at least the majority — and thank God I have a majority . . . they love me.

Since they were Peronist from birth, precocious "social workers," and part of the *caudillo's* inner circle from the beginning of their careers, it follows that their political trajectory was a smooth, almost natural progression toward the posts they now occupy, the quintessential element of any sociodicy. In the production of the impression of a "sacred compatibility" (to borrow Goffman's apt expression) between them and their positions, deals, negotiations, and difficulties are ruled out: "I was so used to political activism because I was always very close to my father,

I felt obliged to continue his struggle. I never thought I was going to occupy any public position. I didn't do it [work in politics] with that objective. I did it with the objective of taking part in the struggle" (Matilde).

Matilde previously worked as a hairdresser in the center of Cóspito and also supervised the sale of hair-care products in the area, overseeing a network of more than three hundred saleswomen all over the city: "[I was] the leader of the area, and that made me aware of the situation of the majority of the people who were doing this [selling products] as a last resource. And I began to penetrate into the needs of the people. That is why, sometimes, everybody says, 'Matilde, Matilde, Matilde.' They recognize me not only because of politics." Her life "has always been [full of] activities for the people" in a way that prevents the emergence of any obstacle to her public recognition: "As I was raised in this environment [a family of politicians], for me it's not so difficult."

Susana also comes from a family of politicians. Modestly, with no special ambitions, she climbed her way up the local political hierarchy: "That is to say, I was born with Peronism . . . my uncles were all activists. But I started to work in politics when I began working with the mayor. . . . I was working socially in a UB, but I never wanted anything. I used to come to see the mayor and tell him, 'I have this for you, this group of women. We are going to come and visit you, but I do not want anything.'"

It would be difficult to find a better description of the logic of accumulation within the local political arena than that provided by the sharp distinction that Matilde and Susana make between *politics* and *social work*. Both started doing social work; politics, they say, is a natural consequence of that. And *that,* as we just saw, was from the very beginning. You get your start in politics by solving people's problems: by granting small favors, you construct your base; you have, in their words, "your own people." With that base, you assure your continued presence as a problem solver, and you start negotiating on behalf of "your people" within the local political arena. "Tell me how many people you have, and we'll see who you are" — that's the axiom.[8]

But this negotiation, this logic of accumulation of political capital (posts) through a maximization of social capital (networks), is never made part of the public presentation of the brokers. On the contrary, theirs has been a smooth path to the top. The narratives of their histories are saturated with stories of people "asking them to stay," "offering them the post." Their presentation of their political trajectory is not a story of sufferings, obstacles to be overcome, and deals to be made, but one of a steady upward movement. It is not that they deny politics, but politics—understood as the need to bargain and to deal—always happens elsewhere. It is a universe foreign to them. Political deals are one of those undercommunicated aspects of impression management.

How, then, do they explain their transition from one position to another? Because "that thing called politics" just happened and "we" took the vacant place. Their public image never includes the displaced, the fired, the defeated. Their post is "theirs," it was "theirs" from the very beginning because they were born Peronists, they were born social workers, and they were born to support the mayor. The sociodicy is complete, and the sacred compatability between them and their position is proof enough against politics. Only they can occupy their post, a post that—as implied in their sayings—"fits" them (and they fit in it). They are there because of their history, they say, thereby presenting—to me and their clients—their particular sociodicy.

The Manipulation of Identity

Because they were born to care for the poor, these women have a special sensitivity that comes from the heart: "When you have affection for what you do, when there is a feeling for the needy, you know that you have to take care of them. Sometimes the things that they ask for are not so important or difficult to obtain. . . . I think that the official starts when the human being is open. It is simple: when they come to me to solve their problems, I take them on as my own problems" (Susana).

Brokers foster the impression that what makes their actions and their relationships with their clients so special is that there is no distance between them and the poor. They are one of them. "I am identified with the *compañeras de base,*" Susana says.

The permanent shift between *I* and *we* as a rhetorical strategy takes full force here: dissolving the problem solver into the mass of problem holders and making her "one of them." "I am like you; we are all *compa-*

ñeras; we are all Peronists." There is something special because "we" are "part of a family," the "great family of the children's soup kitchen," as a speaker announced at the fourth anniversary celebration, which took place in the municipal building. On this occasion, Susana gave a brief speech that is worth recalling: "*Queridas compañeras,* I hope I have humbly fulfilled my obligations to you. I am one among many. I am here side by side with the mayor, the *compañero Rolo,* because he, truly, is the *compañero,* and not the mayor. I wish to thank you all. I am a worker among many. Thanks *chicas,* thanks."

Neither does the mayor distance himself from the people. As we have just seen, Susana considers him (in public discourse at least) as just one *compañero* among many. It is important to note (following De Ipola 1987) that this type of "inclusive interpellation" has been part of Peronist discourse since the beginning. The benefactors position themselves as members of the same group to which the beneficiaries belong.[9]

The fact that he has been mayor for the last fourteen years allows Rolo publicly to present himself as "someone special," as "the master of mayors." "Rolo is unique. He is the last *caudillo,*" Susana told me. He is the quintessential expression of the personalization of politics and of the public misrepresentation of the removal of social and political distance: always available, always present. Rollo is physically, symbolically, and potentially everywhere. His picture hangs on the walls of his functionaries' offices; it is printed on the face of his officials' wristwatches; it is painted on walls throughout the city; it appears on official government proclamations. His voice too is heard everywhere, broadcast from an airplane flying above the city carrying Christmas greetings ("Rolo wishes you a merry Christmas!") and warning of epidemics ("Rolo saves you from cholera!"). He goes places other, "normal" mayors do not: the stories of how Rolo just "suddenly appeared" in a neighborhood are legion.

"When kings journey around the countryside, making appearances, attending fetes, conferring honors, exchanging gifts, or defying rivals," Geertz (1983, 125) claims, they are marking their realm, "like some wolf or tiger spreading his scent through his territory, as almost physically part of them." Matilde and Susana would agree with Geertz: Rolo's mobility is central to his power. Restlessly searching out contact with "the people," Rolo imparts his own "personal touch" on municipal politics. Matilde and Susana copy him closely: "entering into the passageways of the shantytown"; "traversing the different *barrios* on my bicycle." Both know that "getting in touch with the people" is essential to their success.

While the women bring to the job their "spiritual" resources, the men provide the more concrete resources, a down-to-earth practicality and know-how. They also protect the women's stubborn, passionate purity. As Andrea Andrade, president of the UB Fernando Fontana, puts it:

JAVIER AUYERO: What do you like the most about your work?

ANDREA: As an activist, I feel supported by my leader [*mi conductor*], the mayor. . . . He taught me everything I know, and he is still teaching me. He knocks on my door at eight o'clock in the morning to show me a repair that needs to be done in the street and that I haven't taken care of. He takes me to walk through the neighborhood on Sundays. . . . I entered the shantytown's alleyways with him.

JAVIER AUYERO: And what do you dislike?

ANDREA: Those divisions generated by power.

Then there is Matilde's take on the situation:

JAVIER AUYERO: Did you ever face a special difficulty as a woman in politics?

MATILDE: It's always harder for women. I don't realize that because I work with my family. I am constantly guarded; I am always protected, personally protected. My *compañeros* [male comrades] do not dare cross me [*ponerme el pie*] because they know that, with my four sons and my husband, things could turn bad for them. . . . It's difficult to play games with me.

It is important that Rolo visit the different neighborhoods—poor or not—of the city. That is what both Matilde and Susana consider his "personal style," which "we follow": coming into direct contact with the people, with no barriers erected whatsoever. The mayor and his brokers are "close to the people" because they are "part of them," "one among others." They bridge the gap between themselves and the people in a way that surprises even an observer acquainted with the Peronist tradition. Matilde, for example, always interacts with the people in a very "personal" way, as "Rolo would do it":

> See, you cannot always solve their problems, but what people need is someone who listens to them with their heart. . . . People need someone to listen to them . . . and talk to them as if they were your sons and daughters, your people, the one you love, not only as a problem because you are a politician and you have to look for votes. No . . . you have to talk to people as what they are: people. That is to say, my passion is the people, so I take my time to answer to them. . . .
>
> [The thing I like most about what I do] is being with the people. As difficult as it might be, it is what I like the most. It's the essence.
>
> One thing is the passion, and another is the function. You are, or you are not, and today many politicians are professionals. . . . In the past, you were a politician as a natural thing. Today some people take politics as a profession; it seems to be a good business. I don't know . . . because, for me, it's far from being a good business. . . . I am passionate about the people.

One of the things that surprises the observer is the ease with which you can get access to Matilde and Susana. There are no secretaries shielding them, no doors behind which they can escape the public. Her house, Matilde says, is open to everyone who needs to see her. Her office, Susana proudly admits, throws up no obstacles to her presence; she is always available.

Again, what motivates them—they say—is their love of the people: "They [the adolescents who spend their afternoons in her UB] do not have any instructions. [I do not give them any instructions because you] lose what is natural in you, it does not work. . . . You love the people, or you don't love them, and, if you love them, you have to love them, period. With all that that love implies" (Matilde).

When, in 1991, the mayor appointed her advisor to the secretary of social welfare, Susana "did not want to become a functionary": "I wanted to go on working as if I were an employee, with the difference that there was more responsibility. Because the soup kitchens were created and I assumed the coordination of them. I started to coordinate, and I became so enthusiastic about them I took that responsibility as if the soup kitchens were mine and I loved them. So I started to work with the kitchens, where the *compañeras* responded to me wonderfully. We now work closely with each other, and, when something is lacking, they understand the situation." "People love me," Susana remarks. "People love me because they appreciate the way I treat them, the way I talk to them."

Along with the elimination of bureaucratic distance, the "love of the needy" overcomes all political considerations. They are there, they claim, to "serve everyone." Therefore, "the political work starts when someone lends her helping hand to someone else; there is no better way to play politics. Because the people say, 'Go and see Susana; she is a good girl.' No one asks whether Susana is a Peronist, or a Radical, or a Communist. First, you have to be a human being; politics come afterward."

Mothering the Poor

"She is a bitch! [*Es una bruja!*] . . . She has no idea whatsoever what needs to be done . . . and she uses the people." Rosa, a municipal social worker who supervises the workings of the soup kitchens, told me many awful things about Susana's various manipulative tactics. Later that same day, Rosa was present when I interviewed Susana for the first time. Susana began telling me about the personal difficulties and the health problems involved in her work with the soup kitchens, and (impressed by her story) I asked her why she did not take a break:

> SUSANA: Rosa can tell you what happens every time I want to give up the coordination of the soup kitchens. . . .
>
> ROSA: Everyone comes to her and says: "No, Susana, no, don't give up, please! If you are not here, we cannot do anything." That's how it works. She is the only one who can keep the situation under control.

Obviously, Rosa — as she later, and somehow ashamedly, admitted — was playing the part Susana implicitly asked her to play. She could have been fired if, in front of a stranger (even more so a stranger carrying a tape recorder), she alluded to Susana's incompetence and manipulatory behavior. Not only does this anecdote illustrate Rosa's "hidden transcript" (Scott 1990), but, more important for understanding the brokers' symbolic labor, it exemplifies Susana's teamwork. Susana, with the (un-intended) complicity of Rosa, presents one of the key dimensions of the brokers' routine: She herself is vital to the process.

> I direct the *comedores* as I do my own house. . . . The quality of the food is great because I personally taste it.

> When the mayor offered to appoint me as the director of social action, I told him that I did not want the job. He was really angry because he had counted on me. But I said no, not out of arrogance, but because I wanted to be where I could respond to the people. It is difficult be-cause there are some places where everything is "no" and I am good at saying no. And, besides that, I told him, "I gave birth to fifty sons and daughters, the fifty kitchens. I want to keep on raising them."

Probably struck by the Arendtian analogy between political activity and the act of giving birth, I played along with the metaphor and asked Susana: "So, when you were pregnant with those fifty kids, did you know the amount of work that was forthcoming [*sabía en lo que se metía*]?" She was visibly moved:

> I don't think so. I guess I took care of the soup kitchens with the love you give to your children. You know that you have responsibilities, but, at that time, I was not conscious of the amount of work. . . . That's why, when you do things with love, you might end up having five or six kids instead of one. That's what happened to me. I uncon-sciously began to take care of more and more soup kitchens, and, I thank God, all my children are good. I never had a headache because of them, not even serious problems.

The association between the practice of politics and the practice of mothering is openly displayed. Thinking and worrying about the poor are described as maternal feelings. Worrying, in turn, is taken for granted, and expected part of mothering. As Susana emphasizes: "That's why I say that I must be one of those persons who were born with luck . . . because people love me. . . . We women, we are mothers, and we know about the needs; even if the father knows, he is different; he has to go out and be the breadwinner." They thus claim a natural ability to feel for and take care of the poor.

In explaining how her UB works and what the adolescents do there, Matilde remarks, "Unity and base (referring to what the term *unidad básica* means) . . . family. The UB is a temple, is something sacred. You sometimes have to teach them when they do something wrong. . . . Sometimes they get angry at me because I tell them not to drink, but they still come back because I am the only one who says no. . . . At least they have someone who reprimands them and someone who, if need be, will save them. . . . The day of the *acto* [rally] I give money to them to buy a Coke, but they are here every day of the year. They can knock at my door any time, whatever the problem." But this is not something that she does only for the adolescents in her band: "[When people come with problems,] you have to talk to them as if they were your sons or your daughters."[10]

Through incessant performative work, brokers construct their inner circle of followers as a family, a "united, integrated entity which is therefore stable, constant, indifferent to the fluctuation of individual feelings" (Bourdieu 1996a, 20). This "transpersonal person" of the Peronist family is (constructed and performed as) a "world in which the ordinary laws of the economy are suspended, a place of trusting and giving . . . a place where interest, in the narrow sense of the pursuit of equivalence in exchanges, is suspended" (Bourdieu 1996a, 20).

The everyday construction of family imagery is not only a rhetorical endeavor. Matilde establishes ties of fictive kinship with many of her poor clients. At the request of poor women (who are aware of the benefits of having Susana as their *comadre* [lit., comother]), Susana becomes the *madrina* (godmother) of their sons or daughters. In fact, Susana tells me that she has many *ahijados* (godsons), some of them children who frequent the soup kitchens, but she quickly denies any sort of economic or political interest in this fictive kinship tie: "I tell these mothers that the only thing that I can offer them [her godsons] is love and tenderness."

Mothering the poor, like mothering as such, is understood and performed as natural and unchanging. Not only caring for the poor but sustaining the primary emotional ties with them is perceived as a necessary part of the brokers' activity ("You have to listen to them, treat them well," Matilde says, referring to her young followers). They bring their natural maternal instincts with them from the domestic sphere into the realm of "social work." The reproduction of mothering as a constitutive element of the practices of the women brokers in the arena of political problem solving is central to the production and reproduction of gender differences in politics. In other words, men do politics, women do social work; men deal, women remain pure; men decide, women comply.

Women brokers see their public role as based on "traditional" roles: taking care of the household. They legitimize their role in politics by conceiving of it as that of the mother in a house larger than their own: the municipal building. They are *supermadres* (Chaney 1979). They become so in order to function publicly as Peronists.

In front of the gate where people wait to receive food, Susana performs her maternal role. Something that she says clearly conveys the notion that she is the only one capable of doing this job: "If I am not here, everything goes wrong [*Si no estoy aca, se pudre todo*]." Remarkably sensible, she claims to be, as we saw, indispensable, just like a mother.

Although the brokers claim to obtain satisfaction from the act of public mothering, they also—like every "mother"—"suffer" so badly that their own health is always in jeopardy. Solving problems goes hand in hand with making sacrifices. Having to deal continually with other people's problems, the constant availability and abnegation and hard work are reported to cause health problems:

> The three years [that I was the director of "social action"] were very hard. I was so tired, so stressed. It is a mental exhaustion. It's terrible. (Matilde)

> I am like that, you know. . . . It affects your health because twice a year I am in the hospital because my defenses go down, because of this vocation that one feels for what one is doing. (Susana)

The "special" quality of the relation that these women claim to have with the people is amplified by the association with motherhood. All brokers label their own will and their own practice the will and the practice of the people. But Peronist brokers do what they do, not just "in the name of the people," but in the name of *"their* people," *"their* sons," *"their* daughters."

Matilde and Susana lose themselves among the "people" (and they use not the more populist term *pueblo,* which presupposes its opposite, but the softer *la gente*). They become—as Bourdieu would say—"Nothing." And, "because I am capable of becoming Nothing, of abolishing

myself, of forgetting myself, of sacrificing myself, of dedicating myself
. . . I become Everything" (Bourdieu 1991, 211). They claim to be nothing: "I am only one among others. . . . I am what people want me to be."
"I am," Susana and Matilde seem to be saying, "nothing but a representative of my people. Yet those in whose name I speak are everything.
They are, after all, the 'people.'" On this account, Susana and Matilde
are everything; they are synonyms for the people.

Performing Evita

The act of giving itself assumes very solemn forms. . . . The giver affects an exaggerated
modesty. . . . The aim of all this is to display generosity, freedom, and autonomous
action, as well as greatness. Yet, all in all, it is mechanisms of obligation, and even of
obligation through things, that are called into play. —Marcel Mauss, *The Gift*

When I first entered the third floor of the municipal building of Cóspito,
I came across a woman social worker who, on my request, explained the
myriad programs of aid to the poor that the local government was im-
plementing. When I told her that I was writing the social history of Villa
Paraíso, she asserted: "It is impossible to understand what is going on
there without knowing the way in which the neighborhood is politically
crosscut" (the *atravesamiento político*). Then, without further prompting,
she traced the different key positions within the welfare area of the third
floor of the municipal building, pointing out that Susana was the one in
charge of the soup kitchens in Villa Paraíso and elsewhere. I then asked
her to point out Susana, which she did, saying, "The blonde woman
over there, the Evita type of blonde over there." She then proceeded
to imitate Susana's flamboyant style, adding, "All of them [referring to
the women working in the welfare area of the municipality] want to be
Evita."

More than forty years after Eva Perón's death, this statement might
come as a surprise, revealing an idiosyncratic manifestation on the social workers' part or an anachronism typical of people who are "stuck in
the 1940s." The neoliberal policies of the current Peronist government
are said to be eradicating all that was left of populist Peronism. But to
pronounce Peronism dead is not new in Argentine politics. The same
pronouncement was made when Perón was ousted in 1955. Yet unions—

Peronism's backbone and the main mobilizers of the Peronist masses—gave birth to the Peronist Resistance, which eventually returned Perón to power in 1973." A year later, Perón died, and Peronism was again declared dead. In 1989, however, the Peronist Party defiantly returned to power. *Menemismo* does not embody—as many seem to believe—yet another death of Peronism; rather, it represents a third phase in the life of a remarkably resilient party.

It is in the context of this resilience and the persistence of certain cultural elements within Peronism that I read the broker's public presentation. How are we to make sense of the central traits of that presentation? The working hypothesis that I advance is that, through this performance, through this presentation of the self, someone else's practice and image is being restored, re-created, and reinvented. This someone else is Eva Perón. In other words, the woman broker actualizes, re-presents and reinvents Eva. The Eva Perón that they actualize is neither the image encoded in the Black Myth of anti-Peronism, nor the revolutionary Eva of the leftist and guerrilla groups of the 1970s, but the "Lady of Hope." [12]

Once one gets beyond the melodrama, it is clear that the brokers' performances incorporate what Bakhtin (1994, 324) called "another's speech in another's language," the purpose of such appropriation being "to express authorial intentions but in a refracted way." This "other" is Eva Perón. A "mission in their lives," an "early sense of outrage," a "born Peronist," a "vocation for the poor," a special (i.e., maternal) relationship with them: all the elements present in the brokers' public performances are said to have characterized Eva's identity as an intermediary between President Perón and the masses, as a "bridge of love" between Perón and his people. Like the brokers, Eva Perón was a born Peronist. She too claimed to have been born on another founding day of Peronism: 17 October 1945 (the day on which the masses took to the streets of Buenos Aires to demand the freedom of the then Coronel Perón). She too claimed a vocation, a mission in life. In *La razón de mi vida* (Perón 1995), her ghostwritten autobiography, her "past is subsumed under the flat image of what she had then become, and the character of her acts represented as something outside her personality, a 'mission' mysteriously implanted rather than evolved" (Navarro and Fraser 1985, 5).[13]

In that book, Eva—much like Matilde and Susana—talks about an early "sense of outrage against injustice. As far as I can remember the existence of injustice has hurt my soul as if a nail was being driven into it. From every period of my life I retain the memory of some injustice tormenting me and tearing me apart" (quoted in Navarro and Fraser 1985, 5). Her self-portrayal as a home-loving woman and as "one among others" was also a constant discursive strategy: "I am only a woman . . . without any of the merits or defects ascribed to me." "In this great house of the Motherland, I am just like any other woman in any other of the innumerable houses of my people" (Peron 1995, 71, 125). She constantly presented her identity as collective. She *was* the poor, not just a vehicle for their aspirations and needs. Eva incarnated her people; she—like Matilde and Susana and many other Peronist brokers—was one of them. She was all sacrifice and abnegation, stressing her "own martyrdom for the sake of the Peronist cause," and making explicit a "staunch refusal to take any course of action other than that of fatal self-sacrifice" (Taylor 1979, 57). As she publicly announced a year before her death: "I left my dreams by the wayside in order to watch over the dreams of others, I exhausted my physical forces in order to revive the forces of my vanquished brother. My soul knows it, my body has felt it. I now place my soul at the side of the soul of my people. I offer them all my energies so that my body may be a bridge erected toward the happiness of all. Pass it over . . . toward the supreme destiny of the new fatherland" (quoted in Taylor 1979, 58).

According to Taylor (1979, 75), in the myth of the Lady of Hope was constructed an image of an Eva who knew nothing of politics and who "found in social work a sphere for which her womanly intuition and emotional life qualified her perfectly. She dedicated much of this work to children, as would be expected from such an ideally feminine, thus deeply maternal, woman." According to this myth, she "had no sons and daughters of her own; she was mother to the children of Argentina. More than that, she was mother of the nation as a whole, particularly to the common people and the poor and needy of Argentina. It was maternal devotion that motivated her attendance on the poor, her work to raise money for her cause, her conferences with governors of the provinces, and her meetings with labour delegations. In grateful response, popular Peronism dubbed her its Lady of Hope and Good Fairy."

In *La razón de mi vida,* Eva says that she has borne no children because her real children were those whom she protected—the poor, the needy, the helpless, the children—"together with whom she joined in adoration of Perón, their father. Thus, pure, virginal, without sexual desire, she had come the ideal mother" (Navarro and Fraser 1985, 140).

According to the myth of the Lady of Hope, Eva's love for the common people impelled her to embark on a life of "social action." "Social work" was for her not a job but a mission: her mission in life. As she stated, "More than political action, the women's movement needs to carry out social action. Precisely because social action is something which we women carry in our blood" (quoted in Taylor 1979, 90). The devotion that she felt and expressed toward the people was figured publicly as interchangeable with, if not identical to, a motherly devotion. Her feminine nature was conceived of as a source of physical nurturing and of moral guidance. This is exactly what is encoded in the brokers' association of their political practice with mothering: nurturing and moral guidance. They are the ones who "feed" and "guide" the poor—Susana runs the soup kitchens; Matilde treats the neighborhood youngsters as her own children, "saying no, when necessary."

In June 1948, Philip Hamburger reported in the *New Yorker* that the acts of Perón and Evita are based on *love:* "They are constantly, madly, passionately, nationally in love. They conduct their affair with the people quite openly. They are the perfect lovers—generous, kind, and forever thoughtful in matters both great and small" (quoted in Navarro and Fraser 1985, 110). Of the many titles that Evita had (the Lady of Hope, the Mother of the Innocents, the Workers' Plenipotentiary, the Standard-Bearer of the *Descamisados*), the one that she used most was the one that publicly declares her feelings toward "her *descamisados*": the Bridge of Love.[14]

Dissolution in and passion for the masses—that was the key to Eva's public presentation. As she put it: "Life has its real value not when it is lived in a spirit of egoism, just for oneself, but when one surrenders oneself, completely and fanatically, to an ideal that has more value than life itself. I say yes, I am fanatically for Perón and the *descamisados* of the nation" (quoted in Navarro and Fraser 1985, 113). Rhetorically, at least, she allowed no distance to separate her from "her people." According to Taylor (1979, 41), one of the most enduring traditions associated with the image of the "young blonde woman who received homage and dispensed favors seated at her desk" is that of the "stream of the innumerable poor with their individual problems."

Many other elements of Eva Perón's public image can be found incorporated in those of Susana and Matilde. Solving problems and making sacrifices go hand in hand: "In the world of the Peronist myth [Eva] willingly and even happily undertakes abnegation and sacrifice, recognizing this as the only way to her true self-fulfillment" (Taylor 1979, 95; see also Caimari 1995, 229). Their work (solving problems) is untainted by politics. As Evita used to say, "I will never do politics" (quoted in Bianchi and Sanchis 1988, 72). Their work (problem solving) is performed in collaboration with and under the guidance of a male leader. As Eva put it, "We are only collaborators of General Perón. . . . Being a collaborator of the leader means to renounce to oneself in order to follow the example and the teachings of General Perón" (quoted in Bianchi and Sanchis 1988, 72, 73).[15]

Eva Perón's deeds, her public pronouncements, her image, and the different myths that surrounded and constructed her define the *Peronist woman.* The "authentic" Peronist woman, she used to say, "is the one who lives in the *pueblo* and who everyday creates a little bit of *pueblo*" (Perón 1995, 94). In performing Evita, Matilde and Susana demonstrate that they are authentic Peronists.

The main characteristic of a performance is, according to Schechner (1985, 36), the "restoration of behavior." In fact, *performance* means exactly that: "never for the first time." It means "for the second to the *n*th time. Performance is 'twice-behaved behavior.'" The source of the "restored behavior" may be lost, ignored, contradicted, or—as is the case here—reinvented "even while this truth or source is apparently being honored and observed" (Schechner 1985, 35). Who is the Eva that is being constructed in brokers' practices? The Eva who helps the poor, not the incendiary Eva. The "distributive" Eva, the one who erects a "bridge of love" between Perón and the poor. It is not an antagonist Eva; it is the self-sacrificing martyr. It is the woman who loves her children, the poor, not the woman who points to the causes of their deprivation. In this way, the performance and the original turn into each other, modify each other, and construct a new original.

In Susana and Matilde's public performances is incarnated the authentic Peronist woman. As actors, they personify Peronist values, the

Peronist conception of women in politics: self-sacrificing, hardworking, sensitive, assertive, and, last but hardly least, maternal. We can therefore consider these performances as ceremonies, "an expressive rejuvenation and reaffirmation of the moral values" (Goffman 1959, 35) of Peronism.

Performing Evita, restoring a "constructed" behavior, is not a purposely engineered or cynical action. It is not theatrical. It is a practice in Bourdieu's sense of the term: taken for granted, unreflective, and outside the realm of discursive consciousness. Their practice is the embodiment of the way a woman should behave if she is going to be a public, Peronist woman. It is not that these women consciously assume Evita's role and persona. It is simply that there is no other way in which a Peronist woman can engage in political activity. As Goffman would have put it, the Peronist (woman) broker "will intentionally and consciously express [her]self in a particular way, but chiefly because the tradition of this group or social status requires this kind of expression and not because of any particular response (other than vague acceptance or approval) that is likely to be evoked from those impressed by the expression. Sometimes the traditions of an individual's role will lead [her] to give a well-designed impression of a particular kind and yet [she] may be neither consciously nor unconsciously disposed to create such an impression" (Goffman 1959, 6).

In other words, like playing jazz, like boxing, brokerage—in the case on which I am focusing—is *regulated improvisation.*[16] It is regulated in the sense that it is an activity constrained by the social relations in which it is embedded, by its position within the network of political relations, by the way in which these women see themselves and read their situation (readings founded on sociohistorically generated classifications of the world like Peronist/anti-Peronist, women's work/men's work), and, last but hardly least, by the way in which the social programs of which they are in charge are structured and gendered. (The historical imperative of mothering, of caretaking, is operative here: as Diana Taylor [personal communication] notes, these women "perform Evita," not only out of an affinity and admiration for Eva, but also because, as Eva Perón herself found out, there are few good roles for women in the Latin America public arena.)[17] But their practice is also improvisation. Even though Eva is inscribed in Peronism today—and a woman who wants to be a *referente Peronista* must have some (discursive, attitudinal, aesthetic) resemblance to the original Peronist woman—women brokers are not mere cultural dupes who mechanically reproduce Eva's performance or who enact supposedly unchanging gender roles. Different political and ideological orientations, different histories, different relations with other brokers and patrons, all affect the way in which individuals perform. Some will emphasize their longtime commitment to their neighborhood, others their enduring relationship with and loyalty to the mayor. Within the framework of historical imperative, there is always room for some "more personal" style.

Matilde and Susana are involved in this form of giving; they are committed to the Peronist way; they are taken by a role that to them seems second nature. Their lives are invested in the game of local politics, and it is this game that fosters the *illusio* (Bourdieu 1977) that they enact. Brokers are neither cynical agents nor—merely—utility maximizers; they are absorbed in a game in which they believe wholeheartedly. They perform a strategy that has been inscribed in Peronist practice since the time of Eva. Through these bodily, aesthetic, and discursive strategies, brokers seek to satisfy material and symbolic interests—as much as they are impelled to pursue them as a condition of being a Peronist woman broker.[18]

It was one of Eva Perón's closest collaborators—Father Benitez— who probably best captured Marcel Mauss's dictum quoted at the beginning of this section: for him, the act of giving and the form of the act of giving are inseparable. The form is not an addendum to the concrete act of solving a problem; rather, it constitutes it. According to Benitez, the real importance of Eva's work was not the distribution of objects (shoes, cooking pots, sewing machines, etc.) "but the gestures that went with these gifts. 'I saw her kiss the leprous,' he said, 'I saw her kiss those who were suffering from tuberculosis or cancer. I saw her distribute love, a love that rescues charity, removing that burden of injury to the poor which the exercise of charity implies. I saw her embrace people who were in rags and cover herself with lice'" (Navarro and Fraser 1985, 126).

Again, the truthfulness of Father Benitez's statement does not concern us here; what matters is his insight concerning the interpenetration of act and gesture, of the form and the content of the act of giving. Susana and Matilde know this. The things given are important, but what goes with them is just as important. The presentation that accompanies the provision of goods, the granting of favors, should not separate but bring together the problem solver and the problem holder in an imagined community: the solidaristic community of Peronism.

In addition, Father Benitez's statement wonderfully illustrates one of the central shortcomings in most of the literature on political clientelism. Although some of it has paid attention to the intermediary role played by brokers, the traffic of influences over those who control the goods and services that these brokers exercise, and the brokers' position vis-à-vis their clients, structural location does not tell us much about practice. The brokers are not just intermediaries—"go-betweens"—but, as this chapter contends, cardinal figures in the production and reproduction of a "special" way of distributing goods, services, and favors, in the articulation of the imaginary "bond of love" (an implicit ideology) that relates brokers and so-called clients. The practice of clientelism and the establishment and reinforcing of broker-client ties thus become ceremonial performances, performances in which actors "play particular roles, and their behavior can be seen to contain a variety of meanings and 'messages,' " and their interactions can be thought of as "social rituals and etiquette" (Weingrod 1977, 50–51).

Susana's and Matilde's practices—their words, their appearance, their public gestures—are there to be read. They are special signs that gain meaning in the context of the distributive practices in which they are embedded. The entity signaled here is the favor, and the signs stand for the history of Peronism. When not so contextualized—within this particular history of Peronism—what they say and how they act, the passion they say they feel for their people, their exaggerated modesty, their dissolution in the *gente,* none of this can be understood. Yet what they say and how they act not only replicate a disputed original—in this case, Eva's work and life—but also create a new one.

Their blonde hair is not "phony" (although the color might not be natural), their affected behavior is not "fake," their sacrifice is not "inauthentic"—whatever *phony, fake,* and *inauthentic* mean. All these things are part of the way in which their political practice must be embodied. It is all part of their performance. They are "restoring a behavior," yet they are not simply reenacting an idealized past. Their performances are "conjunctions whose center can be located not in any single time or mood but only in the whole bundle, the full complex interrelations among times and moods" (Schechner 1985, 55). They link the past of Peronism—and specifically the history of Eva Perón—with their own present and with their "mission in life," with their "vocation." In this way, the performance of Evita joins first causes to the present in the process of solving everyday problems.

From birth their destiny has been determined. To me, to all, they present a particular sociodicy. By performing Eva, they are constructing a teleology and linking their past, their present, and their—and "their people's"—future.

Doing Politics, Doing Gender: Exploring the "Domination Effect"

The performance of Eva Perón not only presupposes and creates an arbitrary definition of her life and work—as would any other performance—but also reproduces a distinctive—and also arbitrary—definition of gender. Being a Peronist woman in politics "naturally" implies taking care of or mothering the poor, doing social (as opposed to political) work, and collaborating with the man who makes the decisions. Thus, through performance, not only do brokers do politics, but also they "do gender" (West and Zimmerman 1987) by proposing their own cultural construction of sexual difference in politics. The final section of this chapter explores the interanimation of these two elements of the broker's public performance.

In his analysis of the symbolic violence underlying gift exchange, Pierre Bourdieu (1977, 171) asserts that "the labour required to conceal the function of the exchanges is as important an element as the labour needed to carry out the function." This "symbolic labor" intends to "transmute, by the sincere fiction of a disinterested exchange, the inevitable, and inevitably interested relations imposed by kinship, neighbourhood, or work, into elective relations of reciprocity." Symbolic labor is thus understood as a labor of "dissimulation and transfiguration (in a word, of *euphemization*) which secures a real transubstantiation of the relations of power by rendering recognizable and misrecognizable the violence they objectively contain and thus by transforming them into symbolic power, capable of producing real effects without any apparent expenditure of energy" (Bourdieu 1991, 170). Brokers' presentations of their selves provide a wonderful example of this symbolic labor of euphemization that lies at the center of the workings of modern forms of political clientelism.

On the basis of his research in Rio de Janeiro, Robert Gay introduces a distinction that appears very useful for interpreting the effects of the maternal rhetoric surrounding women brokers' work with the poor. Gay (1995) asserts that the leaders of the "new social movements" of the 1970s and 1980s managed to persuade a "significant proportion of the least privileged elements of the population that the *explicit exchange of votes for favors* is detrimental to their collective long-term interests, regardless of the immediate and often considerable rewards that such an exchange might bring." This strategy, Gay suggests, "has been relatively success-ful in discouraging popular participation in 'thick' clientelist arrange-ments," that is, the explicit exchange of votes for favors. The problem is that "it has been largely ineffective in the face of more *subtle and sophis-ticated* mechanisms of mobilization" (p. 20; my emphasis). While social movement leaders were able to "empty government assistance programs of any explicit political content," Gay points out that they have been less successful "in their attempts to convince the population at large that such programs, meager though they may be, should not be rewarded at the ballot box" (p. 20). Social policies and assistance programs that, on the surface, may appear as an expression of a "pluralist negotiation of citizenship rights" are, in fact, an expression of a veiled form of clien-telism, a form that Gay labels *thin* or, borrowing from the language of race relations in the United States, *institutional* clientelism.

Matilde and Susana never explicitly acknowledge that their aid to the poor is given on a quid pro quo basis. They put to work a much more "subtle and sophisticated mechanism," a form of symbolic labor. Their performance—as self-sacrificing and indispensable—is meant to dem-onstrate that only they can guarantee the flow of goods and services di-rected through the social assistance programs. In performing Evita, the brokers invoke what Bourdieu calls *the oracle effect,* meaning that they posi-tion themselves as synonymous with the goods and services received, thereby establishing dominance.[19] The implied threat is, of course, that the continued flow of those goods and services is contingent on their reelection or reappointment.[20] Thus, all protestations to the contrary aside, they do, in fact, do politics.

At the same time, while doing politics, female brokers also "do gender." Through ceaseless symbolic labor that has at its center the mothering of the poor, the logic of self-interest underlying brokers' practices gets misrepresented as the logic of disinterest. Brokers' symbolic labor transforms the relations of power that objectively link them to their clients into forms of disinterested maternal care. As part of this labor of euphemization, brokers establish a division between social work and political work. This division not only serves clientelist functions but also reinforces an already existing demarcation in the political arena: political work is male, social work female. At the same time, women brokers' identification with gender-differentiated public functions implicitly conveys an essentialization of mothering and of taking care of the poor as women's activities. As we have seen, one is born a social worker, but one is *not* born to politics — although politics *is* constructed as something that women might do, should they so choose.

Taking care of, mothering the poor is thus constructed as part of women's identity, something for which they are perceived by men as well as by they themselves to have a natural propensity. Without a doubt, this is a source of power for these women. By claiming not just the right but the duty to do social work, they carve out one of the few — albeit limited — spaces in which they have autonomy. At the same time, they are serving more than their own ends, however. They are establishing their own autonomous space in the political world, and they are ensuring the continued subordination of the poor to the workings of clientelist politics.

Little is known about the gendered dimensions of clientelist exchanges. By paying attention to the discursive practices of female Peronist brokers, I have attempted to arrive at a better understanding of clientelist practices. The maternal routine that brokers of the Peronist Party perform for their clients is, without doubt, an act of supreme condescension. Brokers derive political profit from the symbolic denial of the objective relation of power that links them and "their people." Thus, the presentation of the broker's self works as an ideology, as an attempt to "mystify reality, obscure relations of power and domination, and prevent people from grasping their situation in the world" (Scheper-Hughes 1992, 171).

Is this ideological construction intended? Here, Goffman can again be helpful. He writes, "While we can expect to find natural movement back and forth between cynicism and sincerity, still we must not rule out the kind of transitional point that can be sustained on the strength of a little self-illusion. We find that the individual may attempt to induce the audience to judge him and the situation in a particular way, and he may seek this judgement as an ultimate end in itself, and yet he may not completely believe he deserves the valuation of self which he asks for or that the impression of reality which he fosters is valid" (1959, 21).

After more than eight months of fieldwork, I found that the line separating sincerity and cynicism is as blurred for Peronist brokers as it is for Goffman's actors. Conceptualizing brokers' public presentations as symbolic labor obscuring the hierarchic relation between them and their clients does not necessarily imply that such dissimulation is intentional (although there surely is intention).

*

Throughout this chapter, I have explored the ways in which consolidated brokers present themselves and their activity to their clients and shown how this public presentation re-creates a powerful tradition in Peronist political culture. This public presentation and this reinvention of a cultural tradition allow brokers to define a personalized way of solving problems and avoid explicitly requesting political support in exchange for solving problems. The performance masks the domination that, as we saw in the previous chapter, brokers exert owing to their structural position and functions.

In order to examine the effect of the problem solvers' public performance on the problem holders (i.e., the "effectiveness" of the oracle [domination] effect), we now need to reconstruct the client's point of view. As we will see in the next two chapters, the performance of Evita and the discourse of love and affection are warmly received within the brokers' inner circles. As a consequence, a particular memory of Peronism is being continuously re-created.

CHAPTER FIVE

The "Clientelist" Viewpoint

How Shantytown Dwellers Perceive and Evaluate Political Clientelism

Introduction

One cold winter morning in Villa Paraíso, Nelida tells me that she and Juancito first became friends more than twelve years ago. Juancito is the president of the UB leader. Nelida tells me that Juancito "is so good. He always lends you a hand. Now I am on medication because I had a hemoplegy, and the medicine is so expensive . . . I can't afford it, and he helps me. He gets the medicine from the municipality. . . . He helps me a lot, and whatever happens at the UB he calls me because I collaborate at the UB." She says that the most important politician in Villa Paraíso is Juancito. "Here, on our block, we have Juancito," she assuredly notes.

"I always show up at Matilde's UB, out of gratitude or because of our friendship. They always call me, and I go," Adela says. Her daughter got her job as a public employee with the municipality through Matilde. Her husband got his as a garbage collector through a letter of recommendation from Angel, Matilde's husband. Adela never misses the political rallies organized by Matilde; she "has to be thankful to her."

Adela and Nelida are what the literature on political clientelism would call *clients:* actors who give their political support to a broker or a patron in exchange for particular goods, favors, and services. While journalistic accounts (see frontispiece) would also refer to them as *clients,* a judgment of political venality is implied. They attend Peronist rallies and support

Fig. 1: The action takes place in a UB. The dialogue translates as follows: "LEFT: We've added something new to the organization of our rallies. RIGHT: Tell me about it. LEFT: At the beginning, we give them a sausage sandwich, as always. After that, we give them a speech by Pierri [president of the Chamber of Deputies] and then a speech by Duhalde [governor of the province of Buenos Aires]. RIGHT: And what's the new stuff? LEFT: After that, we give them an antacid tablet." (*Página12*, 24 November 1996, front page.)

Peronist politicians because of the goods and services that they receive from the party.[1]

The study of political clientelism has reached an impasse.[2] It rehashes certain issues repeatedly, leaving others unexplored. One such unexplored issue is the central concern of this chapter: the views that the clients themselves hold concerning the clientelist network.

Testimony about the workings of clientelism is usually gathered from opposition politicians, journalists, and community leaders. Only occasionally are the clients themselves asked to explain their own behavior, to render their own judgments about what others consider an "antidemocratic" process. The present chapter—following Geertz—breaks with the standard externalist approach by focusing on the opinions and evaluations of those involved in the clientelist exchange.[3] It asks what people who receive goods, favors, and services from Peronist Party brokers—who undoubtedly attempt to win their vote—think of these exchanges, how they evaluate the brokers' activities and politics in general.

The chapter is divided into two parts. First, I present the ethnographic data. My analysis concentrates on the different points of view that circulate within Paraíso concerning the distribution of goods before the rallies organized by the local brokers, the different evaluations that people make about the brokers, and the competing views that they hold about politics and its particular role in the history of the neighborhood.

The image depicted in this section will be that of a heterogenous social universe. Yet, within this heterogeneity, there are sets of actors who hold similar views of politics and of certain politicians, offer similar explanations of their participation in the rallies, and produce similar narratives when recounting the history of the *barrio*. While attempting to retain the richness of these various views, I attempt an explanation that embeds them in interpersonal relations and the problem-solving networks described in chapter 3.

In the second part, I examine the differences uncovered in the first, attempting to explain how individuals with similar attributes (socioeconomic status, age, sex) come to hold such different views of politics, politicians, and history. I also examine the brokers' inner circles as "provinces of meaning" (Schutz 1962) that sustain their own social truth: a narrative of the *barrio* inextricably linked to the brokers' actions and a set of cultural representations concerning politics. This section draws on Tilly's (1978) model of the polity and on Bourdieu's (1977) notion of doxic experience to formulate a hypothesis concerning these differences: the closer a set of actors is to the center of the polity (understood here as the local center of power, i.e., the broker), the more those actors will share the ideology espoused by the brokers, the more they will recount a history of the *barrio* in which the central protagonists are the brokers and the mayor, and the more they will participate in brokers' public performances, rendering the brokers' symbolic labor even more effective.

I also stress the need to reconsider the notion of political clientelism—at least in this particular case. If it is to be applied here at all, it should be restricted to the broker's inner circle. And, if it is applied in this limited sense, the image of a captive electorate in the grip of clientelist politics is exploded since that inner circle is usually restricted in number. As we will see, the notion of political clientelism is a "trope" (in Appadurai's sense of the term — see the introduction) that obscures more than it clarifies when applied to the political culture of the urban poor.

Although I think that it is important to retrieve the clients' point of view, I share the critique that has been made of the purposely "empathetic dissection of the native's point of view." As Wacquant (1995b, 491) points out in his exploration of the "pugilistic point of view," it is debatable "whether one can pinpoint a single, generic, 'native' point of view, as opposed to a range of discrepant, competing, or warring viewpoints, depending on structural location within the world under examination." It is also up for discussion "whether the so-called native may be said to have a 'point of view' at all, rather than *being one with* the universe of which he partakes — and thus bound to it by a relation of 'ontological complicity' that precludes a spectatorial posture."

In short, in what follows I attempt to reconstruct the (diverse and competing) points of view through a network-embedded and contextualized analysis of the "symbolic forms — words, images, institutions, behaviors — in terms of which (so-called clients) actually [represent] themselves to themselves and to one another." I thereby attempt to examine problem solving through political mediation in a way that is "neither imprisoned by [clients'] mental horizons, an ethnography of witchcraft as written by a witch, not systematically deaf to the *distinctive tonalities* of their existence, an ethnography of witchcraft as written by a geometer" (Geertz 1983, 58, 57; emphasis added). It should be noted that, rather than taking clients' statements at face value, I subscribe to the principle of nonconsciousness, according to which the actual cause of such sociocultural political phenomena as political clientelism is to be located, not in individual consciousness, but in the system of objective relations within which brokers and clients are embedded.[4]

To anticipate some results of this reconstruction, I argue that what appears, from the outside, as an exchange of votes for favors is seen from the inside in many different (and, sometimes, antagonistic) ways: as either manipulative or altruistic, as interested action (politics, calculated exchange) or disinterested action (friendship). Furthermore, most of those who receive vital resources on an everyday basis do not see their bond with the broker as a power relationship. For them, clientelism is habitual practical knowledge, a fact that skews their perspective on the relationship.

The "Distinctive Tonalities" of Problem Solving through Political Mediation

The Same Rally: Different Interpretations

"On our block," Susy told me, "Matilde donated the pipes to construct the sewer. Yet she never told us: 'I give you this, but you should do this, go there, or vote for me.' The only thing she told us was that she would like to come and see when we have finished construction." Susy lives across the street from the local school. Esther, the school's director, has another interpretation of the "donation." She agrees that the pipes were supplied by Matilde, but she stresses the exchange aspect of the project. According to Esther, Matilde told those who would benefit from the new system: "Whenever I send the bus to the corner of your house in order for it to be loaded [for a rally] . . . you know what to do." To Esther's mind, Matilde exchanges pipes for attendance at rallies. To Susy's mind—and Susy directly benefits from the new sewer system—this is just another demonstration—one among many—of how helpful Matilde is.

Those—like Esther—who do not live in the shantytown but only work there are the only ones who term the exchange of goods and favors for demonstrations of support *political clientelism.* An architect from a nongovernment organization, for example, refered to political practices inside the shantytown as following a "clientelist logic." In the notion of clientelism, such individuals see an indictment of the manipulative practices of the shantytown's political brokers. That the practice flourishes is evidence of the "innocence" of the shantytown dwellers and/or of their continued reliance on the "traditional ways of doing things." As an activist with Frepaso (the center-left coalition) who lives in a nearby neighborhood tells me as soon as we start our conversation about politics in the shantytown: "You know, we are against political clientelism, the handing out of food so that people go to the rallies." Such outsiders are not alone, however, in denouncing the practice. While they would not use the term *clientelism,* many residents consider the rallies organized by the Peronist party as nothing more than disgraceful examples of the way corrupt politicians use the poor and needy.

Many residents insist that the "*punteros* [brokers] use the people" for the rallies and that this "use" works against the interests of Paraíso residents because, as one of them puts it, "there are not enough rallies in a month to feed a family." Rally attendance is seen as a demonstration of the naïveté of some inhabitants or of their arrested psychosocial development ("Do you see those buses? They are going to pick people up for the rally. . . . I don't understand; we will never grow up," Toni told me.)

How attendance at rallies is secured is no secret (as Toni told me, "Everybody knows")—food, alcohol, and drugs are distributed beforehand. Many residents of Paraíso resent the practice, but for different reasons. For some, such tactics are evidence of how harmful and unprincipled the business of politics can be. In an interchange worth quoting at length, Horacio and his wife, Alcira, Peronists who used to attend the rallies, blame the brokers:

HORACIO: How are you gonna go to an *acto* [rally] in which there are four or five bottles of red wine circulating and they touch your wife's ass? And in which you see that they are drunk and smoking pot? I would like to go because I am a Peronist in spite of the fact that they have defrauded me. I would like to go to a mass for Eva. But I can't; what for? I could got stabbed if I don't drink wine or smoke a joint.

JAVIER AUYERO: And politicians allow that?

ALCIRA: They first give them a bottle of wine and tell them, "See you at the *acto.*" You go to a UB, and you get on a bus, and the first thing that appears is a bottle of wine. . . .

HORACIO: The ones at the top are organizing this. They are in agreement with this type of thing. He [the nearest Peronist broker] is the one who takes fifty people who smoke marijuana and drink wine and go and shout like crazy people, and, if they have to punch someone, they will. . . . Nobody is gonna come for me because I do not smoke or drink and because I will go to the rally to listen to what is being said. . . . I like to bring twenty people who are healthy. They prefer to bring a hundred because they give them wine and pot; they don't go without that. Politics is like that.

So does Toni:

TONI: Inside the shantytown, [Matilde] does whatever she wants. . . .
JAVIER AUYERO: What do you mean?
TONI: She calls the people whenever there is a rally, she uses those guys who are idling around, she takes them to paint walls, she uses them for the rallies, to play the drums, and when the day is over she gives them a packet of food or a joint. . . . That has nothing to do with social justice.

Other residents use these rallies as yet another opportunity to single out the young people involved, holding them publicly responsible for everything bad that happens in the shantytown (an expression of the antagonism between the young people and everyone else explored at greater length in chap. 2).

Attendance at rallies to show support for a candidate or an official is probably the most blatant manifestation of clientelist politics. Yet it expresses deep-seated, usually long-lasting relationships between the participants—the problem holders and the problem solvers.

I now turn to an examination of the ways in which Paraíso residents view their own attendance at rallies, what they think about the brokers, and how they feel about politics in general.

Manipulation or Gratitude/Collaboration?

While recipients of jobs or favors would deny that the brokers asked something of them in return, a more subtle association can be seen. Clients feel compelled to attend the rallies but do not understand that duty as being performed in exchange for something. They would instead characterize their attendance at rallies as either collaboration or an expression of gratitude.

Lucina was Matilde's cleaning lady until she suffered a stroke. She had to give up her job but received a pension through Matilde, who, at that time, was the director of the social welfare section of the municipality. Lucina's medications are very expensive, they are also provided by Matilde. Her physician at the Hospital Evita is a friend of Matilde's;

she therefore receives very good care. Lucina's husband is employed by the municipality—a job he got, needless to say, through Matilde—yet he is currently painting and doing repair work at Paco's (Matilde's son) home. And how does Lucina characterize her relationship with Matilde? "Maybe for the rallies . . . yes [she asked us for something], but she doesn't pay attention to whether someone who got medicine from her really attends the rally. Sometimes she promises the people who go to the *acto* a bag of food."

Mónica agrees. Matilde never explicitly asks people to attend rallies in exchange for what they receive from her (mostly medicine and food, in her case): "Sometimes I invite the beneficiaries [of Plan Vida] to the rallies. Some of them go; others don't. But they are not obliged to go, and Matilde never tells me that I have to bring twenty people. . . . Of all the beneficiaries I have, five or six usually go, but they go because they like it. They think that they have to thank her [*agradecerle*] for what she gives us. I talk to my neighbors about Matilde, and they really appreciate her. I tell them to go and ask for medicine because, if she has it, she will hand it out. And, if she doesn't, she will try to get it or tell you where to look."

Rosa gets expensive medicine for her father through Juancito. She also got her glasses through his intervention with the welfare section of the municipality. About her usual participation in the Peronist rallies, she says, "I say that I have to fulfill my obligation to him [*para cumplir con él*]. If my presence is useful to him, there I go":

JAVIER AUYERO: Rosa, what do you like most about the rallies?
ROSA: No, now that Perón is not here, no. . . . It is the fact that, if one doesn't go, the other doesn't go either, and nobody will be there. . . . Juancito says, "I need people for the rallies." So there we are. Who are the ones who ask things of him? Some of the people ask him something, and then they stay at home. . . . I was a Peronist when Perón was alive, not now. Now I go because of Juancito, because I am grateful to him. It is my way of saying thank you.

Coca is part of the permanent staff at Juancito's UB. She sometimes gets a bonus from Juancito to get food at the municipal building, and she receives milk from the UB for her child. She openly admits that food is distributed before and after the rallies, yet she denies that this is why people attend. Carefully analyzed, her statement helps us distinguish the principles generating people's actions: "We go to the rally, and, after a week or so, Juancito brings food from the municipality, and he distributes it among those who have attended the rally, in gratitude to those who went. Sometimes he buys *chorizos* [sausages], he prepares some sandwiches, he gives out sandwiches. I understand that he does that because people support him; I understand it as a kind of gratitude. I do not think [he does that] to buy people [*comprar a la gente*]. It is a way to show gratitude [*mostrarle el agradecimiento*]."

"Gratitude" goes without saying because it almost always comes without saying. It is part of the performance of Peronist politics. People who receive things *know* that receiving favors implies a return. Such a return is one of the rules of the game, a rule understood as a "scheme immanent in practice" (Bourdieu 1977), as a mandate that exists in the practical state of affairs. As relations between problem holders and problem solvers are practical—insofar as they are routinely "practised, kept up, and cultivated" (Bourdieu 1977, 38) through the distribution of goods and the granting of favors—attendance at rallies is part of the stock of practical knowledge. This practical knowledge is verbalized only when an explanation is explicitly requested. And, even so, the clients are so closely involved with the brokers' distributive practices that for them to take an impartial view of the "exchange" is precluded. Chatting with Coca—and pretending that I do not understand what she is telling me (and probably not really *understanding* it)—I asked her: "So, when Matilde gets the medicine you need, does she come and tell you, 'You have to come with me to the rally'?" "No," Coca explained, "I *know* [*yo sé*] that I have to go with her instead of with someone else. Because she gave me medicine, or some milk, or a packet of *yerba* or sugar, I *know* that I have to go to her rally in order to fulfill my obligation to her [*Yo sé que tengo que ir al acto para cumplir con ella*], to show my gratitude. Because, if I do not go to her rally, then, when I need something, she won't give it to me. [She would say,] 'Go ask the person who went to the rally with you.'"

On a few occasions, attendance is explicitly required. Yet such requests are seldom phrased as orders, obligations; rather, they are usually phrased as invitations. Silvina receives food from Andrea's UB. Silvina got her husband's pension (he is an invalid, afflicted with sclerosis of the liver) through the timely intervention of Andrea. Since then, Silvina attends the Peronist rallies with Andrea: "I always tell him [my husband], we have to be thankful when someone does a favor for you. [Andrea] told me: the only favor I ask from you is that you accompany me to the rallies. And I told her: No problem, of course." Silvina's husband agrees: "We have to thank her."

Adela's daughter, Mariana, tells me that her family was having a hard time because her father had been fired from his job as a carpenter and her sister, Luisa, had lost her part-time job:

> MARIANA: We didn't have any resources at all. So my mother looked for support from Matilde, and Matilde helped her a lot. She helped us with food and with the job for Luisa. That's the reason why, if my mother can help with anything, she will be there, with Matilde.
>
> JAVIER AUYERO: Helping Matilde in which sense?
>
> MARIANA: Showing up for a rally because Matilde always needs people. Or, when she sponsors a festival, she always needs some people to help her organize it.

Mariana's father got his job as a garbage collector through Matilde's husband (the undersecretary of public works). Although he didn't vote Peronist in the last elections, he does attend some of the rallies in which Matilde's group participates. "She is a good lady," he told me. "We don't have a way to thank her. So, once in a while, when she asks for our collaboration, we happily agree."

Few consider their participation in the rallies to constitute the fulfillment of an obligation. Victoria is a *manzanera* of Plan Vida. Her husband, Mario, works full-time at the local health center, a job that he got after participating, for free, in Matilde's Band for six months. "Playing the drums [*los bombos*], you know?" Catalina, Mario's stepdaughter, told me. Victoria explains that Mario "went after Matilde, becoming one of the drum players in her band. She promised Mario a job. After six or seven months he got it, and he has been working there for two years. Matilde really delivers. . . . She also sends powdered milk to the UB around the corner."

JAVIER AUYERO: Does she ask something in exchange for that?

CATALINA: No. Sometimes we go to the rallies, but there's no obligation.

VICTORIA: It is not an obligation. As my husband [Mario] says, "You have to invite them [the beneficiaries of Plan Vida] and tell them that it is through Duhalde, through Rolo, that they are getting the milk. Since they are receiving help, it would be good if they show up for at least one rally.

Attendance at rallies is also often considered "spontaneous," as a way of enlivening everyday life. Consider, for example, Ruli, who lives in the Fifth Road, which, as we have seen, is one of the most destitute, crime-ridden, dangerous sections of Paraíso. She and I were talking about the various places (mostly UBS) where food is distributed, and I asked her whether receiving food is contingent on attendance at rallies. She confidently replied, "The rally . . . I don't know because I know nothing about politics . . . but the rally is inside yourself because we are the ones who call people to the rally. It is the same with the church. The church is the temple, but we are the church. What happens if we do not go to the temple? There is no church. I think it is personal, if you want to go." She and her neighbors also report that they attend the rallies for enjoyment:

> We are inside our homes the whole day, we cannot go out anywhere . . . so when there is an *acto,* we catch the bus, we take a ride, we go to the park, we enjoy ourselves [*nos distraemos*].

> We amuse ourselves . . . but don't ask us what happened at the *acto* because we don't understand anything, that's the truth.

> [During Children's Day] we don't have to pay the fare; they send the bus to our front door. Maybe our children get a toy. . . . So we enjoy ourselves because where else can we go? [*Nos divertimos, porque si no donde más vamos a ir?*]

The entertainment value of the rallies can hardly be underestimated. Life in the shantytowns can be dull (when not "enlived" by violence), and the people who attend the rallies have precious little free time and little to do with what free time they do have. In the extreme material deprivation under which they live, a peso is a lot of money, and a free round trip to the city center of Cóspito is not something to be passed up. Can we blame Juana, then, for attending a rally in the summer of 1989 launching Menem's presidential campaign? The party paid her bus fare to Mar del Plata (Buenos Aires's main beach resort) and put her up at the Transport Union's hotel, where, Juana marveled, "they even have hot water." On this trip, at age thirty-four, Juana saw the sea for the first time.

While the literature on political clientelism focuses mainly on the "negative determinants" (Wacquant 1995b) of the phenomenon—economic deprivation (Menendez Carrión 1986), a culture of dependence—the positive nature of the exchange, for example, the entertainment value of the rallies, should be taken into consideration if we are to make a serious attempt to understand the participants' point of view. As Ruli succinctly summarizes, "We go to the rallies to enjoy ourselves; we really enjoy ourselves [*laughing*]." And, as Juana insists, "I saw the sea. . . . It's so nice." If we are truly to understand Juana, to understand that, were we in her position, we "would doubtless be and think just like her" (Bourdieu 1996b, 34), we must realize what it meant for her—a thirty-four-year-old woman with no stable job, an unemployed husband, and a handicapped baby—to see the sea for the first time and stay in a hotel with hot water. Doesn't she *have* to be grateful to those responsible for sending her to the rally?

Attendance at rallies is also considered a way of showing a broker that one is loyal, responsible, and ready to help out when needed—and therefore deserving of a job if and when one becomes available. Alfonsina, who is in charge of distributing milk under Plan Materno-Infantil at Juancito's UB, told me how she got her job as a cleaning woman at a public school through Juancito: "When there is a rally, we [the people of the party] collaborate in any way possible . . . so maybe we can get a job, but you have to be patient." "And you were patient?" I ask. "Yes," she replies, "I was patient, and with patience I got it."

To the outsider, the clientelist exchanges seem almost Pavlovian, the clients responding mechanically to the stimulus of goods proffered and services rendered.[5] But, from the client's point of view, these exchanges are simply routine, part of the normal way in which everyday survival problems are solved. To understand attendance at rallies and other shows of support as mere products of the personalized distribution of goods and services is "distortion bordering on disfigurement," in the same way in which boxing is reduced to mere physical aggression (Wacquant 1995b). Doing so oversimplifies a complex interaction, reducing it to a single element, usually that most objectionable to outsiders.

Brokers: Good or Bad?

Those who see the clientelist system as manipulating the people hold the brokers responsible for the limited amount of resources that social assistance programs distribute in the neighborhood ("they always keep the goods for themselves") and accuse them of distributing drugs to young people, of "deceiving the people," of being concerned only with their own political careers.[6] But, to many, brokers are not unscrupulous, corrupt politicians but "good," "helpful," "self-sacrificing" people with whom they have a personal relationship—sometimes even friendship.

Rosa points out what an "excellent person" Juancito Pisuti is: "The way he takes care of people, he is an exceptional human being. . . . He suffers because those who go there [the UB] will never leave without a solution to their problems. He has a solution for everyone. He willingly advises everyone. Many people ask him for money . . . and he gives them his own money. He never tells them that he doesn't have any money." He is also "very responsible": "Whenever there is a dinner at the UB, Juancito tells the men of the UB to walk us [women] home." Alfonsina agrees with Rosa: "Everybody appreciates Juancito. He is always keen to serve. He likes to help people. He is very patient." Nelida has known Juancito since 1983 and is also part of his UB staff. He provides her with medicine for her hemoplegy. She agrees with both Alfonsina and Rosa: "Juancito is *so* good, always ready to lend you a hand." She "started a friendship with Juancito" more than twelve years ago, and she "really understands him because, once in a while, I go to the municipality and he is there, in that crazy place, full of people, I'm sure his head must be spinning. . . . Yet he really helps you. He doesn't get nervous; he is really good." Carlitos shares this belief: "Juancito sacrifices himself for the people of the shantytown."

Self-sacrificing and *helpful* are also terms that people use when referring to Matilde. Those who are part of Matilde's circle and who speak about their participation in the rallies that she organizes in terms of "gratitude" or "collaboration" believe that Matilde is the most important politician in the neighborhood. She is also seen as the one who contributes the most to the well-being of its inhabitants: "She is always present when something happens." "She is so good." "Matilde pays attention to every single detail." "She is like a small municipal building; everybody goes there." All remark on her accessibility: "You can go and see her whenever you have a problem, any problem. Medicine? She will get it. . . . If she is able to [solve the problem], be sure, she will do it." Some consider their relationship with Matilde to be a "very good friendship." Most clients also sincerely believe that the brokers truly care about them. It would therefore be impossible for them to distance themselves from the relationship sufficiently to view either side in the exchange as maximizing opportunity through the expression of affection.

Most of the residents of Villa Paraíso also consider the brokers to be personally responsible for the distribution of goods and services. It is not the government that gets them their jobs, grants them their pensions, buys them their medicine, finds them their food. It is Matilde, or Juancito, or Andrea. Hundreds of pages of interview transcripts and field notes testify to this one simple, essential fact. And they are seen as doing so, not because they are under any obligation, but because they truly want to, they truly care. One member of Matilde's Band sums it up nicely: "People think it's her obligation to give out things, and it's not an obligation. She does it because she wants to. What's her obligation? Who is she? Is she your mother? People get confused a lot. You do them a favor, and it seems like it is an obligation. And it is a favor."

According to the *Oxford American Dictionary,* a favor is "an act that is kindly or helpful beyond what is due or usual." Because Matilde personally and willingly delivers the goods—beyond what is customary and without having any obligation whatever to do so—the beneficiary cannot invoke any right as a citizen to the thing given or the favor granted. There is no third party to whom clients can resort in order to enforce their claims (which might constitute rights), only a personalized relationship out of which nothing can be obtained, no problem can be solved.[7]

The high regard in which some people hold "their" brokers does not necessarily extend to the other brokers in the neighborhood. While, for example, Nolo feels that "Juancito is the one who really makes sacrifices for the shantytown," his opinion of Matilde is that she "is bad news; she is like Judas's kiss." Alfonsina is also critical of Matilde: "She is not from the shantytown. I don't think she has ever done something for it. . . . She doesn't even bother to come." Half a block away, Mónica finds that Matilde is "always there whenever you need something. She really helps you; she is very nice. I don't think anybody can complain about her." On the other hand, there is Silvia, whose opinion is that both Matilde and Andrea are "very nice; they help a lot."

What we are witnessing here is evidence of the type of relationship that exists between broker and client. Nolo, for example, is a member of Juancito's inner circle; he has not established a relationship with any other broker in Paraíso. But Silvia has established relationships with both Matilde and Andrea. In other words, sometimes brokers' inner circles remain mutually exclusive, sometimes they overlap, and clients' evaluations of brokers will depend on their position(s) within the network(s).

These differing views of the various brokers have another source—in the type of relation established between broker and client—but, before exploring that source, it will be helpful first to examine the role that politics has played in Paraíso and, a related matter, the different versions of the history of the neighborhood.

Politics: Helpful or Dirty?

I don't work, I do politics. —Old bumper sticker in Villa Paraíso

It is hardly a new observation that party politics is seen as far removed from everyday life concerns. It is a "dirty" activity that makes a sudden appearance at election time and then returns to the realm of unkept promises.[8] Many residents comment on this occasional character of party politics and its essentially corrupt nature. As we have seen, that attendance at rallies is ensured by the distribution of drugs and alcohol is one source of complaint.

There is also a strongly held notion among the shantytown dwellers that there is a "time for politics"—around election time—when demands can be quickly satisfied and goods promptly obtained because politicians are eager to get their votes. Rogelio, president of the Neighborhood Association Emilio Redael, tells me: "Matilde shows up when it is time for politics, when there are elections. That is when politicians show up." Hugo, himself president of one of the many soccer clubs in the area, agrees: "If we want to get something, we will have to wait for the elections. At that time we can demand something. . . . We provide so many [votes] that we might get something in return." This belief that elections offer opportunities to get problems solved is anchored in personal experience. Both Rogelio and Hugo received aid for their respective organizations during the past two elections. "Through politics," Hugo tells me, "we got a plot of land for the club. . . . Now we need the bricks, but I will have to wait for the next election."

Politics is also seen as an intermittent activity. "Today is the anniversary of Perón's birthday," Toni tells me, "and I am sure that all the *punteros* are handing out food in the municipal building." He later adds, "Today you are gonna see the workings of a UB. In that UB across the street, there is a young woman [Andrea] who works at the UB. She is going to look for some elderly people in the neighborhood, and she brings them, she hugs them. She never goes and sees how they are doing." Toni does not reserve his criticism for Andrea alone: "Each time there is a rally or an election, [the people at the UBS] hand out food." Even as politics is disvalued, however, it is seen as a necessary evil: "You know, nobody pays attention to you unless you are a relative or an acquaintance of a politician" (Mabel).

Politics is also considered "dirty," "corrupt." It is a "lucrative business," an "opportunity to get ahead," "deceitful," "manipulative." It is an activity that separates "us" from "them," something that "I don't do" but "others do."

If, however, one "takes the trouble to look closely," as W. F. Whyte (1943) recommends in his seminal study of streetcorner society, one can find strikingly dissimilar evaluations of politics and politicians even in the same neighborhood, on the same block, in the same household, among people with similar attributes whom one would expect to be in agreement. The only common ground that can be found is agreement on the fact that politics exists as a universe of its own, with its own rules, and that, if one is clever or lucky, it can be used to serve one's own ends.

Some residents praise the work that the brokers and the municipality do for the neighborhood: "There is a lot of help. . . . The municipality always has an answer, and not only with food. If you need sheet metal, they'll give it to you. . . . In a UB, they used to give milk with a piece of bread. Here, there is a lot of help; someone who says there is no help is lying. . . . What happens is that you have to go there and wait; everything has its own time." Some residents deny that aid is forthcoming only at election time. For them, "assistance" is an everyday, personalized issue. Estela, for example, gets free birth-control pills from Matilde and stresses that in this way she saves ten pesos a month, "which is a lot." She values Matilde's constant preoccupation with the *barrio*'s problems: "If you ask her for something, she will give it to you."

The following excerpts from interviews that I conducted with Paraíso residents probably best exemplify the continuous character of local politics and the ongoing, intimate relationships that some people maintain with their brokers (as noted previously, Juancito obtains Nelida's medication for her, and Matilde got Adela's husband and daughter their jobs):

JAVIER AUYERO: Who do you call when you need the water truck?
NELIDA: I look for Juancito.
JAVIER AUYERO: And when you have to do some paperwork at the municipal building?
NELIDA: Juancito . . . Juancito. . . . [*Laughing.*]

JAVIER AUYERO: How did you become part of Plan Vida?
NELIDA: [*Laughing.*] Juancito involved me in the program. . . . He registered me.

JAVIER AUYERO: And how did you get involved in Plan Pais?
NELIDA: We registered here, on the corner.
JAVIER AUYERO: Through Juancito?
NELIDA: [Smiling.] Always through Juancito. . . . Juancito [is] always there in the middle.

JAVIER AUYERO: What do you do when people ask you for medicine?
ADELA: I send them to Matilde . . . because they are there in the afternoon.
ADELA'S DAUGHTER: Yes, Matilde also helps.
ADELA: Here we resort to Matilde.
ADELA'S DAUGHTER: Matilde is like a small municipality. Everybody goes there.

JAVIER AUYERO: Is there any place where powdered milk is distributed?

ADELA: Matilde's! [*Laughing.*]

Individuals' perceptions of politics and politicians are reflected—to a certain extent—in the narratives they relate about the history of the neighborhood. Those who see politics as an everyday activity, readily accessible to those with problems in need of solving, and who perceive brokers as always available and ready to help attribute all positive developments to state intervention—in the person of the mayor or a particular broker. Those who view politics as intermittent and unreliable and brokers as corrupt and unscrupulous attribute all improvements to residents' collective action.

The "Statist" Narrative versus the "Epic" Version: Are We Talking about the Same Asphalt?

One of the aims of my research was to trace a history of problem solving in a poor neighborhood of Greater Buenos Aires, with the purpose of illustrating the increasing relevance of clientelist arrangements in the way in which poor people solve their everyday survival problems. With that end in mind, I began to pay particular attention to the stories that people told me about the history of the neighborhood and of their own place within it. I was looking for patterns in the way people solve their problems and expecting to find only one version of history, universally agreed on. What I actually uncovered was conflicting testimony—the church/the mayor was responsible for paving the streets; Rolo/Matilde was responsible for building the health center. I found that there was not one history of Paraíso. But what there was was much more interesting.

According to most residents, the biggest change in Paraíso the last decade was the paving of the streets. Before that, a light rain could turn the whole shantytown into a nightmarish quagmire. Yet, although everybody agrees that paving the streets "made a real difference," there are at least two versions of how that came about.

One version emphasizes collective action. For the first time in its history, the shantytown saw its residents working together toward a common goal: "The streets were paved by the residents. We organized soccer competitions, we sold *chorizos* and *empanadas,* we raised the money,

. . . and the municipality . . . built it. The whole neighborhood was united" (Roberto). In the most extreme versions of the story, such collective action raised the political consciousness of the shantytown dwellers. Other versions stress the role played by the particular organizations with which the narrators were affiliated: "The paving was made possible by the church organizations. The residents organized raffles, street fairs, festivals, soccer competitions. We collected the money and went to the municipality. That is the way Villa Paraíso was paved." While no one denies the role that the municipality played in the process, the emphasis is on the residents' collective pursuit of a common goal. The same collective push is also seen as responsible for the building of the sewer system and the health center.

The most extreme—almost epic—version of the collective action memory can be found in a series of interviews conducted in 1989 by the Grupo Parroquia Nueva—and published as *Making Memory in Villa Paraíso*[9]—in an attempt to record the "collective memory" of the shantytown and to "recuperate our history as part of our identity." (The Grupo Parroquia Nueva was associated with the Third World Priests Movement, which was very much inspired by liberation theology, and had a clear leftist political orientation.) In *Making Memory*, we find Anita—a longtime resident of Paraíso—reporting that the sewer system, the paving of the streets, and the lighting of the alleyways all were carried out "slowly and with the effort of each and every resident; [we were] together." That is the reason why, according to Anita, it can be said that "Villa Paraíso was self-constructed. . . . This was truly *heroic*. . . . all the transformations of the area were due to the *collective effort* of the residents" (my emphasis). Then there is Sergio, another resident, who says, "It was through the [neighborhood association] Coordinadora[10] that we got an incredible number of things: the day-care center, the new school building, the health center, the paving, . . . the free garbage collection." The document ends with a testimony that encapsulates this epic version: "What I remembered most clearly is that, when the people got together, we got things done. . . . That is the way."

Another version emphasizes the role played by the state. In the "statist" narrative, it is the mayor or one particular broker who is responsible for the general improvement in living conditions:

The mayor built the health center, paved the streets. . . . He did a lot for the neighborhood. He tried to improve the neighborhood. . . . We have always gotten aid from the mayor. . . . We go to see him when we need something, and sooner or later we get an answer [to our demands]. (Cristina)

The neighborhood has improved a lot, and many people thank Rolo. The residents put up the money to have the paving done, but, whenever they ask him for pipelines, sooner or later they arrive. He sent the machines to do the paving, although we paid to rent the machines and for the materials. (Mónica)

The president of one of the neighborhood associations told me that he and some of his neighbors began the "struggle" to have the health center built by "pressuring" the mayor. "We built the place," "we painted it," "we got the first physician," he told me. Lili, who lives a block from the president, has another version of the same story: "Matilde was the one who started with the health center at the neighborhood association; she brought the nurse and brought the first desk. Although the president of the association is the one in charge, Matilde always 'lends him a hand.' "

It is a matter of emphasis, of course, but the differences are not to be missed. The epic and the statist histories refer to the same place, to the same material improvements, but they do so in ways that give the central place to different actors. Those who recount statist narratives are the ones who perceive politics as something that might help them, as something that is continuous. The constant presence of politicians in their everyday lives produces a narrative featuring those same politicians. It is probably Josefa who best summarizes this position: "Politics helps a lot. . . . I improved my home through politics. I constructed all the pipelines and the sewage system for my home through politics. . . . The paving was done through politics; it was done by Rolo [the mayor]. The water was installed by Pedro [a broker who works for Matilde]. The municipality helps a lot. Politics helps a lot. When we need them to get drinking water, they are here."

On the other hand, those who recount the collective action narratives are those whose distaste for party politics and whose aversion for local brokers are explicitly stated. As two people were quoted in *Making Memory:* "We are Juancito's lifetime enemies." Or, as the president of the neighborhood association (who, according to his own version of the story, was responsible for the construction of the health center) asserts, implicitly linking Matilde with the distribution of drugs in Paraíso, "Matilde's politics is dirty."

Where Do Differences Come From? Embedding Voices

— *Ya te he dicho, Sancho — respondió don Quijote, que sabes poco de achaque de aventuras: lo que yo digo es verdad, y ahora lo verás. —*M. de Cervantes Saavedra, *El ingenioso hidalgo Don Quijote de la Mancha*

Where does this rich variety of narratives, perceptions, and evaluations come from? What importance do these voices have in local politics? The testimonies quoted above come from people of the same social class and roughly the same age group. These are women and men living in the same destitute and stigmatized neighborhood, some of them often living only half a block from one another. They share similar categorical attributes, and they have different experiences of politics, diverse evaluations of the actions of the political brokers of the neighborhood, and distinct visions of the history of the neighborhood.

For statistical purposes, they are the same people, living in the same "poor" neighborhood. Roughly speaking, they all experienced some degree of improvement in their living conditions during the 1950s, 1960s, and 1970s. Yet, since the 1980s, their living conditions have been deteriorating. Almost all are living below the official poverty line. With their strikingly different opinions and evaluations, they defy all attempts at classification. Diversity is the norm.

The mere fact that there are different points of view emerging from similar social settings leads to an obvious conclusion: there is no categorical explanation for these viewpoints. People with similar attributes do not necessarily share common experiences (Somers 1994; Somers and Gibson 1994). We may stop here—as many of the current attempts to recover the (poor) actor's perspective do—and transform what needs to be explained into a mere recollection of voices. Yet, and although imperfect and far from clear-cut, there is a pattern to be discerned in these viewpoints, a pattern that is rooted not in categories but in the relational milieu, in the structural locations in which these voices are embedded.

In chapter 3, I showed that problem-solving networks consist of a set of concentric circles that surround the broker—the focal point. The different circles consist of groups of actors who have differential access to the goods and services under the broker's control. As we saw, some people receive their daily medication from their brokers. Others have obtained their jobs through them. Still others get packages of food. Some have routine access to their brokers. Others have a more distant, sporadic relationship with them. Still others do not even know them personally. What we have are different degrees of contact with the broker: on a gradient that goes from everyday (and, in extreme cases, vital) contact, to intermittent, to none at all.

Brokers constitute the "paramount reality" (Schutz 1962) of those clients located closest to them. They are part of the everyday, wide-awake, commonsense world. As we have seen in the cases of Nelida and Adela, the first word out of some clients' mouths when asked how they solve their everyday life problems is their broker's name. Borrowing from the language of apprenticeship psychology (Rogoff 1990), we can then characterize some of the ties within the problem-solving network as *hot* relationships, insofar as they involve professed emotions, long-lasting ties, expressed commitments, declared loyalties. Problem solving within the inner circle of hot relationships is not a cold, calculated (although there is surely calculation involved), merely instrumental relationship.[11]

As we have seen, brokers' accumulated political power is directly reflected in the size of their inner circles, and the size of those inner circles depends critically on brokers' public performances. And, while the relation between performer and audience needs to be examined in greater detail, instead of analyzing the audience's "reception" of the broker's performance (as if public presentations are conceived in a vacuum), I focus on the degree to which members of the audience share the worldview put forward by the broker. In other words, I am not interested in whether clients believe what their brokers say. Rather, I am interested in the "dynamics of social interweavings" (Elias 1978, 29) that compel some people to participate meaningfully in the worldview proposed by the brokers.

Drawing on Tilly's (1978) model of the polity (and defining the broker as a local center of power) and Bourdieu's (1977) notion of doxic experience (as the recognition of the legitimacy of a social order through the misrecognition of its arbitrariness), we can formulate the following hypothesis that explains part of the variation found in previous sections: the closer to the broker the resident is, the more positive will be his or her evaluations of the broker's activities and of local politics; the closer to the broker, the more the history of the neighborhood will be recounted in terms of the decisive influence of the state, personified by the broker and/or the mayor. In short, proximity to the center of power (self-perception as "protected by" the broker and narrative identity as neighbors living in a *barrio* that was "made through politics") means that the political order will be perceived as less arbitrary.

To paraphrase Schutz's (1962) brilliant analysis of the "world of truth" created in the interaction between Don Quixote and Sancho Panza, the broker's inner circle constitutes a common "subuniverse" of discourse. This subuniverse of discourse is established, maintained, and cultivated by the interactions that take place between clients and their brokers, both of whom have "good arguments for explaining away discrepancies" (Schutz 1962, 143). Within the "province of meaning" established by brokers and their inner circles, politics is viewed as helpful, the rallies as collaborative efforts and expressions of gratitude, and the brokers as truly caring and the motive force behind anything good that happens in the community. The experiences of members of the inner circles are harmonized and the group's worldview reinforced through the brokers' performances—both one on one with individual clients and at rallies, one of the most elementary forms of political objectification—the brokers' legitimacy established through the narratives locating them at the center of life in Paraíso. In short, within brokers' inner circles there is "uncontested acceptance" (*doxa*) of clientelist politics, a misrecognition of the arbitrary character of problem solving through personalized mediation.

Owing to its narrative emplotment and its paramount presence, the identity—that is, the experience of a shared social relation (Tilly 1995)—that is being forged around the local center of power shows signs of neither active "resistance" nor "hidden transcripts" (Scott 1990). Yet in Paraíso there is—as we saw—active resistance to clientelist practices.

These countervoices are usually located outside the circle of hot relations and, more often than not, complain about the scarcity of resources distributed by the brokers. "They [the brokers] give food to whom they want," "Juancito hands out food once in a while, and people need more than that," "they never keep their promises," "they give things out, but they keep the best for themselves"—these are the most commonly heard complaints, and they usually come from people who are not connected to the network. In other words, most protests concern *the way in which* brokers carry out their duties. Occasionally, one can detect voices that ask *what right* brokers have to exercise control at all.

Those within the inner circle are faced with a paradox (see Bourdieu and Wacquant 1992; and Willis 1981). If they resist the broker's domination, they will lose access to vital resources and thus make their already bad living conditions even worse. Resistance is therefore out of the question (and probably futile). If, on the other hand, they assimilate the broker's worldview—which is what I think they do—they are co-opted by the institutionalized practices of political clientelism and thus partake in the reproduction of the hierarchic relations prevailing in the local political arena and thus in their own subordination.[12]

A Reappraisal of Political Clientelism: The Double Life

The distribution of material resources is a necessary, but in itself insufficient, condition for the smooth operation of the clientelist world. As Robert Merton (1949) argued long ago in his analysis of North American political machines, "it is important to note not only that aid is provided but the manner in which it is provided" (p. 49). The political machine, Merton pointed out, "fulfills the important social function of humanizing and personalizing all manner of assistance to those in need" (p. 74). For the case at hand, the implications of Merton's (functionalist) interpretation are quite clear: what is being given (and received) and how it is being given (and received) are equally important elements in the operation of political clientelism.

As we just saw, the type of good distributed matters. Vital resources distributed on a daily or weekly basis (such as food or medicine) and special favors that require greater skill or effort to deliver (such as public jobs) tend to generate a different type of relationship between broker and prospective client than does, say, the distribution of general goods (i.e., those goods that benefit the whole community and cannot be granted to a single individual and withheld others, such as roadwork). However, as existing research in other geographic settings shows (Guterbock 1980), it is not the good per se that has the capacity to generate one or another type of relationship.

In their everyday acts of giving, brokers tailor these goods and services in special ways. As the extensive literature on the subject insists, trust, solidarity, hope for the future, familistic orientation, and reciprocity (see, among others, Roniger 1990; Günes-Ayata 1994; and Scott 1977) do exist in the relationships established between and verbalized by patrons, brokers, and clients. As we saw in the last two chapters, they are reiterated time and again in brokers' public presentations. Yet, "as the truth of the interaction is never entirely contained in the interaction" (Bourdieu 1977, 81), we should look more closely at the effect of this discursive emphasis on trust, solidarity, reciprocity, caring, and hope. Insofar as the solutions, services, and protection provided by brokers (inseparably material and symbolic exchanges) are inclined to legitimate a de facto state of affairs that is an unequal balance of power (i.e., a domination network), we can describe them, following Bourdieu, as *ideological machines*. The act of giving, the caring actions of brokers, and the trusting response of their inner circles transform, or attempt to transform, a *contingent* social relationship—helping someone who is in need—into a *recognized* (i.e., acknowledged as lasting) relationship. Such recognition is at the basis of problem solving through political mediation. Within an ideological environment of cooperation, companionship, and solidarity, ties are constructed that solidify a particular balance of forces. The more some actors participate as members of the polity, the more they share the ideology proposed by political leaders and brokers alike, and, in turn, the more doxic the relationship will be with respect to the asymmetrical bond between client and broker. Paraphrasing Mauss's (1967, 74) analysis of the gift in archaic societies, through favors "a hierarchy is [re]established."

In a recent article, Pierre Bourdieu (1998, 94) clarifies his differences with Lévi-Strauss's and Mauss's understandings of gift exchange. Bourdieu writes: "Mauss described the exchange of gifts as a discontinuous succession of generous acts; Lévi-Strauss defined it as a structure of transcendent reciprocity of acts of exchange, where the gift results in a countergift":

> What was absent from these two analyses was the determinant role of the temporal interval between the gift and the countergift, the fact that in practically all societies, it is tacitly admitted that one does not immediately reciprocate for a gift received, since it would amount to a refusal. I asked myself about the function of that interval: why must the countergift be deferred and different? . . . *the interval had the function of creating a screen* between the gift and the countergift and allowing two perfectly symmetrical acts to appear as unique and unrelated acts. . . . Everything occurs as if the time interval, which distinguishes the exchange of gifts from swapping, existed to permit the giver to *experience the gift* as a gift without reciprocity, and the one who gives a countergift *to experience it* as gratuitous and not determined by the initial gift. (emphasis added)

Bourdieu places the experience of gift exchange at the center of his argument and considers the time interval, to which many inner-circle members refer ("one or two weeks after the rally Juancito brings the food"), a key factor in the construction of the veil that covers the truth of the exchange. Following Bourdieu's insight, I argue that the way in which "objective exchange" of favors for votes is *experienced* does matter a great deal in the case of Peronist problem solving. As we have just seen, what is being communicated and understood in each favor rejects the very idea of an exchange. Experience matters precisely because there is a contradiction between the objective and the subjective sides of this hierarchic arrangement.

The truth of clientelism is collectively repressed by both brokers and clients. This means that clientelist practices have not only double lives (in the "objective circulation" and in "subjective experiences") but also "double truths" (akin to those that Bourdieu detects in gift exchange). We should bring this duality, this ambiguity, back into the study of clientelism because it is "an ambiguity which is not made by the scientist, but which is present in reality itself, *a sort of contradiction between subjective truth and objective reality*" (Bourdieu 1998, 95; emphasis added).

The only way of understanding "double behaviors, without duplicity" (Bourdieu 1998, 97), is by forsaking the theories of action that have, implicitly, governed the approach to understanding clients' actions. As I have already mentioned, the system of objective relations in which individuals are located — networks, dyads, sets — and the exchanges that take place within those networks are the preferred focus of the overwhelming majority of studies of political clientelism. Scholarly accounts of clientelist practices hardly ever explicitly discuss the theories of social action on which their understandings of clients' actions rest. When attempting to do so, that is, when trying to answer the question, Why do clients follow their brokers? most students of clientelism rely on either normative or rational choice models of social action. The client and the broker are seen as either following a norm — an internalized norm of reciprocity that is the source of the client's and the broker's purposive conduct (Gouldner 1977) — or calculating the best way to maximize their opportunities in a pragmatic, utilitarian response to structural constraints (Menendez Carrión 1986). Scott's (1977) pathbreaking work articulates both approaches to clients' actions in a single perspective.

In "Patronage or Exploitation?" Scott (1977, 25) asserts that the central problem in rural patron-client systems is "whether the relationship of dependence is seen by clients as primarily collaborative and legitimate or primarily exploitative." From the client's point of view, the key element in the evaluation of the legitimacy of the relationship "is the ratio of services he receives to the services he provides: the greater the value of what she receives from her patron compared with the cost of what she must reciprocate, the more likely she is to see the bond as legitimate. For the patron, on the other hand, the level of satisfaction with the bond depends on the ratio of the value of this client's services to the costs of retaining him."

When applied to Peronist clientelist practices, this argument becomes problematic. Certainly, the balance of the exchange determines the legitimacy of the relationship. However, a single-minded focus on the balance prevents our seeing what is central in the Peronist case: *the legitimacy of the clientelist network* as a way of solving pressing problems independent of this or that particular broker or patron.

Cholo (a member of Matilde's inner circle and himself a broker in the most destitute area of Villa Paraíso) clearly illustrates this central point in the workings of Peronist clientelism. After the T-shirt dispute described in the introduction, he stayed with Matilde. But he repeatedly complained about the *balance of reciprocity:* "I am worth more than that," he often told me, referring to the income that he receives thanks to Matilde's intervention. "I am really tired of this thing with Matilde," he pointed out two days after the T-shirt episode. At the time, I was not sure whether he meant it. But, after the many hours we spent talking about his history in Paraíso and in the Peronist Party, I realized that he was likely to end his working relationship with Matilde. During his fifteen years of Peronist activism, he has worked for many other brokers. Matilde is simply one in a long chain of *políticos.* The point here is that Cholo did not look for another way of doing politics; he switched allegiances *between brokers* but still *within the Peronist Party.* He remained Peronist (in spite of other attractive possibilities made available to him, especially after the Radical Party came to power). Moreover, the legitimacy of clientelism was never questioned. For Cholo, and for most members of brokers' inner circles, clientelist politics is taken for granted; it is normal (and normalized) politics.

Giving turns out to be a way in which brokers *possess* the members of their inner circles. But the same relation does not hold between brokers and those less intimately connected with them. Those with less intimate relationships with brokers are able to obtain goods and services when they need them, but they do not always offer loyalty in return. Nevertheless, this outer circle is an important part of the network surrounding the broker. And the distinction between inner and outer circle is a fluid one, more a product of analysis than a reality. Status (inner vs. outer circle) depends on such factors as amount of resources available, number of brokers competing for elected posts, and the opportunity structure in local politics.

Ultimately, the strength of the brokers' position comes from their clients' acceptance of the legitimacy of clientelist practices. At the same time, that acceptance is also the system's major weakness. The broker-client relationship must be constantly nurtured, and its maintenance depends on the brokers' capacity to deliver as promised/expected. But a single broker can accommodate only a limited number of people at any given time. Even Matilde—the most powerful broker in Paraíso—can claim no more than a hundred followers (out of a voting-age population of over seven thousand). And the broker's position is also contingent on his or her continued good standing with the source of goods and services provided (in this case, the mayor of Cóspito).

Thus, the image of an extended "captive" clientelist electorate (stereotypically portrayed by the media and sometimes unreflectively adopted by scholars) does not rest, in this case at least, on firm empirical ground. Although significant, the size of brokers' inner circles can hardly account for the "conquest of the vote" and the "building of electoral consensus" that is usually attributed to clientelism. If we are to use the word *clientelism,* we should therefore restrict it to the inner circle of doxic experience.

This does not mean, however, that we should dispose of the study of political clientelism. Domination and inequality are still constantly reproduced within the inner circles, and the strong ties forged within those circles remain extremely important in local politics. In fact, it is its reliance on the clientelist system that makes the Peronist Party so resilient. While small in numbers, the brokers' inner circles are crucial to the party's success, providing as they do not only the party's hard core of voters but also its political operatives. It is they who maintain the party structure between elections and keep support alive (see Levitsky 1998a, 1998b). On the whole, inner circles are cardinal elements in the organizational strength and territorial penetration of the party.

Thus, we see that clientelism leads an analytic double life—in the circulation of favors, goods, and support and in the interactions between patrons, brokers, and clients. Problem solving through personalized political mediation exists both inside and outside the agents, in the clientelist networks themselves and in the actors' "hearts and minds." One of the central points of the last two chapters has been the ways in which these social and mental structures of political clientelism are "interlinked by a twofold relationship of mutual constitution and correspondence" (Wacquant 1998, 7). Within inner circles, the distribution of material resources is important. Clients are, undoubtedly, interested actors. But interest cannot be taken as the actual cause—the generative principle—of clients' behaviors. Reciprocity and calculation exist, but demands for recognition within the inner circle are more significant. The emphasis that inner-circle members place on their "friendship" with their brokers and on the affective ties so contracted hints at the meanings that emerge from and sustain these ties: clients' desires to be cared for and recognized should be considered the central cause of their behavior.

It seems to me that the solutions to problems that brokers provide explain part of the support that they receive. Yet this is only part of the picture. As I explored in the previous chapter, these brokers claim for themselves the identity of true Peronists. The actors who are part of their inner circles also claim that identity—even those who accuse the brokers of manipulation, of corruption, of "playing their own game." Moreover, many of those who recount the "epic" version of the history of the neighborhood consider themselves as Peronists, but "Peronists of Perón." We will see that a "Peronist identity" means different things to different people. Understanding these different meanings is crucial if we are to obtain a clearer picture of the world of problem solving through political mediation, a subject taken up in the next chapter.

CHAPTER SIX

"They Were All Peronists"

The Remnants of the Populist Heresy

Introduction

When we return to a city previously visited what we perceive helps us to restore a picture, certain portions of which had been forgotten. If what we currently see fits into the framework of our old memories, the converse is also true, for these memories adapt to the mass of present perceptions. —Maurice Halbwachs, *The Collective Memory*

Rosa is a fifty-four-year-old woman who has lived in Paraíso since 1953. Since she is unemployed and her husband works "off the books," she does not have any health insurance. "I didn't have money to buy the glasses that the doctor [in the public hospital] prescribed for me. A neighbor suggested that I go to the UB. . . . This neighbor told me that there, at the UB, I should look for Juan Pisutti. Pisutti would tell me whether I can get the glasses or not." Happily showing me her new glasses, Rosa told me that "it was through Pisutti that I got them." When the soup kitchen opened in the UB, Pisutti asked Rosa to help out. Her response: "While I use these glasses, I have to be grateful to you because I obtained them through you." Rosa usually participates in Peronist public rallies and internal elections: "I have to fulfill my obligation to him [Pisutti]. If my presence is useful to him, I'll be there. . . . It is my way of saying thank you."

During the many hours that we spent talking about her life in the shantytown, Rosa repeated a set of recollections over and over again in great detail. Some concerned life under the first Peronist government (1946–55):

> I clearly remembered when I was a little girl and we got a parcel through the mail. It was a big box . . . in it was my first pair of glasses! Evita sent them to me. In the parcel there were also school aprons. . . . We, in my family, have good memories of Evita. She gave us the bonus in the *Mundo infantil* magazine so that we could go to the post office and get our toys, a pink bonus if you were a girl, and a light blue bonus if you were a boy. They [Juan and Eva Perón] distributed a bag of toys. Every child was able to celebrate the Three Wise Men. And, for Christmas, you had your *panettone* and your cider. . . . I was ten years old."

Rosa's recollections caught my attention as a clear example of Halbwachs's dictum, "Memories adapt to the mass of present perceptions" (Halbwachs 1980, 22). Many events in Rosa's life remain obscure to her, but the memories of the "happy times of Peronism" are not among them. She remembers in great detail the presents bestowed by the Peronist government. She remembers, I will argue in this chapter, because her old experiences of Peronism are, to quote Mary Douglas (1980, 5), renewed "by means of external stimuli" and adapted to her present perceptions. The glasses that Rosa obtained through Pissuti are the lenses through which she views contemporary Peronism.

Recent developments in the sociology of memory emphasize the blurred division between past and present. Just as Durkheim discredited the idea of the lonely, suicidal individual, in exploring the social aspects of the mental act of remembering the sociology of memory rejects the existence of "mnemonic Robinson Crusoes" (Zerubavel 1996, 285). Memory is "a perpetually actual phenomenon," writes Pierre Nora (1989, 9), "a bond tying us to the eternal present." Present and past were also mutually implicated in the writings of Maurice Halbwachs, whom we can now consider the founding father of the sociology of memory. Following his lead (but contesting the sharp division between memory and history), Barry Schwartz (1997, 470) asserts that collective memory vanishes when it ceases to be relevant to current experience; collective memory, Schwartz writes, "the way ordinary people conceive the past, reflects the concerns of the present."

It is common knowledge now that memory of the past is affected by present social environment. Scholars highlight this *structured charac- ter* of past recollections: the relational setting in which individuals are located affects the depth, the tone, the very facts of their memories. We remember as members of "mnemonic communities" (Zerubavel 1996). Memory is, thus, understood as socially and intersubjectively structured (Douglas 1980; Passerini 1987; Boyarin 1994). Memory also has a poli- tics. According to Tilly (1994a), the politics of memory refers to "the process by which accumulated, shared historical experience constrains today's political action and the contestation or coercion that occurs over the proper interpretation of that historical experience" (p. 247). Tilly not only insists on the *structured character* of political memories but also points out their *structuring capabilities:* "An observer — historian, ethnog- rapher, or fellow citizen — cannot account for the shared interests on which people will act without investigating what mnemonic and moral frames they actually had available" (p. 244). The "dead seize the living," as Bourdieu (1977) contends, and structure, as in Tilly's analysis, the way in which people engage in collective action.

This structuring character of collective memory has also been noted by Halbwachs. In Durkheimian fashion, he points out that a shared identity is maintained through the act of remembering. If remember- ing structures social groups, remembering actually "re-members." In re- shaping (and reinventing) memories, members of a group create bound- aries and ties among themselves.[1]

"People," Somers (1994, 614) argues, "construct identities (however multiple and changing) by locating themselves or being located within a repertoire of emplotted histories." Their experiences are "constituted through narratives," and they "make sense of what has happened and is happening to them by attempting to assemble or in some way to inte- grate these happenings within one or more narratives." Past recollec- tions are always incomplete. The ability to remember and publicly re- tell a story is entangled with the "partial renewal of the old experiences by means of external stimuli. . . . We remember when some new re- minder helps us to piece together small, scattered and indistinct bits of the past" (Douglas 1980, 5). Narratives and memories about Peronism are embedded in sets of relationships that help us understand them better.

Brokers' public performances (analyzed in chap. 4), the official discourse on food-distribution programs (examined in chap. 3), and the constant interactions between brokers and members of their inner circles (chaps. 3 and 5) will be examined as the *relational support* that acts as the "new re-minder" for a certain memory and a particular narrative of Peronism. To anticipate the argument: those individuals who are members of the brokers' inner circles will—almost invariably—stress different aspects of Peronism than those not so intimately involved.

*

In the last presidential elections (May 1995), nearly 60 percent of the population of Villa Paraíso voted for the Peronist Party (Menem).[2] A year and a half later, under conditions of skyrocketing unemployment and significantly reduced income, almost 40 percent of the population of Paraíso admitted that they would vote for a Peronist candidate again if elections were held that day (12 percent for President Menem, 27 per-cent for Governor Duhalde). Peronism is still the dominant force within this enclave of urban poverty. As the local priest told me: "This is a very Peronist shantytown." And as state officials (gladly) admitted: "Paraíso is a stronghold of the Peronist Party." In the parliamentary elections of 1997, the electoral district in which Villa Paraíso is located was one of the few places in Greater Buenos Aires where Peronism did not lose to the centrist coalition known as La Alianza. More than 50 percent of the (mostly poor) population of this electoral district voted for the Partido Justicialista in what turned out to be one of Peronism's worst electoral defeats in its fifty-year history. Despite Alianza's sweeping victory, then, the majority of poor people—in Paraíso as elsewhere in Buenos Aires— continue to vote Peronist.

According to Adelman's (1994, 91) analysis of the "funeral of popu-lism," the current Peronist government has brought "the country full circle—reopening the class nature of the Argentine state which Perón had sought to elide with a populist alliance. . . . If Peronism and popu-lism aimed to obscure class rule by absorbing contradictory interests of civil society within the ambit of the state, *menemismo* expunges this legacy. . . . [T]he current design leaves little doubts about the allegiances of state power."

The political positions that Peronism had advocated when it was in the opposition (from 1983 to 1989)—mainly a greater role for the state as the guarantor of "social justice"—were surreptitiously abandoned by Menem (Sidicaro 1995; Borón et al. 1995). As Levitsky (1997, 1) asserts, "Historically one of the region's most powerful labor-based movements, Peronism had long been a staunch opponent of liberal economic policies. Nevertheless, since 1989, the Peronist government of Carlos Menem has successfully implemented a neoliberal program that clashes with both party tradition and the interests of the party's trade union allies." With respect to labor and unions, Menem's neoliberal shift entailed, among other things, bans on wage increases not linked to productivity and on strikes in much of the public sector, the encouragement of firm-level collective bargaining, and the "flexibilization" of shop-floor labor relations (see chap. 1).[3] Through its resolute adoption of neoliberal structural adjustment policies, the Peronist government is dismantling the semi–welfare state. Since 1989, Peronism has ceased to be the party of "social equality" (Sidicaro 1995); it has changed, "from a populist party dominated by trade unions into the country's most important market-oriented party" (Levitsky 1997, 1). In organizational terms, the party has also mutated "from a union-based party into something resembling an urban machine" (Levitsky 1996, 21; see also Gutierrez 1998). As Levitsky (1998a, 45) clearly puts it: "The party's linkages to the mass base were transformed, as corporatist, union-based linkages to the party's urban base were replaced by territorial, patronage-based linkages. . . . Rather than an electoral-professional or catch-all party, then, [the Peronist Party] transformed into a mass, increasingly patronage-based, 'party of the poor.' Such a party organizational structure is a far better fit with an urban base characterized by high unemployment, informal sector employment, and social segmentation."

Considering shantytown dwellers' voting patterns and the policy orientations of the Peronist government, the question immediately arises, What does it mean for a destitute shantytown dweller to be Peronist in a context in which a Peronist government has implicitly declared war on the poor? To be a Peronist means, and always has meant, many different and competing things. This final chapter will explore the diverse meanings of Peronism within Paraíso and show that these different meanings are anchored in different relational settings, entailing diverse narratives and memories. In other words, the chapter will explore the meanings, the relational support, and the representational form of Peronist identities.

One of the few works that has paid close attention to the ambiguous meanings of the experience of Peronism for Argentine workers is Daniel James's *Resistance and Integration* (1988). This chapter begins with a brief analysis of that book. James's exploration of (Peronist) working-class "common sense" — of the Peronist identity — will serve as the background to an examination of the remnants of that "strong oppositional culture" among Peronist workers and poor shantytown dwellers.

In the second section of the chapter, I analyze the "official emplotment" of Peronism by trying to answer the following questions: What does Peronism/*menemismo* mean for leaders of the Peronist Party and for officials of the Peronist government? How do they establish the link between the Peronist tradition and current neoliberal orientations? How do they *encode* Peronism? The third section looks at the obverse process, examining the (competing) meanings that Peronism (still) has for shantytown dwellers. How do residents of Villa Paraíso *decode* this public narrative? How do they locate themselves in the official narrative of Peronism? How do they understand Peronism? What does Peronism mean for them?

Although some residents remember Peronism as the truly "heretical experience" analyzed by James, only a few judge the current Peronist experience according to those standards. Others recall Peronism as an epoch in which "a lot of goods were distributed." Interestingly enough, from both standpoints *menemismo* is almost always defined as "non-Peronist." In ideal-typical terms, there are not one but two memories of Peronism. On the one hand, the *heretical memory* narrates the history of Peronism in terms of social justice. The *distributionist memory,* on the other hand, narrates the history of Peronism in terms of "what we got from the government." As in the case of the different histories of Paraíso and the diverse evaluations of politics and brokers (chap. 5), these different memories and narratives are neither clear-cut nor mutually exclusive: the difference is mainly a matter of emphasis within a master narrative of Peronism as a "wonderful time."

What Being a Peronist Once Meant

Daniel James's *Resistance and Integration* (1988) is a deep and insightful analysis of the relation between the Argentine working class, the unions, and Peronism. He criticizes previous understandings of that relation using the general notion of populism because of their level of abstraction. "The specificity of concrete social movements and historical experience," he points out, "have escaped through the broad mesh of such (macro-explanatory) framework." Here, I will not recapitulate his detailed analysis but instead focus on his discussion of the meaning(s) that Peronism had for the workers. These meanings will then be contrasted with the perceptions and evaluations that residents of Paraíso hold about Peronism, a political movement that has the "phoenix-like quality of arising strong and unspoiled from [the] ashes" that Merton (1949, 71) detected in the operation of political machines.

According to James (1988, 263), the political and social movement that erupted in Argentina in the mid-1940s promoted as one of its constitutive elements the belief in the essential virtue of the people. Far from merely representing higher wages, the generalization of a system of collective bargaining, greater levels of unionization, and better living conditions, Peronism also—and more fundamentally—embodied a "political vision which entailed an expanded notion of the meaning of citizenship" and a "'heretical' social component which spoke to working-class claims to greater social status, dignity within the workplace and beyond, and a denial of the elite's social and cultural pretensions." In other words, with all its limitations and contradictions, Peronism challenged the sense of limits of working-class life by giving public recognition to the private experiences of humiliation, resignation, and stigmatization that had characterized it during the 1930s.[4] Decency, pride, and self-esteem were at the center of the social meaning that Peronism had for the working class. In this sense, Peronism became a truly "heretical power."

Peronist moral economy had as its central tenet an affirmation of the workers' rights within society and within the workplace and a collective claim for equality and dignity that was ready to call into question certain social and cultural hierarchies. In short, Peronism expressed a "diffuse social challenge to accepted forms of social hierarchy and symbols of authority" and "remained in a fundamental way, a potentially heretical voice, giving expression to the hopes of the oppressed both within the factory and beyond, as a claim for social dignity and equality" (James 1988, 39).

The traditional way of doing politics, dominated by fraud and clientelism (characteristic of Argentine politics since the turn of the century), was among those uncontested forms of social hierarchy and authority. At the center of the heretical Peronist voice was an uncompromising challenge to the machinelike character of politics.

The political machines of Radicals and Conservatives, their reliance on local political bosses, the Conservatives' widespread use of fraud, and the Radicals' use of state jobs for the construction of its basis of electoral support have all been well documented (see Folino 1971; Luna 1958; Rock 1972, 1975; and Walter 1985).[5] The techniques used by Conservatives and Radicals to build political support were said to be based on "the distribution to individuals of concrete rewards, such as bureaucratic offices, charity donations and petty personal privileges" (Rock 1972, 233). Although Conservative or Radical "clientelism" never existed as the *sole* means of mobilizing political loyalty, the urban political boss (*caudillo de barrio*) became a typical figure in urban politics during the first four decades of the twentieth century. As Rock asserts,

> In return for a biennial vote, the caudillo de barrio performed a multitude of petty favors for his constituents, of a kind which won him and his party a not wholly-undeserved popularity within the barrio. By guaranteeing his supporters immunity from the police for their petty transgressions, by organizing local charity services, and by acting as the occasional dispenser of providential loans, the ward boss acted as an intermediary between the individual and the oppressive tentacles of officialdom, and became, with the Union and the Church, a main agent for relief against almost any kind of unforeseen calamity. It was he also who provided the most effective link between the Government, the upper echelons of the Party and the electorate, greatly facilitating the important task of giving both an attractive human face. (p. 247)

The paternalistic measures were said to be effective in breaking down group solidarity and in "atomizing the electorate and individualizing the voter" (Rock 1975, 79).[6] Radicals' clientelism can be counterpoised with the innovation introduced by Peronism: "Peronism, on the other hand, premised its political appeal to workers on a recognition of the working class as a distinct social force which demanded recognition and representation as such in the political life of the nation. This representation would no longer be achieved simply through the exercise of formal rights of citizenship and the primary mediation of political parties. Instead, the working class as an autonomous social force would have direct, indeed privileged access, to the state through its trade unions" (James 1988, 18).

According to James (1988), Perón addressed the workers as a "social force whose own organization and strength were vital if he were to be successful at the level of the state in asserting their rights" (p. 18). This is not to deny the personalistic and "caudillistic" elements within Peronism. Yet I want to stress James's point that "this personalist element was not present entirely at the expense of a continued affirmation of the social and organizational strength of the working class" (p. 19)—so much so that the sheer "existence and sense of identity" of the Argentine working class "as a coherent national force, both socially and politically, can be traced back to the Perón era" (p. 37).

In all their ambiguity, Peronist ideological tenets (its nationalism and corporatism, its emphasis on class harmony, on the ubiquitous role of the leader, and on the overwhelming presence of the paternalist state) did not preclude the "possibility of working-class resistance and the emergence of a strong oppositional culture among workers." This oppositional culture is the "dynamic substratum" of "the rank-and-file resistance to the post-1955 regimes and [lays] the basis for the reassertion of Peronism as the dominant force within the Argentine workers' movement" (James 1988, 262, 40).

In the period 1955–73, Peronism remained "a sort of protean, malleable common-place of working class identification." Being a Peronist was "almost an accepted part of working-class 'common sense'" (James 1988, 262). This was an extremely ambiguous common sense, one that contained more or less antagonistic, more or less classist elements (Nun 1994; Rubinich 1991). Within the "beliefs *in* Peronism," there were many different beliefs about the potentialities of the movement (what Nun calls "beliefs *that*"). For some, Peronism implied social mobility within a well-established social order; for others, it meant a complete transformation of the social order, whether by constitutional means or not (Nun 1994).

The death of Perón, the calamitous experience of Isabel Perón's government (1974–76), which spiraled into a maelstrom of violence culminating in the military terror of the "dirty war" (1976–83), and Menem's neoliberal frenzy harshly affected the "meaning of Peronism." Although the majority of the working and lower classes continue to vote Peronist, in contemporary Argentina "being a Peronist" is not coterminous with the poor's and workers' "common sense," as it used to be from the mid-1950s to the mid-1970s. As I explored in chapter 2, other social antagonisms dominate and organize the experience of the shantytown dwellers. And no political identity can overcome these pervasive sociocultural oppositions, which constitute the paramount everyday reality of the inhabitants of Paraíso. The Peronist/non-Peronist distinction does not divide the shantytown dwellers into opposing camps, nor does it unite them in the face of the larger society. In other words, even in the context of the "very Peronist" Villa Paraíso, being Peronist is not as important to identity as it was through the mid-1970s. Peronism has lost its relevance as an organizer of everyday experience.

Yet, as clearly emerges from the voting patterns cited above and from a superficial review of the electoral results of the last fourteen years (since the return of democracy), Peronism is still the most important political force among the poor and the working classes (Sidicaro 1995). Since the return of democracy in 1983, Peronism has garnered the majority of its votes from the popular sectors (Sidicaro 1995).[7] However, today "being a Peronist" means many different things. These different meanings stem from distinct narratives and memories and are anchored in different webs of relations.

In what follows, I explore the different meanings of being a Peronist. My argument runs as follows: much like the unions' rank-and-file "resistance" was the specific social universe in which the (Peronist) "opposition culture" was reproduced from 1955 until the early 1970s, the (Peronist) problem-solving networks are now the most important webs of relations in which the remnants of a strong Peronist identity are kept alive.

The fact that this strong identity is embedded in survival problem-solving networks and active in the everyday life of some shantytown dwellers makes the distinction between public and routinely embedded identities problematic (Tilly 1995). In point of fact, the actors involved in the problem-solving networks experience a shared social relation (an identity) that pivots explicitly and implicitly between public life and routine social existence. As the public performances of political brokers (analyzed in chap. 4) and the official point of view on the food-distribution programs (examined in chap. 3) attest, there is no clear division between being a Peronist in public life and solving everyday survival problems in a Peronist way.

What Being a Peronist Means Today

With the same caution that Daniel James chooses the lyrics of the tango to best convey the sense of humiliation, bitterness, and resignation prevailing among workers in the *década infame* of the 1930s, a historian in the year 2050 will probably choose the lyrics of the rock-and-roll band Los Redonditos de Ricota to examine the beliefs and perceptions of the urban poor in the 1990s. "So much sorrow, you get used to it," the historian will read in those lyrics. Ethnographic works (Kuasñosky and Szulik 1996; Auyero 1992) attest to the fact that those lyrics resonate among their listeners. When I asked Coqui—a young resident of nearby Villa Herrera—what his plans were for the future, he told me (quoting the lyrics of that same rock band): "The future . . . what future? *The future is already here. . . .*" The feeling of fatality and gloom is not limited to youngsters but is spreading to most of the population of Villa Paraíso and other shantytowns, working-class neighborhoods, and squatter settlements. As I explored in chapter 2, most shantytown dwellers feel abandoned by the state, socially isolated, and terrorized by social predators and drug dealers. This generalized feeling feeds the three dominant antagonisms that organize the everyday experience of shantytown dwellers and divide the population.

In point of fact, much of the sense of resignation, humiliation, stigmatization, and bitterness that, as James asserts, pervaded popular life in the 1930s can be found in today's territories of urban exclusion. Against the background of this generalized feeling of abandonment and resignation (and the social antagonisms to which this sentiment gives birth) stands the social meaning of contemporary Peronism.

The Official Validation of Peronism

There is probably no better summary of the official meaning of Peronism — that is, the point of view of Peronist leaders as expressed in the party's official discourse — than that offered by the master of ceremonies at a rally organized by the Peronist party of Cóspito City to pay homage to Eva Perón on 26 July 1996, the anniversary of her death. Nearly one thousand people attended the rally. Before introducing the speakers (Mayor Rolo Fontana and his adviser in the welfare section, Susana Gutierrez), the emcee said: "Eva Perón . . . as soon as you took power, you were food, shoes, roofs for a dignified life, sewing machines. . . ." He was not alone in so encoding the history of Peronism: the official Peronist narrative stresses the association of Peronism and the provision of goods to the needy.[8] The official discourse (re)presents Peronism mainly as a response to economic grievances.

In his public speeches, the "very Peronist" mayor of Cóspito — as his (also Peronist) aides define Rolo Fontana — makes the most of this official narrative. On 24 September 1996, the governor's wife came to Cóspito to donate refrigerators, ovens, and cookware to the forty-seven soup kitchens that function in the city. It is worth quoting at length an excerpt from the mayor's introductory speech because in it he explicitly states what good government is and he associates this "good government" with the Peronist tradition:

> We, the Argentines, need sensitive and tender government officials who feel love for those who are unprotected. See . . . the governor's wife comes to the city of Cóspito, to our humble people, and she tells us: "We are going to hand out all these things to the soup kitchens." You can see the ovens, plates, saucepans, frying pans . . . all the necessary things so that the soup kitchens can prepare the meals for our children. . . . This reminds me that forty-five years ago social action was developed by another government, this same social action that you [referring to Ms. Duhalde] are now carrying out. I have to say it, I cannot keep it inside: in this gathering, I am witnessing what I witnessed fifty years ago when another woman, another woman like you

[referring to Ms. Duhalde], who was born in the province of Buenos Aires, also developed social action. That woman was Eva Perón.

"Every time I come to Cóspito," Chiche Duhalde—the governor's wife—replies, addressing the audience of more than five hundred women, "Rolo makes me feel embarrassed because he compares me with Evita." In her public speech, she explicitly dissociates herself from the "Standard-bearer of the Humble," but she implicitly presents herself as the "Bridge of Love," as "a humble woman among others," thereby constructing the image of togetherness and caring that, as we saw in chapter 4, lies at the center of the aid to the poor provided by Eva and by the local Peronist brokers:

> I always say that, as the tango lyrics go, "There will never be anyone like her" [*No habrá ninguna igual, no habrá ninguna*]. I honestly feel that: there is not going to be someone like Evita. . . . The women who have learned [*mamado*] that [Peronist] doctrine, who have truly felt Peronism, take her as a model; but we know that the circumstances are different and that there is not going to be another Evita [*Evita es irrepetible*]. Times have changed; the history of the country is different. . . . So one tries to do the best one can, sometimes making mistakes, other times doing it successfully, in this task that is so important for the humble men and women of our *barrios*. These soup kitchens. . . .

After briefly recounting the history of the soup kitchens, locating their origins in the 1989 riots and lootings, she links her activity with "true Peronism":[9] "The other day, I saw a documentary on the history of Peronism. It was called *Juan Perón: A Passion*. We saw two hours of the documentary. It was a history of Peronism that showed everything that Perón and Evita did in those places [referring to the soup kitchens] where the most humble children of our neighborhoods were being cared for. These were beautiful, dignified places with adequate infrastructure. Why can't we aspire to that? Why can't we have dignified soup kitchens?"

"Dignity"—a central element in the "Peronist moral economy" analyzed by James—is now found in the soup kitchens. Against the traditional Peronist emphasis on "social justice," the need for public soup kitchens is never presented as the product of the unjust distribution of wealth and the increasing marginalization of the poor.

Much like the mayor, Chiche Duhalde also emphasizes the association of Peronism and the delivery of essential goods to the poor. As we saw in chapter 3, her pet plan is considered by her—and by her collaborators and *manzaneras*—to be good and effective government action, "true Peronism." "True Peronism" and "good (Peronist) government" are continuously equated with goods and public works. The more you deliver, the more Peronist you are; the more you inaugurate public works, the better a (Peronist) governor you are.

"In order to win an election, there's no better thing than a bit of Peronism," a mayor of one of the cities of the Conurbano Bonaerense said during a Peronist Party meeting in August 1996 (*Página12*, 25 August 1996, 12). This "bit of Peronism" is what Governor Duhalde has been trying to represent publicly. Although he seldom confronts President Menem in public, he continuously attempts to present himself as the repository of Peronist virtue. His self-presentation recurrently stresses that he is "the true Peronist," the one who is loyal to the legacy of Perón.

According to Duhalde, in order to remain loyal to Perón, the party that he leads in the province of Buenos Aires must become "a mass organization dedicated to solving the problems of the people." Cast in the terms of my analysis in chapters 3, 4, and 5, what he means is that Peronism must become a strong and extended problem-solving network. This is, according to one of the party leaders, the true mission of contemporary Peronism.

Governor Duhalde's portrait is on the cover of the first issue of the Peronist Party magazine *El Bonaerense*. Included in this first issue are two portraits of Perón and Evita. The caption says: "To keep memory alive. Photographs of General Perón and of the *compañera* Evita are included in this issue as a way of keeping alive the legacy of the construction of a Just, Free, and Sovereign Motherland." Eleven pictures of Duhalde are also included (and the issue is only twenty-four pages long). He is photographed at public ceremonies, in party congresses, in homage to Eva Perón, and conferring land titles on the "thousands of residents of Lomas de Zamora." The issue also runs an interview with his wife entitled "Everything for Love" (Partido Justicalista 1996).

Chapters 3, 4, and 5 attest to the fact that "Peronist folklore" has survived the death of populism. In point of fact, the "adaptation" of the party to the "opportunities and constraints posed by a liberalizing world" (Levitsky 1997, 2) *needs* this folklore. Peronist folklore is not a remnant of the past to be further eroded by modern (neoliberal) times but a *residual cultural element* in Williams's (1977, 122) sense of the term: a cultural configuration "effectively formed in the past" but still "active in the cultural process, not only and often not at all as an element of the past, but as an effective element of the present." As a residual cultural element Peronist folklore satisfies two basic "latent functions": the legitimation of current policy orientations and the justification of the brokers' actions.[10]

To be blunt, if in the 1940s Peronism offered a "heretical" (i.e., heterodoxical) reading of social relations of hierarchy and domination embedded in clientelist relations, today the official reading of Peronism reinforces and justifies personalized political mediation as a way of solving everyday problems. From being a heresy (a contestation of, among other things, clientelist arrangements), Peronism has become the orthodoxy (a justification of these institutionalized practices).

Decoding the Official Reading

In his critique of Laclau's analysis of populism, De Ipola (1987) asserts that social discourses do not have an immanent meaning that can be grasped independently of their reception. If we are to avoid the common mistake of identifying the production of a discourse with its effects, we should look at the reception process or, in Stuart Hall's (1993) terms, at the decoding process. In other words, in order to be effective (i.e., believed), the ideological/programmatic validation of true Peronism must be decoded in a particular way. As the production and the reception of political discourses are two sides of the same coin, in order to understand the social meaning of Peronism we must look at the "other side," as James himself does for the adequate comprehension of the Peronist experience.

What do shantytown dwellers do with the Peronist public narrative? How is the official point of view related to what they know or remember about Peronism? Shantytown dwellers remember different things about and verbalize different narratives of Peronism. Some remember Peronism for what the (Peronist) state, personalized in the figures of Perón or Eva Perón, gave them. Their memories nicely dovetail with what the Peronist Party defines as "good Peronism." Others (a minority) recall the "heretical component" of the movement. These recollections of the Peronist experience originate in the particular social milieus in which those who remember are embedded.

For some, Peronism was exactly what the official discourse says it was: Peronism meant *things,* more and better things. When interviewing Paraíso residents, I invariably asked the same questions about Peronism: What do you remember about the Peronist epoch? What was the most important thing that Eva Perón, Juan Perón, or Peronism accomplished? Some answers eloquently express the association of Peronism and goods:

[When Perón went to Formosa (a northern province) at Christmas,] he distributed boxes full of things. On New Year's, [he handed out] toys. It wasn't as they do now . . . [nowadays] they hand out toys, and they keep the toys for those at the top [*para los capos*]. . . . No . . . [they handed out] toys, dolls, bicycles, sewing machines, bicycles for the guys so that they could go to work, balls for those who knew how to play soccer, soccer clothes. Then he and Evita went to Asunción [Paraguay], and they handed out toys. That is something that the Paraguayans will never forget. At Christmas they gave cider, *panettone,* a box, this big, full. . . . Evita was a great woman who loved people from her heart, really from her heart; she loved the elderly, the students, the children. (Ana)

I remember when the people of Perón sent clothes, sneakers, and gave the material that allowed people to repair their homes. . . . I remember that they sent books, pencils, sneakers to my school. . . . A Peronist government should think of the worker, not of those at the top. (Alfonsina)

What really impressed me [about the Peronist epoch], and will keep on impressing me, were the trucks handing out blankets, quilts, and mattresses in the *barrios* . . . boxes full of sneakers. That is missing now. What really impressed me was witnessing how these things were given. We haven't seen that in many years now. . . . [When Perón was in office,] I went and asked for things, and they gave them to me. If you asked for sheet metal, you would get it. If you asked for food, you would get it. (Cholo)

[Under Perón] I used to get my cider and my *panettone* for Christmas. It was different. Now Peronism is in power, but it is different.[11] . . . [When Perón was in power,] you would go to the health center, and they would give you the best powdered milk [Nido]. They used to give me three kilos every fifteen days. . . . There was a lot of help. Now I see the celebrations of Children's Day, and they have nothing to do with those celebrations back in the 1970s: cookies, hot choco-late, candies. . . . Each kid used to get a toy at the end of the day. . . . Now they hold a raffle, and not everybody gets a toy. (Victoria)

These excerpts are only a few of the dozens of testimonies that stress the material goods that Peronism used to distribute. As is clear, all of them set their memories against present conditions and use the oppor-tunity to criticize Menem's government. He is routinely described as "non-Peronist."

Another important element in these recollections is the dichotomy that they point up between "those at the top" and "those at the bottom." What is at issue is not, however, the "elite's sociocultural pretentions" (James 1988, 263) but the fact that most politicians—except those "like us" (the mayor, the local brokers, the governor and his wife)—have aban-doned true Peronist principles. True Peronists "support the poor," Ana tells me. The most important thing that Perón and Evita did was "give houses to the people, hand out sewing machines" (Marta). The abun-dance under Perón is contrasted with today's hard times, true Peronism with *menemismo:* "Menem is not Peronist; he is *menemista.* Under the name of Perón there are a lot of people who are profiting [*Con el nombre de Perón están comiendo todos estos*]. Perón is dead; why don't they do what Perón used to do? They take office in the name of someone who did something good, and then they do whatever they want. In every rally, [there are pictures of] Perón and Evita. Why don't they do something good?"

What does it mean to "do something good"? For those who remem-ber Peronism in terms of what it handed out, *something good* means— obviously—goods and services of the kind the mayor and, especially, the governor and his wife deliver. After admitting that, "when Perón was alive, it was different," Victoria and her daughter told me that, if elec-tions were held that day, they would vote for Governor Duhalde. They both agreed that "he [Duhalde] is helping a lot. . . . This milk program

[Plan Vida] is organized by his wife. And he is improving the streets, he is inaugurating hospitals and schools. He cares about the province." Invariably, Duhalde and his wife are praised for "helping the people." And, as we saw in chapter 3, the people equate that help with them. They are the ones who get the credit for the goods that the state delivers.

The comparison drawn, and the resulting tension that exists, between current (Peronist) government actions and a memory of Peronism is wonderfully expressed in the words of one Plan Vida *manzanera*. For her, Chiche Duhalde is the best Peronist; yet "she will never be like Evita. She is not the Eva Perón of the 1990s because out of one hundred people she helps only one while Evita would have helped all of them" (*Página12 Digital,* 17 March 1997).

The "heretical component" of the Peronist moral economy has been replaced by a "distributionist element." According to many who self-identify as Peronist voters, a *good Peronist* is the one who gives more things. The cultural matrix of many shantytown dwellers, that is, the array of cultural representations according to which they decode their current situation, is dominated by these associations and reconfirmed by the everyday distributive practices of government officials and local brokers.

Rosa—discussed at the beginning of this chapter—offers a typical example of the phenomenon under consideration here: the actions of present Peronism stimulate and color the recall of past Peronism, and vice versa. Rosa's glasses constitute the "mnemonic lenses" (Zerubavel 1996) through which she views Peronism. Her understanding of Peronism is dominated by a broker's performance. A favor granted or an item received in the present brings things full circle. Peronism's "foundational favor" is re-created in each transaction that a broker mediates today.

People also remember that true Peronism stands for social justice. "So do you have any particular recollection of Evita?" I ask Toto, a member of the Peronist Resistance in the 1950s and 1960s (see chap. 2):

My mother used to work in a tannery in Avellaneda, and, when Eva Duarte began to visit the humble people, she went to that factory to see the working conditions of the humble workers. There were people from the countryside, and they were working like animals. Nobody dared talk to Evita, and my mother's fellow workers asked her to tell Evita what was going on in the factory. My mother didn't know how to write or read, and, when she saw [Evita], she was so moved that she started crying. Evita calmed her, and she told my mom that she was a common woman, a woman like her. My mom told Evita that every rainy day the whole ceiling fell down because it was a sheet-metal ceiling. Twenty days later, they had everything renovated.

Toto recalls Peronism as the social and political movement that first treated workers with the dignity that they deserve. Of course he remembers goods and services received, but he also remembers that Peronism meant pride, respect, what James would consider the affirmation of the worker's rights within both the workplace and society at large. As another longtime Peronist, also a member of the Peronist Resistance, told me: "Perón screwed the oligarchy. . . . When Perón took office, everything changed because the worker ceased to be the slave of the rich people. [Perón] awakened [avivó] the workers."

It is hardly a new observation that there are not one but several meanings of Peronism. As I mentioned in the previous chapter, many of those who criticize the actions of the (Peronist) brokers do so in the name of Peronism. At the same time, as we saw in chapters 3 and 4, brokers and government officials perform their roles as "true Peronists." I confronted one of my interviewees with this "enigma": "See, what I don't understand is what you really think. . . . You just told me you are a 'Peronist from the crib.' These people [the neighbors' brokers] who, as you just said, 'use the people' are also Peronists. . . ." His reply eloquently expresses the ambiguity still inherent in Peronism: "No, they are not Peronists. I think that Perón didn't teach us to do this [to 'use the people']. He might have taught us how to maneuver politically [tener muñeca política], but not to do this. He always talked about social justice; nobody practices that anymore. They are not really Peronists. They might kiss the Peronist flag, they might kiss Perón and Evita, but they are not Peronists. Peronism is social justice." Asked what he means by social justice, he refers to the small amount of food distributed at Pisutti's UB. If it were his UB, he tells me, "I would hand out food at least every week."

The Leftovers of the Populist Heresy

As I mentioned in the first section of this chapter, 39 percent of the population of Villa Paraíso would vote Peronist if elections were held today. Once we break down these aggregate data into four age groups, we find that, although there are differences among age groups, these differences are not very significant. Thirty-four percent of those between twenty and twenty-nine years of age, 37 percent of those between thirty and forty-four, and 36 percent of those over sixty would vote Peronist. The most significant difference shows up among those forty-five and fifty-nine: 46 percent would vote Peronist. Thus, Peronism is still the preferred option of the poor, regardless of age. Older people who lived through those "marvelous years" of the first and second Peronist governments tend to be more loyal to Peronism than the younger generations.

Within these votes *for* Peronism, there are different beliefs *about* Peronism. As we saw, regardless of age, sex, and length of residence in Paraíso, residents tell different stories about Peronism. Different "Peronist identities" are constituted through these narratives. What is the source of this variation?

Undoubtedly, there is a public validation of true Peronism that both constrains the emergence of other possible meanings of Peronism and facilitates the consolidation of the association between true Peronism and the delivery of goods and services. Such validation comes from the public pronouncements of politicians, but it also comes from their actual practices. Brokers' ready availability to their clients and politicians' distribution of goods and services are key elements in the public validation of true Peronism, reinforcing this emplotment of Peronism.

Yet such representations of the meaning of Peronism are decoded differently according to the relational and cultural matrix in which clients are embedded, and Peronist identities do not exist outside these complexes (see Somers 1994). In other words, the relational setting in which the public narrative is received determines its interpretation. In some settings, that narrative is warmly received and unknowingly reproduced. In others, it is not.

Within their inner circles, the brokers' incessant performative work has created an especially receptive atmosphere. Within these networks, no ambiguity adheres to the meaning of Peronism. Peronism is the receipt of goods and services, the distribution of those goods and services is the best and, indeed, only possible response to economic hard times, and there is no break, no difference between past and present Peronism.

Beyond the brokers' sphere of influence, things are not so straightforward. Former members of the Peronist Resistance recall the "populist heresy." Others consider Peronism the benchmark against which political action is to be judged morally. Most curiously, still others long for "the return of Peronism"—even though the Peronist party currently controls all levels of government.

But, however the public narrative is received, the fact remains that Peronism (however interpreted) remains the standard against which a government and its representatives and policies are judged. Whatever the reason, Peronism still holds enormous appeal for the residents of Villa Paraíso.

Remembering/Forgetting

People's memories of Peronism are truly effective in the present because they constitute a politics. They fulfill the important function of legitimating brokers' current positional centrality; in other words, they justify brokers' power. And that centrality is conferred, not only because brokers are perceived as historical protagonists in the improvement of the shantytown, but also because they are seen as fulfilling the function that the Peronist government once fulfilled: distributing goods and services. They are seen as today's Perons.

The brokers' way of doing politics resembles a form of political activity that Peronism has attacked in the past (i.e., Conservative and Radical clientelism). However, those closest to the current centers of power consider this new clientelism "true Peronism" because what they remember of Peronism is what the brokers are doing today. It is as if the history of Peronism is constantly being retold/rewritten in the present tense by the everyday enactment of political clientelism. As a Peronist activist tellingly puts it: "Peronism is about helping poor people, and that's what we are doing here. The economic situation is terrible and people are needy. So we give them bags of food, medicine, maybe even a job. That's what Peronism is all about" (quoted in Levitsky 1998a, 35).

Within brokers' inner circles, there are traces neither of the collective-action version of the history of the slum nor of the heretical memory of Peronism. Such memories are anathema to current political arrangements because they offer other possible scenarios. And personalized problem solving works better when its arbitrary nature is not being continually pointed out. Following a functionalist line of reasoning, we could say that problem solving through personalized political mediation does not need the presence of counterfactuals. It is presented as a social arrangement that has been in existence for a long time, since the time of the Perons, since the time when the brokers were working hard to improve the shantytown.

*

"Memory, then, no matter how small the piece remembered, demands my respect, my attention, and my trust," writes Toni Morrison (1996, 214). The seemingly insignificant story of Rosa's glasses commands our sociological imagination because it can help us link the "the personal troubles of milieu" and the "public issues of social structure" of which C. Wright Mills so perceptively talks. The Rosas who constitute the clientelist inner circles are not "mnemonic Robinson Crusoes"; they are embedded in "remembrance environments" (Zerubavel 1996, 284–85) that structure what is to be remembered and what is to be forgotten. As do other social actors, they tend to idealize the past as part of their moral work; their golden past is located in the first and second governments of Perón.

Although people remember different things about the "first Peronism," its idealization always contains an implicit critique of present conditions. Seen from the standpoint of that idealized past, "this"—Menem's politics—"is not Peronism." The generalized belief seems to be that, under a "truly Peronist" government, the poor would not be living like they are.

This idealization not only hints at a critique of the conditions of existence that the poor must endure; it also implies a social construction of forgetting/remembering. The participation of brokers and clients in problem-solving networks gives specific relational support to this process of remembering/forgetting. Within Peronist problem-solving networks we can detect the (re)invention of tradition, to the end of legitimizing existing social arrangements. Although Peronism (still) means different things to different people, within broker's inner circles, within the *manzaneras'* pyramidal network, there is one meaning of Peronism that tends to dominate. Peronism is the distribution of goods and services.

The doxic acceptance of political mediation as a way of solving survival problems analyzed in chapter 5 coexists with a certain memory of Peronism. In point of fact, the misrecognition of the arbitrariness of the order of political mediation and the (re)invention of the Peronist tradition are mutually reinforcing processes.

In the context of deproletarianization, widespread material deprivation, and symbolic rejection, food is the new utopia among the poor. For many shantytown dwellers, Peronism is not a heretical voice, a challenge to sociocultural boundaries, but a promise of food that holds no one responsible for its scarcity. Amid an undeclared war on the poor, the (Peronist) problem-solving networks are now the most important webs of relations in which the remains of a strong Peronist identity are kept alive. Based as they are on the distribution of food and other vital goods, the remnants of the populist heresy embedded in those networks look very much like the leftovers of a golden time.

Problem Solving through Political Mediation as a Structure of Feeling

Half Peronist, Half Journalist

The aspects of things that are most important for us are hidden because of their simplicity and familiarity. (One is unable to notice something—because it is always before one's eyes.) The real foundations of his enquiry do not strike a man at all. Unless that fact has at some time struck him.—And this means: we fail to be struck by what, once seen, is most striking and most powerful. —L. Wittgenstein, *Philosophical Investigations*

Eight months into the course of my fieldwork in Paraíso, Peronist folklore had become for me reality. Governor Duhalde, his wife, and the mayor had become in my mind "El Negro," "Chiche," and "Rolo." I was on familiar terms with "Matilde" and "Juancito." Even Juan and Eva Perón were for me "Pocho" (or "El General" or "El Macho") and "Evita." I was not a convert to Peronism, but the trappings of Peronism—wristwatches with Rolo's picture printed on them, the blonde hair of the female brokers, the daily distribution of food at the UBS—had become unremarkable parts of my normal, everyday life. Such things had lost the capacity to surprise me. I had become so involved with the Peronist "maelstrom" that I was losing the distance—what Elias (1987) calls *detachment*—necessary for the analysis of the complex interrelations between Peronism, survival strategies, and urban poverty, my professed objective.[1] Direct experience was becoming my primary epistemological obstacle.

At about the same time, another—less theoretical—obstacle to my work emerged. One of the mayor's closest friends and political associates was implicated in a corruption scandal, his actions caught on tape by a hidden camera. The whole structure of municipal government was shaken by the scandal. From the mayor down to the brokers, all public officials were suspected of corruption and subjected to intense public scrutiny. And, in the atmosphere of suspicion that resulted, my access to local politicians and brokers was severely restricted.

I had, over the previous eight months, slowly built up the trust of these people. My relationship with Matilde, for example, had gained a certain fluidity. While I never obtained free access to her person and was never given complete notification of all her activities—probably owing to the fact that, as one resident informed me, she had "things to hide"[2]—she did not seem to view me as any kind of threat, at least not initially. Early on in my work, I patiently explained to her the object of my research (a history of Villa Paraíso). And, while having a sociologist around is not something to which it is easy to adjust, she eventually felt comfortable enough with the situation to introduce me to her close followers and associates—and without that introduction much of my work would have been impossible. My presence was also sometimes a source of prestige for her and furthermore offered her an unprecedented performance opportunity—I was a captive audience, always eager to hear more about her hard work and her mission in life.

The corruption scandal changed all that. Where formerly I had been eagerly invited into her house, now Matilde would not talk to me—according to her cleaning lady, she was "too busy." I was no longer invited to attend rallies with her and her band. She and the others seem to have decided that I was an undercover journalist in search of further instances of corruption. Although I was not expelled from the field, my operations were thereafter greatly curtailed.[3]

Reflexivity as a Tool

But as fieldwork progressed and I witnessed such performances a number of times, I began to take them largely for granted. They increasingly became part of my stock of knowledge, part of my world. —Paul Rabinow, *Reflections on Fieldwork in Morocco*

"Scholarly self-reflection often degenerates into narcissistic celebrations of privilege," writes Phillipe Bourgois (1995, 14).[4] I discuss my loss of distance and the abrupt end of my fieldwork not as an exercise in self-knowledge (a sort of "knowing yourself through fieldwork," unwarrantedly fashionable nowadays), but because both experiences foster the exercise of a necessary reflexivity. In particular, they illustrate the type of bias control that I have been attempting throughout this book.

In his comment on Bourdieu's original take on epistemic reflexivity, Wacquant (1992, 39; emphasis added; see also Bourdieu 1998) asserts:

> The *intellectualist bias* which entices us to construe the world as a *spectacle,* as a set of significations to be interpreted rather than as *concrete problems to be solved practically,* is more profound and more distorting than those rooted in the social origins or location of the analyst in the academic field, because it can lead us to miss entirely the *differentia specifica* of the logic of practice. Whenever we fail to subject to systematic critique the "presuppositions inscribed in the fact of thinking the world, of retiring from the world and from action in the world in order to think that action," we risk collapsing practical logic into theoretical logic. (emphasis added)

The firsthand experience of (and immersion in) the everyday practice of Peronism as a prerequisite—and, at the same time, as an obstacle—to adequate knowledge and the confused identity as a practical problem illuminate certain aspects of this type of bias that always threaten to blur the sociological gaze. I would like to conclude with a reflection on the implications that the *conflation* of the ethnographer and the journalist and the *immersion* in the Peronist world of truth have for the sociological knowledge of problem-solving networks and of the cultural representations embedded in them.

That I was taken to be a journalist is offered as far more than an amusing anecdote. The hidden-camera scandal activated in a dramatic form a confusion that was always present as I conducted my fieldwork. People in Paraíso constantly assumed that I was a journalist. Although this is not the place for an extended consideration of this confusion, it seems to me that, in terms of that indispensable reflexivity, the mistake merits some attention.

"People called me TV Crónica, and they call her Channel 27," Nelida told me. After an accident in which a bus nearly killed a five-year-old child, "people called Rosa by the name of Channel 2." So began a series of conversations that I carried out with two residents of the worst sector of Paraíso, the Fifth Road. The comparison that Cacho made between Villa Paraíso and (the mediatic image of) the Bronx on the first day of my research (see chap. 2), the presentation of the self as a television channel, the recurrent misperception that I was a journalist, all seem to validate the opinions of those who talk about the almost complete mass mediatization of society in the era of globalization. Yet there is another key dimension to such media identification. Not only do the shantytown dwellers constitute an audience for the media; they also establish an instrumental relationship with them. "People called me Channel 27 because, when the accident happened, I was the one who called them, and they came to the shantytown," Ruli told me. She called the police and network television.

The media—television, radio, the popular press—are part of shantytown dwellers' everyday lives not simply because they are consumers but also—and probably more importantly—because they see the media as a means (the only means?) for drawing attention to themselves and their concerns. From their space of relegation, from their position of stigmatization and neglect, the media offer them a means of communicating with the outside world. When Ruli calls the television station to report an accident, she gets the attention of an outsider, someone who is willing to come into the shantytown, listen to what she has to say, and convey that message to the outside world. In all probability, the shantytown dwellers viewed me as an ethnographer in the same light. And that "confusion" tells us a great deal about the commonsense universe of the residents of Villa Paraíso. What they need is to be listened to, to be paid attention to, to be allowed to have a voice.

My loss of objectivity is important as well because, in order to maintain the integrity of my research agenda, I was forced to resort to conceptual tools foreign to most studies of Peronism. My explorations and analyses of problem-solving networks as a set of ongoing relationships between positions, of the different ideal-typical trajectories of brokers (chap. 3), of their public performances (chap. 4), of the problem holders' readings of those presentations (chap. 5), and of the memories that are being re-created within brokers' inner circles (chap. 6) were my ways of breaking with preconceived notions and—as this "break with apparent relations presupposes the construction of new relations among the appearances" (Bourdieu, Chamboderon, and Passeron 1991, 57)—constructing anew the object of research. At the same time, my dissatisfaction with academic studies of contemporary Peronism/*menemismo* increased.

The detachment needed to construct an object out of the "Peronist maelstrom" does not inexorably lead to the detached point of view that prevails in many of the understandings of contemporary Peronism (see, e.g., Borón et al. 1995; Palermo and Novaro 1996; Sidicaro and Mayer 1995). This conventional science of Peronism/*menemismo* is dominated mostly by a political science approach that—in its obsession with the party system, the separation of powers (or the absence thereof), the corporations, the "type" of democracy that is being consolidated, etc.— pays attention neither to the ways in which the "actors" and "structural processes" examined affect people's everyday lives nor to the active engagement that people establish with those processes of transformation. No wonder these analyses do a magnificent job of explaining "everything but" the fundamental elements (or the enigma) of contemporary Peronism, namely, the continuous support that it gets among the poor (despite its electoral setbacks). The sophistication that many of these analyses exhibit vanishes when they are forced to tackle the bases of Peronism: its capacity to retain the loyalty of the destitute. In none of the most-cited studies of *menemismo* do the authors trouble to conduct primary field research in the areas evincing the highest support for Peronism[5]—a curious absence, especially considering the ambitious objective of "understanding *menemismo,* and through it, contemporary Argentina" (Hora and Trímboli 1995, 9). Serious ethnographic work is replaced by the poor substitute of survey opinion polls, as if the reasons why some poor people still "keep memory alive" when voting can be comprehended by the question, "Why do you vote for X?"

This book does not claim to explain the support that Peronism still finds among the masses. Yet it does explore one of the ways in which the party reproduces its organizational strength and reinvents the Peronist tradition on a daily basis. While the continuous presence of the party as a problem-solving center at the grassroots level is certainly not the only reason for its resilience (and, anyway, there is no *one* reason), the detailed analysis of the phenomenon helps us understand this support in a way that current studies of Peronism/*menemismo* do not. Either because they take this support for granted or because they (wrongly) assume that surveys are a good instrument with which to gauge that support, current analyses of Argentina politics have avoided any sort of contact with the Peronist world of truth.

"Clientelism" in the Making

The analysis of performances, representations, and memories (chaps. 4, 5, and 6) is grounded in the general context of deepening marginalization, growing inequality, and the retrenchment of the welfare component of the populist state (chap. 1), in the history of the shantytown and in the experiences of shantytown dwellers (chap. 2), and in the specific social universe of the problem-solving network, (re)constructed in chapter 3. This universe expresses the organizational strength of the Peronist Party at the mass level. Discussions with colleagues in the United States and in Argentina alerted me to an unintended emphasis on the "fixity" and "finished" character of my analysis. It is true: embedding performances, representations, and memories in the general process of social destitution and in a specific network runs the risk of giving an impression of fixity that does not do justice to what is actually happening in the dynamic social universe of problem solving through personalized political mediation.

My way of proceeding was guided by the one-sided accentuation of some properties and elements found during the course of my fieldwork and by the synthesis of concrete individual phenomena into an analytic construct that I label *problem solving through personalized political mediation.*[6] It is true that this procedure of reasoning by "moving to the limits" gives the impression of a fixed and coherent social universe, risking a loss of fidelity to the real for the sake of theoretical coherence. Yet I chose it, not only as a way of attempting to maintain a certain level of objectivity, but also as a way of revealing the dynamic structure of the operation of this universe of practices. The extreme form that I (re)constructed in this book is a privileged point of departure for revealing the forms and functions of a whole set of isomorphic cases that abound in contemporary Argentina. Furthermore, this way of proceeding allowed me to show the ways in which the content and form of social relationships affect the formation of political attitudes and behaviors.

Reasoning by "moving to the limit," by analytic accentuation and synthesis, does not necessarily preclude a consideration of the processual character of the universe under study. As Raymond Williams (1977) notes, "In most description and analysis, culture and society are expressed in an habitual past tense. The strongest barrier to the recognition of human cultural activity is this immediate and regular conversion of experience into finished products" (p. 128). Institutions, relationships, and formations in which people are still involved in contemporary life—and through which, as in the case of this study, they solve pressing everyday problems—are converted "into formed wholes rather than forming and formative processes," thus feeding the fundamental error in the analysis of contemporary culture and society, namely, reducing "the social to fixed forms" (pp. 128, 129). The notion *structure of feeling* attempts to come to terms with this processual, not fully articulated character of reality. "We are talking," says Williams,

> about characteristic elements of impulse, restraint, and tone; specifically affective elements of consciousness and relationships: not feeling against thought, but thought as felt and feeling as thought: practical consciousness of a present kind, in a living and interrelating continuity. We are then defining these elements as a "structure": as a set, with specific internal relations, at once interlocking and in tension. Yet we are also defining a social experience which is still in process, often indeed not yet recognized as social but taken to be private, idiosyncratic, and even isolating, but which in analysis (though rarely otherwise) has its emergent, connecting, and dominant characteristics, indeed its specific hierarchies. (p. 132)

In conceptual terms, structures of feeling are "social experiences in solution," that is, cultural forms that have not yet precipitated out. In methodological terms, a structure of feeling is a "cultural hypothesis." The analytic accentuation and synthesis of certain aspects of reality performed throughout this book offer a "guidance to the construction"

(Weber 1949, 90) of a cultural hypothesis that emphasizes the processual character of the reality under analysis.

With the processes of deepening marginalization fostered by growing unemployment and state neglect, the concomitant organizational desertification in enclaves of urban poverty, and a governing party with a strong organization in those spaces and with low-cost access to state-funded programs of social assistance, personalized political mediation (as a way of solving pressing survival needs) is gaining strength and spreading throughout territories of urban relegation. In this book, I showed that, much like the patron-client ties in rural Southeast Asia analyzed by Scott and Kerkvliet (1977, 443), problem solving through personalized political mediation should be taken seriously and "cannot be merely dismissed as vestigial remains of old structures." On the contrary, as a way of solving pressing survival needs, it should be "analyzed as a type of social bond that may be dominant under some conditions and marginal under others." Furthermore, taking into consideration the process of deepening marginalization of the population living in shanty-towns, squatter settlements, and poor *barrios* in Argentina, it would not be risky to venture that the personalized and lopsided forms of exchange analyzed in the preceding chapters might crystallize into new forms of clientelism.

The increasing significance of clientelist forms does not mean that the solution of survival problems through the personal intervention of Peronist Party members comes to supplant other ways in which Peronism has established links to the poor during the past fifty years (unionism, "charismatic" following, etc.). On the contrary, clientelism is constructed out of Peronism; it is superimposed on it; it imbues this resilient political party with new life, with a new form of power. The UBS are the sites of this convergence of Peronism and clientelist politics, providing Peronism its most crucial support. Curiously enough, these seemingly unimportant popular institutions have been persistently neglected in most studies of contemporary Peronism.[7]

The cultural hypothesis that, I think, emerges from this process runs as follows: With the strengthening of local centers of power that mediate between the poor and those who have the resources to solve their problems, a cultural definition of the way of handling survival problems is being hammered into the mental schemes of those problem holders who are close to the local centers of power. The idea that pressing problems can be solved through personalized political mediation and that there are good *referentes* to be had—that is, brokers who are generous, hardworking, caring, and kind—is becoming an uncontested aspect of life in the shantytowns, at least among members of the brokers' inner circles. As Scheper-Hughes (1992, 108) asserts for the case of the population of the Brazilian Alto do Cruzeiro, "For people who live their lives so close to the margins of survival, the idea of a benefactor is soothing. To admit the opposite, to entertain the idea that patronage itself is exploitative, is to admit that there is no structural safety net at all and that the poor are adrift within an amoral social and economic system that is utterly indifferent to their well-being and survival."

The notion that the exchange of votes for favors is at the core of political clientelism does not do justice to the much more complex reality of the enduring and long-lasting relationships, narratives, and identities that are constructed within the problem-solving networks. By choosing the awkward term *problem solving through personalized political mediation* I did not intend to obliterate the analysis of political control that the distribution of favors, goods, and services fosters (and that the notion of political clientelism does highlight). On the contrary, it is in the collusion between the elites' attempts to control the poor and the problem-solving strategies that the destitute operationalize that the most interesting aspects of the reproduction (and, yes, sometimes, the challenge) of this political order occurs.

Several authors (Scott and Kerkvliet 1977; Silverman 1977; Burgwald 1996; Scott 1977) have studied the processes by which clientelist bonds are broken down and the tactics of resistance crafted to ward off the grip of clientelist politics in diverse social, geographic, and historical settings. My opposite emphasis on the process of the consolidation of personalized political mediation, on the mechanisms of its reproduction, and on its undisputed acceptance is not dictated by rigid theoretical options. Fidelity to what I saw and heard during an intensive year of fieldwork gives this work the "reproductivistic" accent that some colleagues have criticized.

The uncontested acceptance of problem solving through personalized political mediation, however, is not understood here as a finished cultural product. It is, rather, a structure of feeling that is emerging from the ashes of the populist heresy. Problem solving through personalized political mediation is thus a *structured* and *structuring* process, a cluster of relationships with its own rules, its own things to say and not to say, its own trajectories, all giving birth to particular performances, identities, and memories.

Marcel Mauss ([1947] 1989, 7) once wrote that "what may appear as futile detail is in fact a condensation of principles" (quoted in Wacquant 1996c, 1). Throughout this book, I have paid close attention to the apparently trivial. My obsession with such minute details of life in Paraíso was my way of shedding light on the operation of politically mediated problem solving, that is, on the hows and whys of problem solving in contexts of material deprivation. The anecdotal interactions on which I focus my attention illustrate, paraphrasing Marx's famous formula, how an increasing number of men and women—living under conditions of material and symbolic relegation—actively solve their survival problems. The "futile details" also show us that shantytown dwellers do not solve those pressing problems through material means and symbolic categories of their own choosing.

Last Rally

While carrying out my fieldwork and writing this book, the terms *clientelism* and *asistencialismo* became part of the journalistic and political discourse in a way that I could not have fathomed when I set out to research this topic three years ago. During the last electoral campaign (1997), the opposition persistently accused the Peronist government of exchanging "favors for votes," of "using the needs of the people," of "doing *asistencialismo* in order to get votes." The *manzaneras* became the objects of media attention (newspaper reports and television programs covered the many facets of their work) as well as the focus of the attacks of the political opposition. Not only did Eva Perón become a best-seller, but, more important, her legacy was also constantly discussed as a source of Chiche Duhalde's public image.

In the last Peronist rally I attended (on 26 July 1997), Chiche launched a new (and short-lived) internal faction within the Peronist Party called the Evitismo in order to promote her candidacy for a seat in the national parliament (she was the first candidate on the Peronist ticket in the province of Buenos Aires). More than twenty thousand women—among them the more than twelve thousand *manzaneras*—attended that rally, which also commemorated the death of Eva (on 26 July 1952). In that rally, a singer, her hair bleached and dressed like Eva's, sang "Don't Cry for Me Argentina," Eva Peron's grandniece gave a speech highlighting the role of women in politics, and an ex-actress and member of the

Peronist Party read a poem in homage to Eva ("Volveré y Sere Milliones" [I will return and I will be millions]). Chiche, in turn, delivered a perfect public performance as the Eva of the 1990s while acknowledging that "it is very usual that, each time a woman works in social work, people will say, 'Look, she wants to be like Evita; she likes to imitate her.' Tell those who say so that Evita was unique, that there is not going to be another one like her. This rally shows that the prophecy has been fulfilled. She has returned, and she is millions. *All of you, all of us, are Evita. . . .*"

Herbert Gans (1997, 506) points out that, "before we social scientists let a new concept loose on the world, especially one to be applied to the poor and other stigmatized populations, we should think about whether it could be turned into a pejorative, by journalists or social scientists." Although he is referring to the ill-defined notion *underclass,* his comments can just as aptly be applied to the notion *clientelism.* Politicians' and journalists' evaluations of the Evitista rally and of many other Peronist rallies attest this pejorative manipulation of the notion *clientelism.* Chiche's followers are depicted as "passive participants," as "not spontaneous attendants," as "carried by the *punteros,*" as the product of "clientelist mechanisms used by Duhalde" (*La Nación Digital,* 27 July 1997).

As I finish writing this book, a new electoral map dominates Argentine politics. After a sweeping victory in the last elections, the centrist Alianza defeated the Peronist Party in the last presidential elections (1999). This, some observers point out, would prove the declining relevance of clientelism. Old, and useless, dichotomies die hard: the "modern" way of doing politics (presumably expressed in La Alianza—never mind that the Radical Party, the central party in this coalition, has a long history of clientelist practices—will defeat the old, clientelist, way, that is, the Peronist way). As the sociologist and opinion pollster Mora y Araujo asserts, "The weight of the clientelist vote has diminished. The new mechanisms of communication and determination of the vote are more independent. There is not such a tight relationship between those [the government] who give and those [the governed] who receive" (*Clarín Digital,* 10 November 1998). As should be clear by now, this book made an argument, not about electoral results, but about the workings of certain types of relations between *políticos,* brokers, and poor people. I even questioned the vote-getting capacity of clientelist mechanisms, even in a place where these practices are as generalized and normalized as they are in Villa Paraíso. Not being tempted by the prophecies of which the pundits and political analysts are so fond these days, I cannot help but express many doubts about Araujo's claim. How do we know about the past "weight of the clientelist vote"? How do we recognize its decreasing relevance? No survey can give us the answer here. More historically informed ethnographies of places in which clientelist practices are said to be gaining strength or losing their hold are badly needed. We would then be able to make informed judgments. In this sense, this book is an invitation to further research. It is also a call for reintroducing into the discussions of social movements and "civil society" in Latin America (a discussion somewhat bland and usually closed to poor people's experiences of politics) a close examination of the way in which politics is also deeply embedded in the lives of those destitute people who do not *mobilize* in the usual sense of the term, without, however, being in any way *passive*.

In reference to the journalistic use of social scientific concepts, Gans observes that, if the concepts that we use are "catchy and sufficiently attention-getting," the media may pick them up, "transforming them into lay terms." As the concepts that we invent or use are not our own private property, we cannot prevent these transformations. In a society with a free press, journalists can distort social scientific concepts at will. As Gans (1997, 506) notes, we "have the right, as individuals and as a discipline, to protest loudly when journalists alter our terms—but then we should also refrain from tampering with journalists' terms." Throughout this book, I have tried to do what many people would deem impossible; I used the notion of clientelism while simultaneously criticizing some of its assumptions and shortcomings and warning the reader of its most common misuses. Sharing Gans's warning, it seems to me, is that the "contamination" of sociological concepts is, sometimes, a risk worth running. Ultimately, it is the expression of our dialogue (our way—always mediated, always truncated—of doing politics) with publics that are outside the restricted and restricting confines of academe.

Notes

Introduction: The Day of the Rally

1 The Conurbano Bonaerense includes the nineteen districts in Argentina's industrial heartland surrounding the federal capital of Buenos Aires. Except for the names of the governor of the province of Buenos Aires and his wife, all the names of people and places used throughout this book have been changed to ensure anonymity.

2 All translations from my fieldwork notes are my own. The biggest problem that I confronted while writing this book was translating transcripts of conversations and interviews from the original Spanish into an appropriate form of English. My initial impulse was to use the street language that I had learned, not only from living in New York, but also from conducting interviews with New York–born Puerto Ricans for another study and from reading ethnographic works. But my informants wound up sounding like residents of "El Barrio" (East Harlem). So I chose instead to use the most neutral language possible. That is why, to someone familiar with the kind of Spanish spoken in Argentina, the transcripts may sound artificial, lacking as they do the expressive richness of popular language. I have attempted as far as is possible to retain the original grammatical form of the transcripts, sometimes noting the original Spanish for clarification.

3 Goffman refers to the situation in which the stigmatized person "may be led into placing brackets around a spate of casual interaction so as to examine what is contained therein for general themes" (1963, 111).

4 Fieldwork was carried out from December 1995 to February 1996 and from July 1996 to January 1997 as part of my doctoral dissertation project. In 1991, I worked in Villa Paraíso as an assistant researcher/social worker in the shantytown's Centro de Jubilados, under the auspices of a project funded by the Inter American Foundation, and my initial contacts in Paraíso came from this work. The original aim of my fieldwork was to reconstruct a history of problem solving in a poor neighborhood in Buenos Aires, with the implicit purpose of illustrating the increasing relevance of clientelist arrangements to the way in which poor people solve their everyday survival problems.

5 For a recent insightful analysis of the relation between the pervasiveness of clientelism and the "meanings of democracy" in a different sociocultural context, see Schaffer (1998).

6 Robert Gay's recent work (see, e.g., Gay 1998) exposes and discredits most of the false and simplistic antinomies that populate the literature on clientelism in Latin America.

7 For a seminal treatment of the relational character of social inquiry, see Bourdieu, Chamboderon, and Passeron (1991), Bourdieu and Wacquant (1992), and Tilly

(1997, 1998). Emirbayer (1997) provides a comprehensive overview of the foundations and implications of such a perspective.

8   To my knowledge, the only study that deals specifically with the role of women within Peronism is Bianchi and Sanchis (1988).

9   In the case of women's participation in human rights movements, the debate focused on the reproduction or subversion of traditional gender divisions. The growing involvement of women was "often derived from an attempt to fulfill, rather than subvert, the traditional gender divisions" (Chinchilla 1997, 218). In this same vein, Feijoo (1989) sustains that, analytically, a defense of human rights based on women's reproductive roles reinforces the conventional sexual division of labor.

10   For similar arguments concerning the key role of women in "making ends meet" among the poor in the United States, see Stack's (1970) pathbreaking work and Edin and Lein's (1997) outstanding recent research.

11   This double character of institutions is analyzed by Friedland and Alford (1991). For a seminal treatment of the symbolic aspects of institutions, see Douglas (1986).

1 "They Were Mostly Poor People"

1   Despite its many conceptual flaws (Mollenkopf and Castells 1991), the "dual city" metaphor on which I am drawing has the virtue of directing attention to the deepening inequality that is the defining feature of Argentina at the turn of the millennium. As Sassen (1998, xxxiii) puts it: "The disparities, as seen and as lived, between the urban glamour zone and the urban war zone have become enormous. The extreme visibility of the difference is likely to contribute to further brutalization of the conflict: the indifference and greed of the new elites versus the hopelessness and rage of the poor."

2   Following Wacquant (1996a), I understand *territories of urban relegation* as those spaces in which multiple deprivations accumulate, reinforcing each other.

3   With the necessary precautions concerning the different macroeconomic forces at work and the central place of race in his analysis, I am borrowing the notion *regime of urban marginality* from Wacquant (1996d). As will later become clear, the notion of marginality occupied a central place in the analyses of poverty in Latin America.

4   For the sake of the argument that I develop in the following chapters, and owing to the availability of data, my examination of the new regime of urban marginality concentrates on the Conurbano Bonaerense.

5   According to a government-funded research institute, the increase in unemployment since the launching of the Convertibility Plan in 1991 was 300 percent (CEB 1995). Carbonetto (1997) examines the problems involved in measuring unemployment/underemployment. He also provides some clues about the "informalization" of formal employment.

6   Several surveys show that the fear of losing one's job is widespread among the Argentine population (Murmis and Feldman 1996; Galli and Malfé 1996).

7   On the relation between formal education and rates of unemployment, see Feijoo (1997).

8   Greater Buenos Aires comprises the Conurbano Bonaerense and the federal capital.

9   See, e.g., Germani (1966, 1980) and DESAL (1969, 1970). For a review of different approaches to the study of marginality in Latin America, see Perlman (1976), Portés (1972), Peattie and Alderete-Hass (1981), and Kay (1989).

10   This behaviorist and value-centered approach to marginality seems strikingly similar to the current emphasis on the alleged emergence of an underclass of urban—usually black—poor in the United States. Although I will not tackle the issue here, the thorough criticism to which this approach to marginality was subjected (Portés 1972; Perlman 1976) can be a useful tool with which to contest the academic pitfalls and political dangers (Gans 1995) of the ambiguous notion of the underclass.

11   The marginality school sparked a wave of criticism (e.g., Kay 1989; Cardoso 1971; and Roberts 1978; see also Roberts 1996; and Belvedere 1997). My point here is neither to vindicate this approach nor to provide a full-fledged review of the critics but to acknowledge the fact that the relation between marginality and un/underemployment has been the object of serious consideration by Latin American social scientists. Current levels of un/underemployment prove that, at least in what concerns the (mal)functioning of the labor markets, the proponents of the notion of marginality were right on target.

12   As Carlos Vilas (1996, 25) reports, "The biggest surge in employment is taking place in the informal sector, which offers work that is precarious and low-paying. Of the 15.7 million jobs created in all of Latin America over the past five years, 13.6 million came from the informal sector."

13   The official discourse on the subject stresses that, owing to the "success of the economic plan," people are raising their expectations and looking for new and better jobs.

14   For an examination of flexibilization as the new ideological faith of neoliberalism, see Bourdieu (1996c). Testa and Figari (1997) analyze the relation between flexibilization, working conditions, and social exclusion. Marshall (1997) provides an interesting comparative analysis of labor reforms (and the flexibilization of labor relations) and their effect on labor markets in Latin America.

15   For an exploration of the correlation between unemployment and poverty in Argentina, see Murmis and Feldman (1996).

16   In 1993, the poverty line for a family of four was $420 a month (Minujin and Kessler 1996, 63).

17   This figure includes part of the expenditures on clothing, housing, and health care of four people in Greater Buenos Aires.

18   Unemployment insurance covers only 5 percent of those unemployed in the whole country; only a neligible percentage of the (chaotic) national employment programs are located in the Conurbano (CEB 1995). This means that, following Thernborn (1986, quoted in Mingione 1996, 26), Argentines face a punitive form of un-

employment (accompanied by low or no subsidies) as opposed to the compensated forms (accompanied by sufficient subsidies) that prevail in some advanced societies.

19   As do children growing up in the ghetto in the United States, poor youngsters in Argentina face "a separate and unequal set of educational opportunities that continues throughout their schooling. One could easily argue that their educational experiences are not intended to and cannot prepare [them] to function in the same society and the same economy" (Orfield 1985, 176, quoted in Wacquant 1994a, 262; see also Devine 1996).

20   In terms of Sen's (1981, 3) notion of entitlement, increasing income inequality and the decreasing purchasing power of income mean that the "exchange entitlement" of what some people own has worsened; the set of alternative bundles of commodities that these persons can acquire in exchange for what they own decreases. There has been a vast change in what the author calls *the exchange-entitlement mapping*.

21   Even a cursory reading of current studies of poverty in Argentina will reveal that spatial metaphors (*la caída, la rodada, cuesta abajo,* "the fall," is the one most used) dominate the understanding of the fate of the poor. The local academic debate seems to revolve around a sort of arithmetic of misery and to be dominated by a variables-oriented approach buttressed by positivism and methodological individualism. The discussion always revolves around the same issues: how many people are "above or below" the official poverty line, how many households have "unmet basic needs."

22   For a conceptual elaboration of this argument, see Mingione (1991).

2 "Most of Them Were Coming from Villa Paraíso"

1   According to Smith (1987, 297): " 'Places' are replete with well-established human associations deriving from the fact that particular communities frequent or reside in them. 'Spaces' are areas perceived in terms of their *potential* for being acquired or occupied by members of either your own group or some other potentially threatening group or category. Crudely, 'places' are 'full' and 'fixed,' stable arenas; 'spaces' are 'potential voids,' 'possible threats,' areas to have to be feared, secured or fled. The shift from a politics of place to a politics of space is encouraged by the weakening of territorially-based communal bonds in the city. It is also fostered by a tendency to retreat into the privatised household and by the strengthening of feelings of vulnerability arising in the course of the pursuit of fulfilment or security." The change from *place* to *space* is one of the underlying shifts in the process of hyper-ghettoization analyzed by Wacquant (1994a, 1996d, 1996a). I am also taking the idea of organizational desertification from Wacquant (1996d).

2   For this section, I rely heavily on various secondary sources: Lazcano (1987), De Luca (1976), and municipal documents as well as several life histories that I conducted with the older residents of Paraíso.

3   One need not agree with the movie's political intent (it was intended as a denunciation of the "demagoguery" of the Peronist government and of the misery that it had allegedly fostered) to consider it a precious document. The dialogues that I

selected from the film represent the best synthesis of what I heard during hours of interviews and talks with older residents.

4 For a general description of the formation of shantytowns in Latin America and elsewhere, see Lloyd (1979).

5 The track is located in front of Villa Paraíso.

6 In my analysis of the interaction between state policy and shantytown dwellers' organizations, I follow Lazcano (1987) and Yujnovsky (1984).

7 For an analysis of this period in Argentine history, see James (1988).

8 For a description of the activities of the Resistence, see Baschetti (1988, esp. 26–27).

9 For an analysis of this (mostly ineffective) program, see Yujnovsky (1984).

10 For an analysis of the process of shantytown eradication in the federal capital, see Oszlak (1991).

11 In order to grasp the notion of the shantytown as an urban configuration (the subject of the previous section), it might be useful to compare the shantytown to another form of urban settlement: the *asentamiento* (Grillo, Lacarrieu, and Raggio 1995; Merklen 1991; Izaguirre and Aristizabal 1988). Between 1978 and 1989, 101 squatter settlements (*asentamientos*) seized approximately thirteen hundred blocks (one block is equivalent to one hundred square meters) of land in Greater Buenos Aires. In all, 173,000 people participated in these "land invasions." The social contexts in which the shantytown and the *asentamientos* emerge are strikingly different. As we saw, the former emerged in a context characterized by upward mobility, reasonably high income levels, and increasing employment opportunities. The latter emerged in a context of general downward mobility, lowering of income, and escalating unemployment. The shantytowns are associated—as we saw—with rural migration to the city. The *asentamientos* are linked to (intra)urban movement, with participants emerging from the predominantly urban experience of industrial work. The predominant strategy that dominated the growth of the shantytown is individualistic and linked to family networks. In the case of Villa Paraíso, there was initially no need for collective organization, and improvements were pursued by individual households. The *asentamientos,* however, were the products of collective land takeovers in which external agents (political and religious activists) often took part. Although both types of settlement are illegal, the *asentamiento*'s streets and blocks follow urban zoning regulations (what is known as the *forma damero*), while the shantytown's alleyways and passages do not. The relation to the state is also different: in principle, the shantytown dwellers expected the state to provide housing, while from the onset the *asentamiento* is conceived as a permanent form of settlement, built with the explicit intention of *not* becoming a shantytown.

12 The experience of the residents of what Clark termed *the dark ghetto* can be applied only metaphorically to that of the residents of the shantytown. Insofar as we understand the ghetto, not just as an accumulation of poor people, but as "a particular institutional configuration or *clustering of exclusionary mechanisms*—in the housing,

labor, marriage, and cultural markets—*based on skin color*" (Wacquant 1995a, 558; emphasis added), the shantytown is *not* a ghetto (see Auyero 1997b).

13　This is not to suggest that a community's struggles to better its lot (Castells 1983) are unimportant. As many studies of Third World low-income populations point out, these struggles have animated (and still encourage) class and/or community action in many settings and have won important material gains (sewers, electricity, water, schools, streets, etc.). (See, e.g., Gay [1994] for Rio de Janeiro, Burgwald [1996] for Quito, Eckstein [1990a, 1990b] for Mexico City, Kowarick [1988] for São Paulo, and Grillo, Lacarrieu, and Raggio [1995] and Merklen [1991] for Buenos Aires. For a recent overview, see Gilbert [1994].) As the brief section above on the history of the shantytown shows, such collective struggles were responsible for substantial material gains. The analogy to the *Titanic* points to the structural connections (or, better, the structural dislocations) between the space of the shantytown and the rest of society.

14　According to INDEC (1993b), the indicators of privation are considered to be overcrowded housing (more than three people to a room), inadequate housing (e.g., in rented rooms or in shantytown construction), unsanitary living conditions (homes without toilets), nonattendance at school of school-age children, an income level inadequate for basic subsistence (four or more nonworking household members to one working member), and a household head who has attained only a low level of education.

15　The *rancho* is typical in rural areas. It generally has walls of sun-dried clay bricks, floors of dirt, and a metal or straw roof. The *casilla* is typical of urban areas and is normally constructed with low-quality materials or debris. Type B houses are those that do not meet at least one of the following conditions: water provision through pipelines inside the house, no toilet with water discharge, floors of dirt or any other material except wood, carpet, plastic, cement, fixed bricks, ceramic, tile, or mosaic.

16　In the city center, 0.1 percent live in *ranchos/casillas*, and only 1.7 percent live in type B houses. While 14 percent of the houses in Greater Buenos Aires are type B and 8.7 percent *casillas*, in Paraíso 20.1 percent are type B houses and 30 percent are *casillas*.

17　More than half (51.5 percent) of the women between fifteen and nineteen years of age who had jobs in 1991 were working in domestic service (30 percent of those between twenty and thirty-four and 48 percent of those between thirty-five and forty-nine).

18　As will become clear in chap. 5, there are differing opinions about who gets the credit for paving the streets and for other improvements.

19　A street in the center of the federal capital, an area populated by movie theaters, coffee shops, and bookstores.

20　The following discussion of the sense of indignity felt by the residents of Paraíso and of the social divisions within the shantytown draws on Wacquant's examination of stigma and division in the North American and French territories of urban relegation (Wacquant 1993).

21   As Wacquant asserts in his analysis of the ghetto, the drug economy "creates an environment of poor health and high risk of death at an early stage, strains family relationships, and severely weakens local social cohesion. And it causes rampant violence and a sharp decline in neighborhood safety" (Wacquant 1994a, 249).

22   This is not to imply that the 1950s and 1960s were a "golden age" but to stress the different context in which poverty and destitution used to exist in the shantytown. In his comments on Wilson's pathbreaking work, Michael Katz (1997, 165) points out that earlier urban poverty in the United States "coexisted with urban growth and with the expansion of opportunities for unskilled and semiskilled work. Prospects for modest social or economic mobility, especially for one's children, remained widespread. As a result, poverty existed in a context of hope." By contrast, nowadays poverty exists "within a context of hopelessness," fueled by deindustrialization. Chapter 1 above points out that these new conditions are also present in Argentina. Today, poverty in the shantytown exists in a context of deindustrialization and generalized downward mobility (Minujin 1992; Minujin and Kessler 1996). As a consequence, it is no longer perceived as transitory, and social or economic mobility is unthinkable. Both perceptions mark a real departure from past beliefs and point to a commonality with the kind of poverty that now prevails in advanced societies.

23   Curiously enough, this was the exact same question posed by the proponents of the marginality school (see chap. 1) when analyzing the structural character of the then-incipient unemployment problem.

3 "They Knew Matilde"

1   Marijuana, cigarettes, wine, and barbecues are—as far as I know—the most common rewards that the members of the band obtain from Matilde. The expectation of a public job with the municipality and general protection against the police also lure many members of the band. As another youngster from the neighborhood told me: "They [Matilde's Band] are there [at her UB], so the police don't come for them."

2   Plan Materno-Infantil targets poor mothers and children and is mostly funded by a World Bank loan. For an analysis of the program, see Martinez Nogueira (1995).

3   There are of course significant differences among the various species of broker. As was suggested to me by Robert Gay, one important difference is that some are tied to a specific political party (or to a specific patron), as is the case with the *punteros peronistas*. As Gay (1990, 1994) shows, the allegiance of the *cabo eleitoral* to a specific political party is much less solid. For a review of the representations of brokers, *caciques,* and other types of bossism in Latin American literature, see Nason (1973).

4   Brokers "put interested actors in touch with one another so that they can strike a deal. A brokerage relation involves at least three actors, in which the intermediary smooths the transactions between other actors who lack access to or trust in one another" (Knoke 1990, 144).

5   Walking in Paraíso during an election, you can see many more UBs, almost

one per block. These are what the political jargon labels *mushrooms*. They suddenly appear during an election, and they disappear soon after the campaign is over.

6   In Argentina, blocks are called *manzanas*. Block delegates or representatives are thus called *manzaneras*.

7   At a more general level, Uehara (1990, 521) notes that "intangible and material aid provided by family members and others operating outside of the professional and bureaucratic arenas is a viable, central part of contemporary social life."

8   Singerman's (1995) study of the popular sector in El Cairo (the *sha'b*) constitutes a provocative exception. In her extremely detailed investigation of the way in which informal networks "connect" the household and the extended family to the public bureaucracy and private institutions, she signals a new direction in our understanding of popular politics. According to her analysis, we should delve beneath the veneer of formal institutions if we are to understand the political culture of popular groups. For her, informal networks constitute heretofore unacknowledged "avenues of participation" of the *sha'b* in the Egyptian public space.

9   By *political networks,* I mean (following Knoke 1990) a set of regular contacts or similar social connections among individuals or groups in which at least one of those involved is a member of a political party or an official of the state. Survival strategies are thus embedded in a political problem-solving network because they are expressed in the interactions between party agents or local officials and shantytown dwellers.

10   During the months of September and October, I surveyed a random sample of three hundred individuals (stratified according to sex, age group, and place of residence), asking about most recent jobs, occupation status, the places to which or the persons to whom resorted when specific problems arise, length of residence in Paraíso, best-known politician in Paraíso, and voting preferences.

11   The scope of Caritas's activities is also expanding at the national level. According to its director, Monsignor Rafael Rey, the number of children whom Caritas is feeding in its soup kitchen has increased from 50,000 to 400,000 (an eightfold increase) in the last three years (see *Clarín Digital,* 19 November 1996).

12   This does not mean that, in rural settings, patron-client relationships are not contested. For an examination of the way in which patron-client relationships acquire or lose legitimacy, see Scott (1977) and Scott and Kerkvliet (1977). In *Peasant Society and Culture* (1956), Redfield observes the existence of *hinge groups* that are similar to Wolf's brokers. A hinge group is a cluster of administrative or cultural intermediaries who constitute a link between the local life of a peasant community and the state of which it is part. For Silverman (1965, 294), the concept of mediator is also central to understanding the relation of a community in central Italy with the larger society during a particular period. The concept, she asserts, "refers to a status which functions as a link between a local system and a national system. In interactional terms, the mediator may be seen as one to whom action is originated from the national system and who in turn originates action to the local system." According to Silverman, the two basic features of mediators can be described as follows:

"the functions which those who are defined as mediators are concerned with must be 'critical', of direct importance to the basic structures of either or both systems," and "the mediators 'guard' these functions, i.e., they have near-exclusivity in performing them."

13   Social relations are resources for individuals. Coleman (1990, 302) also labels these resources *social capital*. According to him, "Like other forms of capital, social capital is productive, making possible the achievement of certain ends that would not be attainable in its absence. . . . Unlike other forms of capital, social capital inheres in the structure of relations between persons and among persons. It is lodged neither in individuals nor in physical implements of production." As Wacquant (1993, 39) points out: "Among the resources that individuals can draw upon to implement strategies of social mobility are those potentially provided by their lovers, kin, and friends and by the contacts they develop within the formal associations to which they belong—in sum, the resources they have access to by virtue of being socially integrated into solidary groups, networks, or organizations, what Bourdieu calls 'social capital.'"

14   Yet, as noted by R. Gay (personal communication, September 1997), informal access to public resources could be seen as criminal. Although some of the *referentes* have some sort of relationship with the drug economy, they are far from being gang leaders or party bosses.

15   On the difference between *strong* and *weak ties* (time, intimacy, and emotional intensity involved in the relationship), see Granovetter (1973).

"Fictive kinship" ties are established when a *compadre* (godfather)/*comadre* (godmother) sponsors a child at baptism, thereby becoming the spiritual parent of the child and the spiritual relatives of the child's parents.

16   This state-funded program was intended to develop microenterprises in poor neighborhoods. The provincial government distributed small cash subsidies among different groups so that they could buy the machinery necessary to produce certain commodities, which they would then sell in order to supplement their cash income. The original intention of the program was to "strengthen community organization." In Cóspito, part of the funds of the program were captured by brokers, becoming an extra source of income for their inner circles. Matilde obtained one of those subsidies and organized a group of women to work at the cultural center. She still provides Lucina and her *comadre* with the raw materials to work even though their artisanal mode of production does not allow them to compete with cheaper imported puppets. As Lucina told me, "Imports screwed us up. . . . But we are still making puppets whenever it's necessary, for example, for Children's Day." In an interview I carried out with Analia Mat, the coordinator of Plan País in Cóspito, she agreed that the *punteros* attempted to take over the program. For obvious reasons, she did not admit that they partially succeeded. The scant research done on social programs demonstrates that Cóspito is a particularly "hot" area in which Peronist *punteros* have an important effect on the implementation of social programs (see Prévot Schapira 1996).

17 As if to add a stronger element to Briggite's already strong relation with the "big woman," Matilde almost bestowed Briggite with her present name. Briggite's real name is Beatriz, but "Matilde knew me as a child when people called me Briggite. Since Matilde calls me by this name, the whole neighborhood now knows me as Briggite. Everybody knows me as Briggite."

18 Since privatization, the cost of phone service in Argentina is among the five most expensive in the world.

19 A tie, according to Tilly (1996, 20), is a "continuous series of transactions to which participants attach shared understandings, memories, forecasts, rights and obligations." The next two chapters analyze the perceptual consequences of these ties and the social identities with which they dovetail.

20 On the relation between lack of knowledge and lack of connections, see Erickson (1996).

21 This power "derives from networks of structural relations and it exists apart from actors' knowledge or ignorance about the larger opportunity structures within which their positions are embedded" (Knoke 1990, 10).

22 This constant effort to acquire and control most of the links between the community and the government is one of the main characteristics of other types of political brokers. As Cornelius (1977, 347) describes, the Mexican urban *cacique* "seeks to monopolize all links between the community under his control and political and bureaucratic structures in the external environment."

23 Mexican urban *caciques'* relationships with supralocal agents (politicians and government officials) are also key power resources. As Cornelius (1977, 341) points out: "The *cacique*'s relationships with external political actors are extremely important to understanding the influence he exerts within the community. 'Derivative power' flowing from sources outside the *cacique*'s domain can be used effectively to consolidate his position within the community and discourage challenges to his authority."

24 *El viejo es un zorro* (the old man is sly like a fox) is the expression that better captures his tactics, meaning that he is a wise, cunning politician. It was used repeatedly during my fieldwork in the municipality.

25 Although UBS are formally part of the party bureaucracy, "in practice, they operate almost entirely outside of the formal party organization. Anyone can open up a UB at any time, and most UBS are not registered with the party leadership. Local party authorities possess no means by which to convey instructions to UBS or to ensure their compliance, and UBS possess no effective mechanisms with which to either channel local demands to higher level bodies or to elect local leaders into those bodies. Despite their informal nature, however, UBS play a central role in base-level Peronist organization" (Levitsky 1998a, 15).

26 As Elson (1992, 26) notes, "In the context of economic crisis and structural adjustment, women are particularly valued for their ability to devise and implement survival strategies for their families, using their unpaid labor to absorb adverse effects of structural adjustment policies."

27   "Everything for Love" is the title of an interview with Chiche Duhalde published in the first issue of the journal of the Peronist Party of the province of Buenos Aires (see Partido Justicalista 1996). The title is ambiguous because it does not specify whose love it refers to: is it the *manzaneras'* love for their beneficiaries or Chiche's love for "her" *manzaneras?*

28   On "strategies of condescension" as a way of symbolically strengthening social hierarchies, see Bourdieu (1991, 66–89).

29   For an illustration of pervasive party favoritism in the implementation of social assistance programs, see Graham's (1991) analysis of the PAIT program in Lima, Peru. For an analysis of "clientelist distribution" of job programs, see Cetrángolo and Golbert (1995).

30   I elaborate on the implicit character of these exchanges in chap. 5.

31   Murphy (1988) offers further analysis of this type of domination.

32   *Domination,* in this sense, means "the situation in which the manifested will (*command*) of the *ruler* or rulers is meant to influence the conduct of one or more others (*the ruled*) and actually does influence it in such a way that their conduct to a socially relevant degree occurs as if the ruled had made the content of the command the maxim of their conduct for its very own sake. Looked upon from the other end, this situation will be called *obedience*" (Weber 1968, 943).

4 "We Will Fight Forever, We Are Peronists"

1   In one of the few serious ethnographic studies of the subject, Guterbock (1980, xviii) shows that this presumption is incorrect. In his words, "The services distributed by party workers have no direct effect on the political loyalties of the voters who receive them." Whether this conclusion can be applied to other settings is an open empirical question. As I showed in chap. 3, brokers act on the basis of this presumption.

2   For a summary of voting studies in the United States, especially the Michigan model and the Columbia voting studies, see Knoke (1990, 31–34).

3   For a description of these and other ideal types of brokerage relationships, see Gould and Fernandez (1989). For a summary, see Knoke (1990).

4   Neither Goffman nor Taylor asserts that performance is always a "conscious" activity. As will become clear later, I am attempting theoretically to link—and empirically to utilize—the notions *performance* and *practice* so as to account for the *doxic* adjustment between the brokers' dispositions and the (male-) gendered political field in which they act.

5   At the beginning of my fieldwork, my mental picture of political brokers (or, better, my established prejudice against them, men and women alike) was very close to the overwhelmingly negative image that pervades both journalistic and literary accounts in Argentina (see, among others, Guido 1958; Lynch 1962): mindless, unscrupulous, manipulative, and easily corrupted politicians who, in their quest for power, use people. If, as elsewhere in Latin America (Heredia 1996), politics was seen as distant from everyday life concerns, as a *dirty* activity that shows up during

an election and then disappears, leaving behind only unfulfilled promises, *they* were, to my mind, responsible. With that not easily removed epistemological obstacle, I made my way to the municipal building in the city of Cóspito to interview the mayor's adviser in the welfare area, Susana Gutierrez.

"Oh . . . here you are. . . . Nice to see you again. Today is not a good day. I am so tired; it is kind of hectic here with all these soup kitchens." Those were Susana's opening remarks. Seeing that I hesitated to step into her office, she told me: "Wait a couple of minutes for me, and I'll be right with you." During the first interviews and informal conversations I had with both Susana and Matilde, they constantly reminded me of the physical and mental price they were paying for what they call their "vocation." They were, to borrow from Goffman (1959), "making invisible costs visible." Despite their professed fatigue, they were extremely kind. Always ready to talk, they provided me with contacts in other areas of the municipality, invited me to rallies, and offered me their followers to be interviewed. At the beginning of my fieldwork, it seemed, not only that they had no secrets to hide, but also that they were eager to share every single aspect of their arduous activities. At that time, I felt that I had gained the good rapport necessary to conduct sound fieldwork without any remarkable effort on my part. Needless to say, I began to feel extremely uncomfortable. While gaining what I then wrongly took as a good rapport, my prejudices were being shattered. As I wrote in one of my first fieldnote entries: "These women are not what I expected. They look like nice people, truly concerned with the fate of the poor. Even more, they are the only politicians available to poor people; they devote much effort and time to delivering goods to individual poor voters."

Much as in the seemingly trivial interactions of everyday life analyzed by Goffman (1959, 1967), in politics "first impressions" define the situation. Only after various face-to-face encounters with Matilde and Susana did I become aware of the patterned way through which they were (re)presenting their public selves and their activities to others. Only after realizing that their way of "getting off on the right foot" (Goffman 1959, 12) was a more complex and richer strategy of "impression management" than I had at first thought did I recognize that the "face" that they presented—i.e., the "image of self delineated in terms of approved social attributes" (Goffman 1967, 5)—was crafted, not just to seduce me, but also (and more importantly) to make an impression on everyone.

In recounting his experiences in Argentina interviewing the military and human rights activists, the anthropologist Antonius Robben (1995) comments that "certain interviewees did not try to dominate or overpower" him but, instead, "disarmed" him "by showing their vulnerabilities" (p. 88). Seduction, for him, is an important dimension of fieldwork, and he perceptively distinguishes between ethnographic seduction and good rapport. Seduction, he asserts, "makes us feel that we have accomplished something profound in the encounter, that we have reached a deeper understanding and have somehow penetrated reality. We are in a state of well-being, and have a we-feeling with our informants that we mistakenly interpret as good rapport. It is only when we look back at our meeting and review the information gathered that we realize that we displayed a personal inhibition to break our rapport with critical questions. We realize that we have mistaken seduction for empathy" (p. 86).

As will be seen, Matilde and Susana display the kind of weakness that, according to Robben, is a central element in this seduction. "Playing along with" this seduction and grasping "its meaning from the inside" is, according to Robben, one way in which we can subvert it. In the case at hand, we need to comply with Matilde's and Susana's professed weakness and vulnerability in order to understand the symbolic richness of the political practice of clientelist brokerage.

6   The maintenance of the impression fostered by the performance involves the overcommunication of some facts and the undercommunication of others. Which facts are overcommunicated? The successful solutions to problems. A scholarship to summer camp obtained, a driver's license earned, a soup kitchen opened, food distributed: such accomplishments are pointed out time and again in order to foster the impression of effective performance. "We solve problems," both Matilde and Susana say, "and we do it in our own way." And, as will be seen, the details of how such solutions were obtained—the political nitty-gritty—are downplayed.

7   As Robert Merton (1949, 74) noted long ago in his brilliant functional analysis of political machines, in the machine "politics is transformed into personal ties."

8   This does not mean that the relationship between a broker and his or her clientele is the only basis for reelection or reappointment. The broker's history within the party and his or her relationship with the mayor and with other political patrons are also important elements to be taken into account.

9   As De Ipola (1987) shows, there is a permanent ambivalence, a tension, between inclusion and exclusion that can be traced to Perón's own rhetoric.

10   The association between the Peronist Party and a "great family" was a central element in Perón's own discursive strategies (see Bianchi and Sanchis 1988).

11   For an analysis of this period, see James (1988).

12   For an analysis of the three versions of the myth of Eva Perón, see Taylor (1979).

13   Caimari's (1995, esp. chap. 7) excellent analysis of the religious connotations of the image of Eva Perón, her "redemptive actions," and the tensions with the Catholic Church that they fostered also focuses on *La razón de mi vida* in order to examine the ways in which Eva attempted to "construct an identity" of her own "social work."

14   Peron's supporters came to be known as the *descamisados* (shirtless ones). As bestowed by the opposition to the Peronist masses, this epithet was meant to be derogatory. But it was soon transformed and "adopted in proletarian pride as a handy variant of the French *sans-culottes*" (Navarro and Fraser 1985, 68).

15   For a full examination of Eva Perón's thoughts about the role women should play in politics, see Bianchi and Sanchis (1988). This work also documents the origins and development of the Feminine Peronist Party. Caimari (1994, 217) also notes the relation between participation and subordination. For an examination of the Fun-

dación Eva Perón, see Plotkin (1993). There are, in fact, key continuities between the brokers' practices and those analyzed by Plotkin.

16   The idea of "regulated improvisation" is taken from Bourdieu (1977, 1990a). See also Bourdieu and Wacquant (1992) and Wacquant's numerous works on boxing (e.g., 1994b, 1995b).

17   Diana Taylor (personal communication, February 1997) notes that Evita resolved a structural problem for Perón (as the brokers analyzed here continue to do for Peronism) by gendering the division of labor: "The General [Perón] could remain strong, tough, and rational, in charge of important matters such as the economy, the military, and international relations, while Evita picked up, and actually came to embody, *excess*—that which overflowed institutional structures and could not be officially mandated. Her passionate intervention on behalf of the poor, especially women and children, could be construed as 'soft,' 'maternal,' a complementary *plus* or add-on to the national well-being."

18   *Interest* here is understood, following Bourdieu, not as a rational calculation made by rational subjects who attempt to maximize capital. Rather, it is defined in relation to a system of "objective potentialities, immediately inscribed in the present, things to do or not to do, to say or not to say, in relation to the forthcoming reality which—in contrast to the future conceived as 'absolute possibility' . . . —put[s] itself forward with an urgency and a claim to existence excluding all deliberation" (Bourdieu 1977, 76). *Strategy*, on the other hand, is understood, not as an intentional and always conscious act, but as "objectively oriented lines of action that obey regularities and form coherent and socially intelligible patterns, even though they do not follow conscious rules or aim at the premeditated goals posited by a strategist" (Bourdieu and Wacquant 1992, 25). In other words, the brokers' presentation of self is the enactment of a constant and persistent way of organizing the Peronist act of giving. For an interesting analysis of strategies and interests in a game other than politics, see Wacquant (1995b).

19   "The oracle effect, a limiting form of performativity, is what enables the authorized spokesperson to take his authority from the group which authorizes him in order to exercise recognized constraint, symbolic violence, on each of the isolated members of the group. . . . I take my authority from the group, and that group authorizes me to impose constraints on the group" (Bourdieu 1991, 213). The contrast between brokers synonymity with the goods distributed and the way in which the local church carries out food distribution is striking. In the latter case, there is an explicit dissociation between the things distributed and the person in charge of distributing them. As Nora (who runs Caritas) explains, "We have to make them [the people who collaborate with Caritas] understand that what we hand out does not belong to us. . . . We are here to collaborate." Far from idealizing church charity, I am merely noting the difference between it and political brokerage.

The effect of the oracle effect—the domination effect—will be explored in the next chapter through an examination of the relationship that the performance establishes between the performer and the audience.

20   Threatening deprivation in order to control the behavior of others is a central aspect of a relationship of domination as understood by Knoke (1990, 4–6). As he asserts, domination is a "relationship in which one actor controls the behavior of another actor by offering or withholding some benefit or harm . . . one actor promises or actually delivers a *sanction* (reward or punishment) to an actor in order to gain compliance with commands. Sanctions may be physical events (a salary increase, a new highway, execution at sunrise), but may also involve primarily intangible symbols (redesigned flag, a benediction, ridicule on the editorial page). Obviously, domination can occur only if the dominee is responsive to the sanction. . . . Domination is clearly relational, because it involves one actor exchanging some valued (or abhorred) resource for obedience by another actor" (p. 4).

5 The "Clientelist" Viewpoint

1   See, e.g., the (almost denigrating) newspaper and television accounts of the Peronist rally organized on the occasion of the anniversary of Eva Perón's death, 26 July 1997.

2   I am taking the idea of impasse from Thrift's (1993) analysis of the "urban impasse" in the study of the Western city.

3   For a discussion of the study of culture from the actor's point of view as one of Geertz's major contributions, see Ortner (1994).

4   "The meaning of the most personal and 'transparent' actions does not belong to the subject who performs them but to the complete system of relations in which and through which they are enacted. . . . [T]he principle of non-consciousness requires one to construct the system of objective relations in which individuals are located, which are expressed more adequately in the economy or morphology of groups than in the subjects' opinions and declared intentions" (Bourdieu, Chamboderon, and Passeron 1991, 17–18).

5   Such a characterization is, of course, overly reductive. Most of the literature relies on either normative or rational choice models of social action (see the final section of this chapter), both of which are insufficient guides to understanding clientelist practices as carried out by the Peronist Party because they inadequately conceptualize the unreflective, routinized, taken-for-granted, and learned character of those practices and the extent to which they are rooted in cultural and political traditions. Clientelist practices are, in the context on which I am focusing here, neither normative nor the product of rational calculation but practical choices learned over time. Clients solve their problems, and, in the process, they learn subordination, limits, what to say and not to say, what to do and not to do. Sometimes (see Burgwald 1996), clients develop both a public explanation of their actions (a *public transcript*) and a private one (a *hidden transcript* in Scott's [1990] formulation). Likewise, clients sometimes learn that calculation can improve their chances in the clientelist game (Gay 1995), a calculation that should be carefully distinguished from resistance. Other times, the clientelist exchange is seen as (constructed as) "the only game in town" (see, e.g., Scheper-Hughes 1992).

6   The charge of the "political use" of food programs has been leveled in other *barrios* (Golbert 1992).

7   According to Tilly (1997, 198), a right is an "enforceable claim, the reciprocal of obligations." Rights are "enforceable claims on the delivery of goods, services, or protections by specific others. Rights exist when *one party can effectively insist that another deliver goods, services, or protections, and third parties will act to reinforce (or at least not to hinder) their delivery.*" When the "object of claims is a state or its agent and the succesful claimant qualifies by simple membership in a broad category of persons subject to the state's jurisdiction," those claims—or entitlements—become citizenship rights (Tilly 1997, 98; my emphasis).

8   Other works (Kuasñosky and Szulik 1996; Auyero 1992) have shown that, in many other lower-class neighborhoods of the Conurbano Bonaerense, politics is experienced as something distant, linked to delusion and trickery, especially among the young. The practice of distributing drugs and alcohol among young people in poor neighborhoods by local politicians is also widespread (Kuasñosky and Szulik 1996), especially at political rallies.

9   Of course the title of the pamphlet uses the real name of the shantytown, not *. . . Villa Paraíso. Making Memory . . .* was published without date by the Centro Urbano Nueva Parroquia in Buenos Aires.

10   Coordinadora was an umbrella organization representing fourteen neighborhood associations. It was formed in 1967 in response to flooding (see chap. 2).

11   According to Rogoff (1990), thinking and cognition must be understood as problem solving: "Problem solving involves interpersonal and practical goals, addressed deliberately (not necessarily consciously or rationally). It is purposeful, involving flexible improvisation toward goals as diverse as planning a meal, writing an essay, convincing or entertaining others" (p. 8). Her problem-solving approach, to which much of my perspective is indebted, "places primacy on people's attempts to negotiate the stream of life, to work around or to transform problems that emerge on the route of attaining the diverse goals of life" (p. 9). Acting, feeling, and thinking are integrated: "Thought . . . is not born of other thoughts. Thought has its origins in the motivating sphere of consciousness, a sphere that includes our inclinations and needs, our interests and impulses, and our affect and emotion. The affective and volitional tendency stands behind thought. Only here do we find the answer to the final 'why' in the analysis of thinking" (p. 282). Intersubjectivity is at the basis of problem solving, involving cognitive, social, and emotional interchange. Problem solving, Rogoff recurrently points out, "is not 'cold' cognition, but inherently involves emotion, social relations, and social structure" (p. 10).

12   The dominated, as Bourdieu repeatedly notes, "are very often condemned to such dilemmas, to choices between two solutions which, each from a certain standpoint, are equally bad ones" (Bourdieu and Wacquant 1992, p. 82).

6 "They Were All Peronists"

1   It is probably Barry Schwartz's (1996, 1997) analysis of commemorative symbolism that has contributed the most to our thinking about the structuring capacities of memory. According to his analysis, the contrast between memory and history as formulated by Halbwachs is not so clear-cut. Collective memory is "a representation of the past embodied in both commemorative symbolism and historical evidence." His analysis of the changing image of Lincoln among African Americans shows that commemoration "adds to history," affecting the way in which we imagine the past. Commemoration is thus "a *structuring process* that partially overrides the qualities of its objects and imposes upon them its own pattern" (1997, 471, 489; emphasis added).

2   Data come from one of the voting centers in the shantytown and from my own survey (see chap. 3, n. 10).

3   Contrary to what the neoliberal creed sustains, the "flexibilization" of working conditions has not expanded employment opportunities. Under the Peronist government, unemployment has increased 200 percent in Argentina. In the Conurbano Bonaerense, there was a 277 percent increase in the number of unemployed people between 1991 and 1995 (see chap. 1).

4   As James (1988, 34) notes, "much of the Peronist state's efforts between 1946 and its demise in 1955 can be viewed as an attempt to institutionalise and control the heretical challenge it had unleashed in the earlier period and to absorb this challenge within a new state-sponsored orthodoxy. Viewed in this light Peronism was, in a certain sense, a passive, demobilising social experience for workers. It stressed increasingly in its official rhetoric the controlled, limited mobilisation of workers under the aegis of the state."

5   For a literary approach to the life of a political patron, see Guido (1958).

6   The "atomizing and individualizing" effects of clientelist practices are a contested issue in the literature on the subject. As Burgwald (1996) shows in his analysis of clientelism in a squatter settlement in Quito, clientelist practices can coexist with a specific repertoire of collective action (see also Escobar 1994, 1997).

7   Although there has been an increase in "electoral volatility" during the last decade, "such 'de-freezing' has occurred almost exclusively on the anti-Peronist side of the Peronist/anti-Peronist cleavage. . . . [T]he Peronist electorate, both in terms of its size and its composition, has remained relatively stable" (Levistky 1996, 4).

8   The Peronist narrative is a *public narrative* in the sense in which Somers (1994, 619) uses the term. Public narratives are "those narratives attached to cultural and institutional formations larger than the single individual, to intersubjective networks or institutions, however local or grand, micro- or macro-stories about American social mobility, the 'freeborn Englishman,' the working class hero, and so on. Public narratives range from the narratives of one's family, to those of the workplace (organizational myths), church, government, and nation." It is in this sense that Peronism can be understood as a grand public narrative.

9   In a series of unplanned protests over rapid price increases, thousands of people took to the streets of major cities in Argentina (Buenos Aires, Rosario, Cor-

doba) by the end of May 1989, looting hundreds of stores, supermarkets, and food-processing plants. By official count, fourteen people died in the *saqueos* (eleven men, two women, and one nine-year-old boy), eighty were seriously injured, and twenty-one were arrested. Over fifty-two thousand people participated in the *saqueos;* fifteen of the twenty-two provinces reported looting.

10   Following Robert Merton (1949, 72), we can say that these "residual" cultural elements are most likely attaining certain "latent functions." According to Merton, functional analysis tells us that we should ordinarily (although not invariably) expect that persistent social structures and patterns perform some positive functions, functions that "are at the time not adequately fulfilled by other existing patterns and structures."

11   According to Caimari (1995, 226), the distribution of large amounts of cider and *panettone* is one of those rituals firmly associated with Peronism in the popular collective memory.

Conclusions

1   I use the term *maelstrom* in acknowledgment of Elias's (1987) exploration of the dialectic between "involvement" and "detachment," which takes as its inspiration Edgar Allan Poe's story "A Descent into the Maelstrom." It is worth quoting at length the opening passage of Elias's "The Fishermen in the Maelstrom" because it illustrates the role that detachment plays in theory formation: "One may remember that the fishermen, while they were slowly drawn into the abyss of the whirlpool, for a while still floated, together with other pieces of wreckage, around the walls of its narrowing funnel. At first, both brothers—the youngest had been lost in the storm already—were too overcome by fear to think clearly and to observe accurately what was going on around them. After a time, however, one of the brothers, so Poe tells us, was able to shrug off his fears. While the elder brother cowered helplessly in the boat, paralysed by the approaching disaster, the younger man collected himself and began looking around with certain curiosity. It was then, while taking it all in almost as if he were not involved, that he became aware of certain regularities in the movements of the pieces that were being driven around in circles together with the boat. In short, while observing and reflecting, he had an 'idea'; a connecting picture of the process in which he was involved, a 'theory,' began forming in his mind" (p. 45).

2   That she distributed drugs among the members of her band is one of the more obvious things that she might wish to keep hidden from me.

3   Confusion about the identity of the ethnographer in the field is part and parcel of his work (see, e.g., Bourgois 1995).

4   I am very much indebted to Alejandro Grimson for some of the main ideas in this section (see Auyero and Grimson 1997).

5   For a recent exception, see Martuccelli and Svampa (1998).

6   For a full exploration of the logical function and structure of social scientific concepts, see Weber (1949).

7   For an exception, see Levitsky (1998a, 1998b).

Bibliography

Acuña, Carlos, ed. 1995a. *La nueva matriz política Argentina.* Buenos Aires: Nueva Vision.

———. 1995b. Politics and Economics in the Argentina of the Nineties (or, Why the Future No Longer Is What It Used to Be). In *Democracy, Markets, and Structural Reform in Latin America: Argentina, Bolivia, Brazil, Chile, and Mexico,* ed. Carlos Acuña, Eduardo Gamarra, and William Smith. New Brunswick, N.J.: Transaction.

Adelman, Jeremy. 1994. Post-Populist Argentina. *New Left Review,* no. 203 (January/February): 45–69.

Appadurai, Arjun. 1988. Putting Hierarchy in Its Place. *Cultural Anthropology* 3, no. 1:36–49.

Auster, Paul. 1992. *Leviathan.* New York: Penguin.

Auyero, Javier. 1992. *Otra vez en la via: Notas e interrogantes sobre la juventud de sectores populares.* Buenos Aires: Espacio Editorial.

———. 1996. La doble vida del clientelismo político. *Sociedad* 8:31–56.

———. 1997a. Evita como performance: Mediación y resolución de problemas entre los pobres urbanos del Gran Buenos Aires. In *Favores por votos? Estudios sobre clientelismo político contemporáneo,* ed. Javier Auyero. Buenos Aires: Losada.

———. 1997b. Wacquant in the Argentine Slums: Comment on Loïc Wacquant's "Three Pernicious Premises in the Study of the American Ghetto."

International Journal of Urban and Regional Research 21, no. 3:508–11.

Auyero, Javier, and Alejandro Grimson. 1997. Se dice de mi: Notas sobre convivencias y confusiones entre etnógrafos y periodistas. *Apuntes de Investigacion del Cecyp* 1:81–93.

Bakhtin, Mikhail. 1994. *The Dialogic Imagination.* Austin: University of Texas Press.

Baschetti, Roberto. 1988. *Documentos de la resistencia peronista, 1955–1970.* Buenos Aires: Puntosur.

Beccaria, Luis, and Nestor Lopez. 1996. Notas sobre el comportamiento del mercado de trabajo urbano. In *Sin trabajo: Las características del desempleo y sus efectos en la sociedad argentina,* ed. Luis Beccaria and Nestor Lopez. Buenos Aires: Losada.

Bellardi, M., and A. De Paula. 1986. *Villas miseria: Origen, erradicación, y respuestas populares.* Buenos Aires: CEAL.

Belvedere, C. 1997. El inconcluso proyecto marginalidad. *Apuntes de Investigación* 1:97–115.

Benjamin, Walter. 1968. Theses on the Philosophy of History. In *Illuminations.* New York: Schocken.

Bianchi, Susana, and Norma Sanchis. 1988. *El partido peronista femenino.* Buenos Aires: CEAL.

Bitran, R., and A. Schneider. 1991. *El gobierno conservador de Manuel A. Fresco en la provincia de Buenos Aires (1936–1940).* Buenos Aires: CEAL.

Bodeman, M. 1988. Relations of produc-

tion and class rule: The hidden basis
of patron-clientage. In *Social Structures:
A Network Approach,* ed. B. Wellman
and S. Berkowitz. Cambridge, Mass.:
Cambridge University Press.

Boissevain, Jeremy. 1977. Factions,
Parties, and Politics in a Maltese
Village. In *Friends, Followers, and
Factions: A Reader in Political Clientelism,*
ed. S. Schmidt, L. Guasti, C. Landé,
and J. Scott. Berkeley: University of
California Press.

Borges, Jorge Luis. 1974. El aleph. In
Obras completas. Buenos Aires: Emece.

Borón, Atilio, et al. 1995. *Peronismo y
menemismo.* Buenos Aires: El Cielo por
Asalto.

Bourdieu, Pierre. 1977. *Outline of a
Theory of Practice.* Cambridge, Mass.:
Cambridge University Press.

———. 1990a. *The Logic of Practice.*
Stanford, Calif.: Stanford University
Press.

———. 1990b. *In Other Words: Essays
towards a Reflexive Sociology.* Stanford,
Calif.: Stanford University Press.

———. 1990c. The Scholastic Point
of View. *Cultural Anthropology* 5,
no. 4:380–91.

———. 1991. *Language and Symbolic Power.*
Cambridge, Mass.: Harvard University
Press.

———. 1993. Concluding Remarks:
For a Sociogenetic Understanding
of Intellectual Works. In *Bourdieu:
Critical Perspectives,* ed. Craig Calhoun,
Edward LiPuma, and Moishe Postone.
Chicago: University of Chicago Press.

———. 1996a. On the Family as a Realized Category. *Theory, Culture, and
Society* 13, no. 3:19–26.

———. 1996b. Understanding. *Theory,
Culture, and Society* 13, no. 2:17–37.

———. 1996c. La verdadera ideología
de la flexibilización. *Clarín* 30:16–17.

———. 1998. *Practical Reasons.* Stanford,
Calif.: Stanford University Press.

Bourdieu, Pierre, Jean-Claude Chamboderon, and Jean-Claude Passeron.
1991. *The Craft of Sociology.* New York:
de Gruyter.

Bourdieu, Pierre, and Jean-Claude
Passeron. 1977. Reproduction. In
Education, Society, and Culture. London:
Sage.

Bourdieu, Pierre, and Loïc Wacquant.
1992. *An Invitation to Reflexive Sociology.*
Chicago: University of Chicago Press.

Bourgois, Philippe. 1995. *In Search of
Respect: Selling Crack in El Barrio.*
Cambridge: Cambridge University
Press.

Boyarin, Jonathan, ed. 1994. *Remapping
Memory: The Politics of Time and Space.*
Minneapolis: University of Minnesota
Press.

Burgwald, Gerrit. 1996. *Struggle of the Poor:
Neighborhood Organization and Clientel-
ist Practice in a Quito Squatter Settlement.*
Amsterdam: CEDLA.

Burt, Ronald S. 1992. *Structural Holes:
The Social Structure of Competition.*
Cambridge, Mass.: Harvard University
Press.

Caimari, Lila. 1995. *Perón y la Iglesia
Católica: Religión, estado, y sociedad en
la Argentina, 1943–1955.* Buenos Aires:
Ariel Historia.

Calvino, Italo. 1986. *The Uses of Literature.* New York: Harcourt Brace
Jovanovich.

Carbonetto, Daniel. 1997. El sector informal y la exclusión social. In *Empleo
y globalización: La nueva cuestion social en
la Argentina,* ed. Ernesto Villanueva.

238 *Bibliography*

Buenos Aires: Universidad Nacional de Quilmes.

Cardoso, F. H. 1971. Comentarios sobre os conceitos de superpopulacao relativa e marginalidade. *Estudio CEBRAP* 1:99–130.

Cardoso, Ruth. 1992. Popular Movements in the Context of Consolidation of Democracy. In *The Making of Social Movements in Latin America,* ed. Arturo Escobar and Sonia Alvarez. Boulder, Colo.: Westview.

Carlos, Manuel, and Bo Anderson. 1991. Political Brokerage and Network Politics in Mexico: The Case of a Dominance System. In *Networks, Exchange, and Coercion: The Elementary Theory and Its Applications,* ed. David Willer and Bo Anderson. New York: Elsevier.

Castells, Manuel. 1983. *The City and the Grassroots: A Cross-Cultural Theory of Urban Social Movements.* Berkeley and Los Angeles: University of California Press.

Castells, Manuel, and John Hull Mollenkopf. 1991. Conclusion: Is New York a Dual City? In *Dual City: Restructuring New York,* ed. John Hull Mollenkopf and Manuel Castells. New York: Russell Sage.

Centro de Estudios Bonaerenses (CEB). 1995. *Informe de Coyuntura 51-1.* Buenos Aires.

Cetrángolo, Oscar, and Laura Golbert. 1995. Desempleo en Argentina: Magnitud del problema y políticas adoptadas. *CECE: Serie Estudios* 8:1–30.

Chaney, Elsa. 1979. *Supermadre: Women in Politics in Latin America.* Austin: University of Texas Press.

Chinchilla, Norma. 1997. Marxism, Feminism, and the Struggle for Democracy in Latin America. In *Materialist Feminism: A Reader in Class, Difference, and Women's Lives,* ed. Rosemary Hennessy. New York: Routledge.

Cieza, Daniel, and Verónica Beyreuther. 1996. De la cultura del trabajo al estado de malestar: Hiperdesocupación, precarización, y daños en el Conurbano Bonaerense. *Cuadernos del IBAP* 9:1–32.

Clark, Kenneth. 1965. *Dark Ghetto: Dilemmas of Social Power.* New York: Harper and Row.

Coleman, James. 1990. *Foundations of Social Theory.* Cambridge, Mass.: Belknap.

Conniff, Michael L. 1981. *Urban Politics in Brazil: The Rise of Populism, 1925–1945.* Pittsburgh: University of Pittsburgh Press.

Cornelius, Wayne A. 1973. Contemporary Mexico: A Structural Analysis of Urban Caciquismo. In *The Caciques: Oligarchical Politics and the System of Caciquismo in the Luso-Hispanic World,* ed. Robert Kern. Albuquerque: University of New Mexico Press.

———. 1977. Leaders, Followers, and Official Patrons in Urban Mexico. In *Friends, Followers, and Factions: A Reader in Political Clientelism,* ed. Steffen Schmidt, Laura Guasti, Carl Landé, and James Scott. Berkeley: University of California Press.

Davis, J. 1973. Forms and Norms: The Economy of Social Relations. *Man* 8, no. 2:159–76.

DeCerteau, Michel. 1997. *The Capture of Speech and Other Political Writings.* Minneapolis: University of Minnesota Press.

De Ipola, Emilio. 1987. *Ideología y discurso populista*. Mexico: Plaza and Janes.

De la Torre, Carlos. 1992. The Ambiguous Meanings of Latin American Populisms. *Social Research* 59, no. 2:385–414.

De Luca, J. 1976. *Teología concreta*. Buenos Aires: IRE-APE-CUNP.

DESAL (Centro para el Desarrollo Social en América Latina). 1969. *Marginalidad en América Latina: Un ensayo de diagnóstico*. Barcelona: Editorial Herder.

———. 1970. *Marginalidad, promoción popular, e integración latinoamericana*. Buenos Aires: Troquel.

Devine, John. 1996. *Maximum Security: The Culture of Violence in Inner-City Schools*. Chicago: University of Chicago Press.

Dominguez, Virginia. 1986. *How Institutions Think*. Syracuse, N.Y.: Syracuse University Press.

———. 1989. On Ritual Uncertainty. In *People as Subject, People as Object*. Madison: University of Wisconsin Press.

Douglas, Mary. 1966. *Purity and Danger*. New York: Routledge.

———. 1980. Introduction: Maurice Halbwachs. In *The Collective Memory*, by Maurice Halbwachs. New York: Harper and Row.

Durkheim, Emile. 1984. *The Division of Labor in Society*. New York: Free Press.

Eckstein, S. 1990a. Poor People versus the State and Capital: Anatomy of a Successful Community Mobilization for Housing in Mexico City. *International Journal of Urban and Regional Research* 14:274–96.

———. 1990b. Urbanization Revisited: Inner-City Slum of Hope and Squatter Settlement of Despair. *World Development* 18, no. 2:165–81.

Edin, Kathryn, and Laura Lein. 1997. *Making Ends Meet: How Single Mothers Survive Welfare and Low-Wage Work*. New York: Russell Sage.

Eisenstadt, Samuel. 1995. *Power, Trust, and Meaning*. Chicago: University of Chicago Press.

Eisenstadt, Samuel, and Luis Roniger. 1984. *Patrons, Clients, and Friends*. Cambridge: Cambridge University Press.

Elias, Norbert. 1987. *Involvement and Detachment*. New York: Blackwell.

———. 1994. *The Civilizing Process*. Oxford: Blackwell.

Elson, D. 1992. From Survival Strategies to Transformation Strategies: Women's Needs and Structural Adjustment. In *Unequal Burden: Economic Crises, Persistent Poverty, and Women's Work*, ed. Lourdes Beneria and Shelley Feldman. Boulder, Colo.: Westview.

Emirbayer, Mustafa. 1997. Manifesto for a Relational Sociology. *American Journal of Sociology* 103, no. 2:281–317.

Emirbayer, Mustafa, and Jeff Goodwin. 1994. Network Analysis, Culture, and the Problem of Agency. *American Journal of Sociology* 99, no. 6:1411–54.

Engbersen, Godfried. 1989. Cultures of Long-Term Unemployment in the New West. *The Netherlands' Journal of Social Sciences* 25, no. 2:75–96.

Epstein, A. L. 1969. The Network and the Urban Organization. In *Social Networks in Urban Situations*, ed. Clyde J. Mitchel. Manchester: Manchester University Press.

Erickson, Bonnie. 1996. The Structure of Ignorance. Keynote address, Sunbelt XVI: International Sunbelt

Social Network Conference, Charleston, S.C., 22 February.

Escobar, Arturo, and Sonia Alvarez, eds. 1992. *The Making of Social Movements in Latin America*. Boulder, Colo.: Westview.

Escobar, Cristina. 1994. Clientelism and Social Protest: Peasant Politics in Northern Colombia. In *Democracy, Clientelism, and Civil Society*, ed. Luis Roniger and Ayse Günes-Ayata. Boulder, Colo.: Lynne Reinner.

———. 1997. Clientelism and Citizenship: The Limits of Democratic Reforms in Colombia. Paper delivered at the meeting of the Latin American Studies Association, Guadalajara, Mexico, 17–19 April.

Farinello, Luis. 1996. *La mesa vacía: Desocupación y pobreza en la Argentina*. Buenos Aires: Carlos Serrano Editor.

Feijoo, M. 1989. The Challenge of Constructing Civilian Peace: Women and Democracy in Argentina. In *The Women's Movement in Latin America: Feminism and the Transition to Democracy*, ed. Jane Jaquette. Boston: Unwin Hyman.

———. 1997. Inglés y computación. In *Empleo y globalización: La nueva cuestión social en la Argentina*, ed. Ernesto Villanueva. Buenos Aires: Universidad Nacional de Quilmes.

Fernandez, Roberto, and Roger V. Gould. 1994. A Dilemma of State Power: Brokerage and Influence in the National Health Policy Domain. *American Journal of Sociology* 99, no. 6:1455–91.

Fine, Gary Alan. 1996. Reputational Entrepeneurs and the Memory of Incompetence: Melting Supporters, Partisan Warriors, and Images of President Harding. *American Journal of Sociology* 101, no. 5:1159–93.

Folino, Norberto. 1971. *Barceló y Ruggierito, patrones de Avellaneda*. Buenos Aires: CEAL.

Foster, George. 1977. The Dyadic Contract: A Model for the Social Structure of a Mexican Peasant Village. In *Friends, Followers, and Factions: A Reader in Political Clientelism*, ed. Steffen Schmidt, Laura Guasti, Carl Landé, and James Scott. Berkeley: University of California Press.

Fox, Jonathan. 1994. The Difficult Transition from Clientelism to Citizenship. *World Politics* 46, no. 2:151–84.

Fraser, Nancy. 1989. *Unruly Practices: Power, Discourse, and Gender in Contemporary Social Theory*. Minneapolis: University of Minnesota Press.

Friedland, Roger, and Robert R. Alford. 1991. Bringing Society Back In: Symbols, Practices, and Institutional Contradictions. In *The New Institutionalism in Organizational Analysis*, ed. Walter W. Powell and Paul J. DiMaggio. Chicago: University of Chicago Press.

Friedman, John, and Mauricio Salguero. 1988. The Barrio Economy and Collective Self-Empowerment in Latin America: A Framework and Agenda for Research. *Power, Community, and the City* 1:3–37.

Friedrich, Paul. 1977. The Legitimacy of a Cacique. In *Friends, Followers, and Factions: A Reader in Political Clientelism*, ed. Steffen Schmidt, Laura Guasti, Carl Landé, and James Scott. Berkeley: University of California Press.

Galli, Vicente, and Ricardo Malfé. 1996. Desocupación, identidad, y salud. In

Sin trabajo: Las características del desempleo y sus efectos en la sociedad Argentina, ed. Miguel Murmis and Silvio Feldman. Buenos Aires: Losada.

Gans, Herbert J. 1992. Sociological Amnesia: The Noncumulation of Normal Social Science. *Sociological Forum* 7, no. 4:701–11.

———. 1995. *The War against the Poor: The Underclass and Antipoverty Policy.* New York: Basic.

———. 1997. Uses and Misuses of Concepts in American Social Science Research: Variations on Loïc Wacquant's Theme of "Three Pernicious Premises in the Study of the American Ghetto." *International Journal of Urban and Regional Research* 21, no. 3:504–7.

Gay, Robert. 1990. Community Organization and Clientelist Politics in Contemporary Brazil: A Case Study from Suburban Rio de Janeiro. *International Journal of Urban and Regional Research* 14, no. 4:648–65.

———. 1994. *Popular Organization and Democracy in Rio de Janeiro: A Tale of Two Favelas.* Philadelphia: Temple University Press.

———. 1995. Between Clientelism and Universalism: Reflections on Popular Politics in Brazil. Connecticut College. Typescript.

———. 1998. Rethinking Clientelism: Demands, Discourses, and Practices in Contemporary Brazil. *European Review of Latin American and Caribbean Studies* 65 (December): 7–24.

Geertz, Clifford. 1973. *The Interpretation of Cultures.* New York: Basic.

———. 1983. *Local Knowledge.* New York: Basic.

Gellner, Ernest, and John Waterbury, eds. 1977. *Patrons and Clients in Mediterranean Societies.* London: Duckworth.

Germani, Gino. 1966. *Política y sociedad e una época de transición: De la sociedad tradicional a la sociedad de masas.* Buenos Aires: Paidos.

———. 1980. *Marginality.* New Brunswick, N.J.: Transaction.

Gilbert, Alan. 1994. *The Latin American City.* London: Latin American Bureau.

Goffman, Erving. 1959. *The Presentation of the Self in Everyday Life.* New York: Doubleday.

———. 1963. *Stigma: Notes on the Management of Spoiled Identity.* New York: Simon and Schuster.

———. 1967. *Interaction Ritual: Essays on Face-to-Face Behavior.* New York: Doubleday.

———. 1971. *Relations in Public: Microstudies of the Public Order.* New York: Basic.

Golbert, Laura. 1992. La asistencia alimentaria: Un nuevo programa para los argentino. In *La mano izquierda del estado: La asistencia social según los beneficiarios,* ed. Susana Lumi, Laura Golbert, and Emilio Tenti Fanfani. Buenos Aires: Miño y Dávila.

———. 1996. Viejos y nuevos problemas de las políticas asistenciales. *CECE: Serie Estudios* 12:1–41.

Gould, Roger, and Roberto Fernandez. 1989. Structures of Mediation: A Formal Approach to Brokerage in Transaction Networks. *Sociological Methodology 1990,* 89–126.

Gouldner, Alvin. 1977. The Norm of Reciprocity: A Preliminary Statement. In *Friends, Followers, and Factions: A Reader in Political Clientelism,* ed. Steffen Schmidt, Laura Guasti, Carl Landé, and James Scott. Berkeley: University of California Press.

Graham, C. 1991. The APRA Government and the Urban Poor: The PAIT Programme in Lima's Pueblos Jóvenes. *Journal of Latin American Studies* 23, no. 1:91–130.

Granovetter, Mark. 1973. The Strength of Weak Ties. *American Journal of Sociology* 78, no. 6:1360–80.

Granovetter, Mark, and Richard Swedber, eds. 1992. *The Sociology of Economic Life.* Boulder, Colo.: Westview.

Grassi, Estela. 1997. Políticas sociales, necesidades, y la cuestión del trabajo como capacidad creadora del sujeto humano. In *Empleo y globalización: La nueva cuestion social en la Argentina,* ed. Ernesto Villanueva. Buenos Aires: Universidad Nacional de Quilmes.

Graziano, Luigi. 1977. Patron-Client Relationships in Southern Italy. In *Friends, Followers, and Factions: A Reader in Political Clientelism,* ed. Steffen Schmidt, Laura Guasti, Carl Landé, and James Scott. Berkeley: University of California Press.

Grillo, Oscar, Monica Lacarrieu, and Liliana Raggio. 1995. *Políticas sociales y estrategias habitacionales.* Buenos Aires: Espacio Editorial.

Guasti, Laura. 1977. Peru: Clientelism and Internal Control. In *Friends, Followers, and Factions: A Reader in Political Clientelism,* ed. Steffen Schmidt, Laura Guasti, Carl Landé, and James Scott. Berkeley: University of California Press.

Guido, Beatriz. 1958. *Fin de fiesta.* Buenos Aires: Losada.

Günes-Ayata, Ayse. 1994. Clientelism: Premodern, Modern, Postmodern. In *Democracy, Clientelism, and Civil Society,* ed. Luis Roniger and Ayse Günes-Ayata. Boulder, Colo.: Lynne Reinner.

Gunther, Richard, P. Nikiforos Diamandouros, and Hans-Jürgen Puhle. 1996. O'Donnell's "Illusions": A Rejoinder. *Journal of Democracy* 7, no. 4:151–59.

Guterbock, Thomas. 1980. *Machine Politics in Transition: Party and Community in Chicago.* Chicago: University of Chicago Press.

Gutierrez, Ricardo. 1998. Desindicalización y cambio organizativo del peronismo argentino, 1982–1995. Paper presented at the meeting of the Latin American Studies Association, Chicago, 24–26 September.

Hagopian, Frances. 1992. The Compromised Consolidation: The Political Class in the Brazilian Transition. In *Issues in Democratic Consolidation: The New South American Democracies in Comparative Perspective,* ed. Scott Mainwaring, Guillermo O'Donnell, and J. Samuel Valenzuela. Notre Dame, Ind.: University of Notre Dame Press.

Halbwachs, Maurice. 1980. *The Collective Memory.* New York: Harper and Row.

Hall, Stuart. 1993. Encoding, Decoding. In *The Cultural Studies Reader,* ed. Simon During. New York: Routledge.

Hamburger, Philip. 1948. A Reporter in Argentina: Love, Love, Love. *New Yorker,* 26 June, 15–21.

Harvey, David. 1990. *The Condition of Postmodernity.* Cambridge: Blackwell.

Heredia, Beatriz. 1996. Política, familia, y comunidad. Paper delivered at the Encuentro Internacional de Antropología, IDES, Buenos Aires, 15–17 August.

Herzfeld, Michael. 1992. *The Social Produc-*

tion of Indifference: Exploring the Symbolic Roots of Western Bureaucracy. New York: St. Martin's.

Hintze, Susana. 1989. Estrategias alimentarias de sobrevivencia: Un estudio de caso en el Gran Buenos Aires. Buenos Aires: CEAL.

Hora, Roy, and Javier Trímboli. 1995. Presentación. In Peronismo y menemismo, ed. Atilio Borón et al. Buenos Aires: El Cielo por Asalto.

Hoskin, Gary. 1997. Democratization in Latin America. Latin American Research Review 32, no. 3:209–23.

Instituto Nacional de Estadística y Census (INDEC). 1985. La pobreza en la Argentina. Buenos Aires.

———. 1993a. Censo nacional de población. Buenos Aires.

———. 1993b. Censo 1991: Avellaneda-lanús. Buenos Aires.

———. 1996. Encuesta permanente de hogares. Buenos Aires.

Iñiguez, A., and A. Sanchez. 1995. El Conurbano Bonaerense y la provincia de Buenos Aires: Condensación de la tragedia nacional de la desocupación y la subocupación. Cuadernos del IBAP (Buenos Aires), no. 7:1–23.

Izaguirre, Inés, and Z. Aristizabal. 1988. Las tomas de tierra en la zona sur del Gran Buenos Aires. CEAL, 1–29.

James, Daniel. 1988. Resistance and Integration: Peronism and the Argentina Working Class, 1946–1976. Cambridge: Cambridge University Press.

Jaquette, Jane. 1989. The Women's Movement in Latin America: Feminism and the Transition to Democracy. Boston: Unwin Hyman.

Jelin, Elizabeth. 1985. Los nuevos movimientos sociales. Buenos Aires: Centro Editor de America Latina.

———. 1987. Ciudadanía e identidad: Las mujeres en los movimientos sociales latinoamericanos. Geneva: UNRISD.

———. 1997. Don't Cry for Me, Argentina; or, The Globalization of Peronism. Contemporary Sociology 26, no. 3:302–4.

Katz, Michael. 1997. Inner-City as Place. In Sociological Visions, ed. Kai Erikson. Lanham, Mass.: Rowman and Littlefield.

Katznelson, Ira. 1981. City Trenches: Urban Politics and the Patterning of Class in the United States. Chicago: University of Chicago Press.

Kay, Cristobal. 1989. Latin American Theories of Development and Underdevelopment. London: Routledge.

Kenny, Michael. 1977. Patterns of Patronage in Spain. In Friends, Followers, and Factions: A Reader in Political Clientelism, ed. Steffen Schmidt, Laura Guasti, Carl Landé, and James Scott. Berkeley: University of California Press.

Kessler, Gabriel. 1996. Algunas implicancias de la experiencia de la desocupación para el individuo y su familia. In Sin trabajo: Las características del desempleo y sus efectos en la sociedad argentina, ed. Luis Beccaria and Nestor Lopez. Buenos Aires: Losada.

Knoke, David. 1990. Political Networks. Cambridge: Cambridge University Press.

Kornblum, William. 1974. Blue-Collar Community. Chicago: University of Chicago Press.

Kotlowitz, Alex. 1991. There Are No Children Here: The Story of Two Boys Growing up in the Other America. New York: Doubleday.

Kowarick, Lucio, ed. 1988. As lutas sociais

e a cidade: Sao Paulo, passado e presente. Rio de Janeiro: Paz e Terra.

Kuasñosky, Silvia, and Dalia Szulik. 1996. Desde los márgenes de la juventud. In *La juventud es más que una palabra,* ed. Mario Margulis. Buenos Aires: Biblos.

Lazcano, Cecilia. 1987. Historia de la consolidación de Villa Jardín. Buenos Aires. Typescript.

Lévi-Strauss, Claude. 1963. *Structural Anthropology.* New York: Basic.

———. 1996. Populism Is Dead! Live the Populist Party! Labor-Based Party Adaptation and Survival in Argentina. Department of Political Science. University of California, Berkeley, Typescript.

Levitsky, Steve. 1997. Crisis, Party Adaptation, and Regime Stability in Argentina. Paper delivered at the meeting of the Latin American Studies Association, Guadalajara, 17–19 April.

———. 1998a. From Labor Politics to Machine Politics: The De-Unionization of Urban Peronism, 1983–97. Paper delivered at the meeting of the Latin American Studies Association, Chicago, 24–26 September.

———. 1998b. Institutionalization and Peronism: The Concept and the Case for Unpacking the Concept. *Party Politics* 4, no. 1:77–92.

Lind, Amy. 1992. Power, Gender, and Development: Popular Women's Organizations and the Politics of Needs in Ecuador. In *The Making of Social Movements in Latin America: Identity, Strategy, and Democracy,* ed. Arturo and Sonia Alvarez Escobar. Boulder, Colo.: Westview.

Lloyd, Peter. 1979. *Slums of Hope? Shanty Towns of the Third World.* New York: St. Martin's.

Lloyd-Sherlock, Peter. 1997. Policy, Distribution, and Poverty in Argentina since Redemocratization. *Latin American Perspectives* 24, no. 97:22–55.

Lomnitz, Larissa. 1975. *Cómo sobreviven los marginados.* Mexico, D.F.: Siglo XXI.

———. 1988. Informal Exchange Networks in Formal Systems: A Theoretical Model. *American Anthropologist* 90, no. 1:42–55.

Lo Vuolo, R., and A. Barbeito. 1993. *La nueva oscuridad de la política social: Del estado populista l neoconservador.* Buenos Aires: Miño y Dávila.

Lozano, Claudio, and Roberto Feletti. 1996. Convertibilidad y desempleo, crisis ocupacional en la Argentina. *Aportes para el estado y la administración gubernamental* 3, no. 5:155–88.

Lumi, Susana, Laura Golbert, and Emilio Tenti Fanfani. 1992. *La mano izquierda del estado.* Buenos Aires: Miño y Dávila.

Luna, Felix. 1958. *Alvear.* Buenos Aires: Libros Argentinos.

Lynch, Marta. 1962. *La alfombra roja.* Buenos Aires: Compañía General Fabril Editora.

Margulis, Mario. 1981. Fuerza de trabajo y estrategias de sobrevivencia en una población de origen migratorio: Colonias populares de Reynosa. *Demografía y economía* 15:3–47.

Marshall, Adriana. 1997. Protección del empleo en América Latina: Las reformas de los noventa y sus efectos en el mercado de trabajo. In *Empleo y globalización: La nueva cuestión social en la Argentina,* ed. Ernesto Villanueva. Buenos Aires: Universidad Nacional de Quilmes.

Martinez Nogueira, Roberto. 1995. Devising New Approaches to Poverty in Argentina. In *Strategies to Combat Poverty in Latin America,* ed. Dagmar Raczynski. Washington, D.C.: Inter-American Development Bank.

Martuccelli, Danilo, and Maristella Svampa. 1998. *La Plaza Vacia: Las transformaciones del peronismo.* Buenos Aires: Losada.

Mauss, Marcel. [1947] 1989. *Manuel d'ethnographie.* 3d ed. Paris: Bibliothèque Payot.

———. 1967. *The Gift.* New York: Norton.

Mayer, Adrian C. 1977. The Significance of Quasi-Groups in the Study of Complex Societies. In *Friends, Followers, and Factions: A Reader in Political Clientelism,* ed. Steffen Schmidt, Laura Guasti, Carl Landé, and James Scott. Berkeley: University of California Press.

McAdam, Doug, Sidney Tarrow, and Charles Tilly. 1995. To Map Contentious Politics. *Working paper* no. 222. New School for Social Research, Center for Studies of Social Change.

McFate, Katherine. 1995. Introduction: Western States in the New World Order. In *Poverty, Inequality, and the Future of Social Policy,* ed. Katherine McFate, Roger Lawson, and William Julius Wilson. New York: Russell Sage.

McFate, Katherine, Roger Lawson, and William Julius Wilson, eds. 1995. *Poverty, Inequality, and the Future of Social Policy.* New York: Russell Sage.

Menendez Carrión, Amparo. 1986. *La conquista del voto en el Ecuador: De velazco a roldos.* Quito: Corporación Editora Nacional.

Merklen, Denis. 1991. *Asentamientos en La Matanza.* Buenos Aires: Catalogos.

Merton, Robert K. 1949. *Social Theory and Social Structure.* Glencoe, Ill.: Free Press.

———. 1987. Three Fragments from a Sociologist's Notebooks: Establishing the Phenomenon, Specified Ignorance, and Strategic Research Materials. *Annual Review of Sociology* 13:1–28.

Mingione, Enzo. 1991. *Fragmented Societies: A Sociology of Economic Life beyond the Market Paradigm.* Cambridge, Mass.: Blackwell.

———, ed. 1996. *Urban Poverty and the Underclass: A Reader.* Cambridge, Mass.: Blackwell.

Mintz, S., and Eric Wolf. 1977. An Analysis of Ritual Co-Parenthood (*Compadrazgo*). In *Friends, Followers, and Factions: A Reader in Political Clientelism,* ed. Steffen Schmidt, Laura Guasti, Carl Landé, and James Scott. Berkeley: University of California Press.

Minujin, Alberto. 1992. *Cuesta abajo.* Buenos Aires: Losada.

Minujin, Alberto, and Gabriel Kessler. 1996. *La nueva pobreza en la Argentina.* Buenos Aires: Planeta.

Mollenkopf, John Hull, and Manuel Castells, eds. 1991. *Dual City: Restructuring New York.* New York: Russell Sage.

Monza, Alfredo. 1996. Evolución reciente y perspectivas del mercado de trabajo en la Argentina. *Aportes para el Estado y la administración gubernamental,* no. 3:65–78.

Morrison, Toni. 1994. *The Bluest Eye.* New York: Plume.

———. 1996. Memory, Creation, and Writing. In *The Anatomy of Memory,* ed. J. McConkey. New York: Oxford University Press.

Mouzelis, Nicos. 1985. On the Concept of Populism: Populist and Clientelist Modes of Incorporation in Semiperipheral Polities. *Politics and Society* 14, no. 3:329–48.

Municipalidad de Lanús. N.d. *Historia de Villa Jardin.* Lanús, Buenos Aires: Secretaría de Difusíon.

Murmis, Miguel, and Silvio Feldman. 1996. De seguir así. In *Sin trabajo: Las características del desempleo y sus efectos en la sociedad Argentina,* ed. Luis Beccaria and Nestor Lopez. Buenos Aires: Losada.

Murphy, Raymond. 1988. *Social Closure: A Theory of Monopolization and Exclusion.* Oxford: Clarendon.

Nason, Marshall R. 1973. The Literary Evidence, Part III: The Caciques in Latin American Literature. In *The Caciques: Oligarchical Politics and the System of Caciquismo in the Luso-Hispanic World,* ed. Robert Kern. Albuquerque: University of New Mexico Press.

Navarro, Marysa, and Nicholas Fraser. 1985. *Eva Perón.* New York: Norton.

Nora, Pierre. 1989. Between Memory and History: Les lieux de mémoire. *Representations* 26 (spring): 7–25.

Novaro, Marcos. 1994. *Piloto de tormentas: Crisis de representación y personalización de la política en Argentina (1989–1993).* Buenos Aires: Letra Buena.

Nudler, Julio. 1996. Trabajo no hay y además es malo. *Página 12* 12/15:5.

Nun, J., J. C. Marín, and M. Murmis. 1968. Marginalidad en América Latina. Working Paper no. 53. Instituto di Tella.

Nun, José. 1969. Superpoblación relativa, ejército industrial de reserva y masa marginal. *Revista latinoamericana de sociología* 5, no. 2:30–53.

———. 1972. Marginalidad y otras cuestiones. *Revista latinoamericana de ciencias sociales* 4:1–25.

———. 1987. Cambios en la estructura social argentina. In *Ensayos sobre la transición democrática en Argentina,* ed. José Nun and Juan Carlos Portantiero. Buenos Aires: Puntosur.

———. 1994. *Averiguación sobre algunos significados del peronismo.* Buenos Aires: GECUSO, Fundación del Sur.

O'Donnell, Guillermo. 1992a. Delegative Democracy? Working Paper no. 172. University of Notre Dame, Helen Kellog Institute for International Studies.

———. 1992b. Transitions, Continuities, and Paradoxes. In *Issues in Democratic Consolidation: The New South American Democracies in Comparative Perspective,* ed. Scott Mainwaring, Guillermo O'Donnell, and J. Samuel Valenzuela. Notre Dame, Ind.: University of Notre Dame Press.

———. 1996a. Illusions about Consolidation. *Journal of Democracy* 7, no. 2:34–51.

———. 1996b. Illusions and Conceptual Flaws. *Journal of Democracy* 7, no. 4:160–68.

Orfield, Gary. 1985. Ghettoization and Its Alternatives. In *The New Urban Reality,* ed. Paul Peterson. Washington, D.C.: Brookings.

Ortner, Sherry B. 1994. Theory in Anthropology since the Sixties. In *Culture/Power/History: A Reader in Contemporary Social History,* ed. Nicholas Dirks, Geoff Eley, and Sherry Ortner. Princeton, N.J.: Princeton University Press.

Oszlak, Oscar. 1991. *Merecer la ciudad: Los pobres y el derecho al espacio urbano.* Buenos Aires: Humanitas.

Padgett, John F., and Christopher K. Ansell. 1993. Robust Action and the Rise of the Medici, 1400–1434. *American Journal of Sociology* 98, no. 6:1259–1319.

Paige, Karen, and Jeffery M. Paige. 1981. *The Politics of Reproductive Ritual.* Berkeley and Los Angeles: University of California Press.

Palermo, Vicente, and Marcos Novaro. 1996. *Política y poder en el gobierno de Menem.* Buenos Aires: Norma.

Partido Justicialista de la Provincia de Buenos Aires. 1996. "Todo por amor." *El Bonaerense* (Buenos Aires) 1:12–13.

Passerini, Luisa. 1987. *Fascism in Popular Memory: The Cultural Experience of the Turin Working Class.* Cambridge: Cambridge University Press.

Peattie, Lisa, and Jose A. Alderete-Hass. 1981. "Marginal" Settlements in Developing Countries: Research, Advocacy of Policy, and Evolution of Programs. *Annual Review of Sociology* 7:157–75.

Perlman, Janice. 1976. *The Myth of Marginality.* Berkeley: University of California Press.

Perón, Eva. 1995. *La razón de mi vida.* Buenos Aires: C.S. Ediciones.

Pinheiro, Paulo S. 1996. Democracies without Citizenship. *NACLA* 30, no. 2:17–23.

Pok, Cinthia. 1997. El mercado de trabajo: Implícitos metodológicos de su medición. In *Empleo y globalización: La nueva cuestion social en la Argentina,* ed. Ernesto Villanueva. Buenos Aires: Universidad Nacional de Quilmes.

Portés, Alejandro. 1972. Rationality in the Slum: An Essay in Interpretive Sociology. *Comparative Studies in Society and History* 14, no. 3:268–86.

Powell, John Duncan. 1977. Peasant Society and Clientelist Politics. In *Friends, Followers, and Factions: A Reader in Political Clientelism,* ed. Steffen Schmidt, Laura Guasti, Carl Landé, and James Scott. Berkeley: University of California Press.

Powers, Nancy. 1995. Popular Discourse about Politics and Democracy in Argentina. Paper delivered at the Latin American Studies Association Conference, Washington, D.C., 28–30 September.

Prévot Schapira, M. 1996. Las políticas de lucha contra la pobreza en la periferia de Buenos Aires, 1984–1994. *Revista mexicana de sociología* 59, no. 2:73–94.

Putnam, Robert. 1993. *Making Democracy Work: Civic Traditions in Modern Italy.* Princeton, N.J.: Princeton University Press.

———. 1995. Bowling Alone: America's Declining Social Capital. *Journal of Democracy* 6, no. 1:65–78.

Rabinow, Paul. 1977. *Reflections on Fieldwork in Morocco.* Berkeley: University of California Press.

Ratier, Hugo. 1985. *Villeros y villas miseria.* Buenos Aires: CEAL.

Redfield, Robert. 1956. *Peasant society and culture: An anthropological approach to civilization.* Chicago: University of Chicago Press.

Robben, Antonius. 1995. The Politics of Truth and Emotion among Victims and Perpetrators of Violence. In *Fieldwork under Fire: Contemporary Studies of Violence and Survival,* ed. Carolyn Nordstrom and Antonius Robben Nordstrom. Berkeley and

Los Angeles: University of California Press.

Roberts, Bryan. 1978. *Cities of Peasants.* Beverly Hills, Calif.: Sage.

———. 1996. The Social Context of Citizenship in Latin America. *International Journal of Urban and Regional Research* 20, no. 1:38–65.

Rock, David. 1972. Machine Politics in Buenos Aires and the Argentine Radical Party, 1912–1930. *Journal of Latin American Studies* 4, no. 2:233–56.

———. 1975. *Politics in Argentina: The Rise and Fall of Radicalism, 1890–1930.* Cambridge: Cambridge University Press.

———. 1987. *Argentina, 1516–1982: From Spanish Colonization to Alfonsin.* Berkeley and Los Angeles: University of California Press.

Rofman, A. 1996. El desempleo en la capital y en el interior: Perfiles actuales del desempleo estructural en la Argentina. In *Desempleo estructural, pobreza, y precariedad,* ed. S. Peñalva and A. Rofman. Buenos Aires: Nueva Visión.

Rogoff, Barbara. 1990. *Apprenticeship in Thinking: Cognitive Development in Social Context.* New York: Oxford University Press.

Roniger, Luis. 1990. *Hierarchy and Trust in Modern Mexico and Brazil.* New York: Praeger.

Roniger, Luis, and Ayse Günes-Ayata, eds. 1994. *Democracy, Clientelism, and Civil Society.* Boulder, Colo.: Lynne Reinner.

Roy, Beth. 1994. *Some Trouble with Cows: Making Sense of Social Conflict.* Berkeley and Los Angeles: University of California Press.

Rubinich, Lucas. 1991. Apuntes sobre nociones de derechos en sectores populares urbanos. *Documentos CEDES,* 1–32.

Sahlins, Marshall D. 1977. Poor Man, Rich Man, Big-Man, Chief: Political Types in Melanesia and Polynesia. In *Friends, Followers, and Factions: A Reader in Political Clientelism,* ed. Steffen Schmidt, Laura Guasti, Carl Landé, and James Scott. Berkeley: University of California Press.

Sanchez Jankowski, Martín. 1991. *Islands in the Streets: Gangs and American Urban Society.* Berkeley and Los Angeles: University of California Press.

Sarlo, Beatriz. 1996. *Instantáneas: Medios, ciudad, y costumbres en el fin de siglo.* Buenos Aires: Ariel.

Sassen, Saskia. 1991. *The Global City.* Princeton, N.J.: Princeton University Press.

———. 1998. *Globalization and Its Discontents.* New York: New Press.

Schaffer, Frederic, 1998. *Democracy in Translation.* Ithaca, N.Y.: Cornell University Press.

Schechner, Richard. 1985. *Between Theater and Anthropology.* Philadelphia: University of Pennsylvania Press.

Scheper-Hughes, Nancy. 1992. *Death without Weeping: The Violence of Everyday Life in Brazil.* Berkeley and Los Angeles: University of California Press.

Schmidt, Steffen. 1977. The Transformation of Clientelism in Rural Colombia. In *Friends, Followers, and Factions: A Reader in Political Clientelism,* ed. Steffen Schmidt, Laura Guasti, Carl Landé, and James Scott. Berkeley: University of California Press.

Schmidt, Steffen, Laura Guasti, Carl Landé, and James Scott, eds. 1977. *Friends, Followers, and Factions: A Reader* in *Political Clientelism.* Berkeley: University of California Press.

Schutz, Alfred. 1962. *Collected Papers.* The Hague: Martinus Nijhoff.

Schwartz, Barry. 1996. Memory as a Cultural System: Abraham Lincoln in World War II. *American Sociological Review* 61:908–27.

————. 1997. Collective Memory and History: How Abraham Lincoln Became a Symbol of Racial Equality. *Sociological Quarterly* 38, no. 3:469–96.

Scott, James. 1977. Patronage or Exploitation? In *Patrons and Clients in Mediterranean Societies,* ed. Ernest Gellner and John Waterbury. London: Duckworth.

————. 1990. *Domination and the Arts of Resistance.* New Haven, Conn.: Yale University Press.

Scott, James, and Benedict J. Kerkvliet. 1977. How Traditional Rural Patrons Lose Legitimacy: A Theory with Special Reference to Southeast Asia. In *Friends, Followers, and Factions: A Reader in Political Clientelism,* ed. Steffan Schmidt, Laura Guasti, Carl Landé, and James Scott. Berkeley: University of California Press.

Scott, Joan. 1988. *Gender and the Politics of History.* New York: Columbia University Press.

Sen, Amrtya. 1981. *Poverty and Famines: An Essay on Entitlement and Deprivation.* Oxford: Clarendon.

Shefner, Jon. 1997. From the Counter-Elites to the Streets: Civil Society Challenges Clientelism in Guadalajara. Paper delivered at the meeting of the Latin American Studies Association, Guadalajara, 17–19 April.

Sidicaro, Ricardo. 1995. Poder político, liberalismo económico, y sectores populares, 1989–1995. In *Peronismo y menemismo,* ed. Atilio Borón et al. Buenos Aires: El Cielo por Asalto.

Sidicaro, Ricardo, and Jorge Mayer. 1995. *Política y sociedad en los años del menemismo.* Buenos Aires: Universidad de Buenos Aires.

Silverman, Sydel F. 1965. Patronage and Community-Nation Relationships in Central Italy. *Ethnology* 4, no. 2:172–89.

————. 1977. Patronage and Community-Nation Relationships in Central Italy. In *Friends, Followers, and Factions: A Reader in Political Clientelism,* ed. Steffen Schmidt, Laura Guasti, Carl Landé, and James Scott. Berkeley: University of California Press.

Silverstein, Michael. 1976. Shifters, Linguistic Categories, and Cultural Description. In *Meaning in Anthropology,* ed. Keith H. Basso and Henry A. Selby. Albuquerque: University of New Mexico Press.

Simmel, Georg. 1971. *On Individuality and Social Forms.* Chicago: University of Chicago Press.

Singerman, Diana. 1995. *Avenues of Participation: Family, Politics, and Networks in Urban Quarters of Cairo.* Princeton, N.J.: Princeton University Press.

Sirvent, Maria Teresa. 1998. Esta política educativa ignora a los pobres. *Clarín,* 2 June.

Smith, D. 1987. Knowing Your Place: Class, Politics, and Ethnicity in Chicago and Birmingham, 1890–1983. In *Class and Space: The Making of Urban Society,* ed. Nigel Thrift and Paul Williams. London: Routledge and Kegan Paul.

Smith, William. 1992. Hyperinflation, Macroeconomic Instability, and

Neoliberal Restructuring in Democratic Argentina. In *The New Argentine Democracy,* ed. E. Epstein. New York: Praeger.

Somers, Margaret R. 1993. Citizenship and the Place of the Public Sphere: Law, Community, and Political Culture in the Transition to Democracy. *American Sociological Review* 58 (October): 587–620.

———. 1994. The Narrative Constitution of Identity: A Relational and Network Approach. *Theory and Society* 23:605–49.

———. 1995. What's Political or Cultural about Political Culture and the Public Sphere? Toward an Historical Sociology of Concept Formation. *Sociological Theory* 13, no. 2:113–44.

Somers, Margaret R., and Gloria D. Gibson. 1994. Reclaiming the Epistemological "Other": Narrative and the Social Constitution of Identity. In *Social Theory and the Politics of Identity,* ed. Craig Calhoun. Oxford: Blackwell.

Stack, Carol. 1970. *All Our Kin: Strategies for Survival in a Black Community.* New York: Harper and Row.

Stein, Steve. 1980. *Populism in Perú: The Emergence of the Masses and the Politics of Social Control.* Madison: University of Wisconsin Press.

Stillwaggon, Eileen. 1998. *Stunted Lives, Stagnant Economies: Poverty, Disease, and Underdevelopment.* New Brunswick, N.J.: Rutgers University Press.

Swartz, David. 1997. *Culture and Power: The Sociology of Pierre Bourdieu.* Chicago: University of Chicago Press.

Taylor, Diana. 1997. *Disappearing Acts.* Durham, N.C.: Duke University Press.

Taylor, Diana, and Juan Villegas, eds. 1994. *Negotiating Performance: Gender, Sexuality, and Theatricality in Latin/o America.* Durham, N.C.: Duke University Press.

Taylor, Julie. 1979. *Eva Perón: The Myths of a Woman.* Chicago: University of Chicago Press.

Testa, Julio, and Claudia Figari. 1997. De la flexibilidad a la precarización: Una visión crítica de las vinculaciones entre el empleo y el sistema de relaciones laborales. In *Empleo y globalización: La nueva cuestión social en la Argentina,* ed. Ernesto Villanueva. Buenos Aires: Universidad Nacional de Quilmes.

Thernborn, Goran. 1986. *Why Some People Are More Unemployed Than Others.* New York: Verso.

Thrift, Nigel. 1993. An Urban Impasse? *Theory, Culture, and Society* 10, no. 2:229–338.

Tilly, Charles. 1978. *From Mobilization to Revolution.* New York: McGraw-Hill.

———. 1990. Where Do Rights Come From? *Working Paper* no. 98. New School for Social Research, Center for Studies of Social Change.

———. 1992. How to Detect, Describe, and Explain Repertoires of Contention. Working Paper no. 150. New School for Social Research. Center for Studies of Social Change.

———. 1994a. Afterword: Political Memories in Space and Time. In *Remapping Memory,* ed. Jonathan Boyarin. Minneapolis: University of Minnesota Press.

———. 1994b. Citizenship, Identity, and Social History. Working Paper no. 205. New School for Social Research, Center for Studies of Social Change.

———. 1994c. Democracy Is a Lake. Working Paper no. 185. New School for Social Research, Center for Studies of Social Change.

———. 1994d. Political Memories in Space and Time. Working Paper no. 165. New School for Social Research, Center for Studies of Social Change.

———. 1995. Political Identities. Working Paper no. 212. New School for Social Research, Center for Studies of Social Change.

———. 1996. Durable Inequality. Working Paper no. 224. New School for Social Research, Center for Studies of Social Change.

———. 1997. *Roads from Past to Future.* Lanham, Mass.: Rowman and Littlefield.

———. 1998. *Durable Inequality.* Berkeley and Los Angeles: University of California Press.

Tilly, Charles, Jeff Goodwin, and Mustafa Emirbayer. 1995. The Relational Turn in Macrosociology: A Symposium. Working Paper no. 215. New School for Social Research, Center for Studies of Social Change.

Torrado, Susana. 1985. *El enfoque de las estrategias familiares de vida en América Latina.* Buenos Aires: Cuadernos del CEUR 2.

———. 1992. *Estructura social de la Argentina.* Buenos Aires: Ediciones La Flor.

Uehara, Edwina. 1990. Dual Exchange Theory, Social Networks, and Informal Social Support. *American Journal of Sociology* 96, no. 3:521–57.

Ugalde, Antonio. 1973. Contemporary Mexico: From Hacienda to PRI, Political Leadership in a Zapotec Village. In *The Caciques: Oligarchical Politics and the*
System of Caciquismo in the Luso-Hispanic World,* ed. Robert Kern. Albuquerque: University of New Mexico Press.

Velez-Ibañez, Carlos. 1983. *Rituals of Marginality: Politics, Process, and Culture Change in Urban Central Mexico, 1969–1974.* Berkeley and Los Angeles: University of California Press.

Verbitsky, B. 1957. *Villa miseria también es América.* Buenos Aires: G. Kraft.

Vilas, Carlos. 1996. Neoliberal Social Policy: Managing Poverty (Somehow). *NACLA Report on the Americas* 39, no. 6:8–15.

Villareal, Juan. 1985. Los hilos sociales del poder. In *Crisis de la dictadura argentina,* ed. Eduardo Jozami. Buenos Aires: Siglo XXI.

———. 1996. *La exclusión social.* Buenos Aires: Norma.

Wacquant, Loïc J. D. 1992. Toward a Social Praxeology: The Structure and Logic of Bourdieu's Sociology. In *An Invitation to Reflexive Sociology,* by Pierre Bourdieu and Loïc J. D. Wacquant. Chicago: University of Chicago Press.

———. 1993. Urban Outcasts: Stigma and Division in the Black American Ghetto and the French Urban Periphery. *International Journal of Urban and Regional Research* 17, no. 3:366–83.

———. 1994a. The New Urban Color Line: The State and Fate of the Ghetto in Post-Fordist America. In *Social Theory and the Politics of Identity,* ed. Craig Calhoun. Oxford: Blackwell.

———. 1994b. A Sacred Weapon: Bodily Capital and Bodily Labor among Professional Boxers. University of California, Berkeley. Typescript.

———. 1995a. The Comparative Structure and Experience of Urban Exclusion: "Race," Class, and Space in Chicago and Paris. In *Poverty, Inequality, and the Future of Social Policy,* ed. Katherine McFate, Roger Lawson, and William Julius Wilson. New York: Russell Sage.

———. 1995b. The Pugilistic Point of View: How Boxers Think and Feel about Their Trade. *Theory and Society* 24:489–535.

———. 1996a. Dynamics of Relegation in Advanced Societies. Paper presented to the International Conference on Globalization and the New Social Inequality, Utrecht, 1 September.

———. 1996b. Elias in the Ghetto. University of California, Berkeley. Typescript.

———. 1996c. Reading Bourdieu's "Capital." *International Journal of Contemporary Sociology* 33, no. 2:151–70.

———. 1996d. The Rise of Advanced Marginality: Notes on Its Nature and Implication. *Acta Sociologica: Journal of the Scandinavian Sociological Association* 39, no. 2:121–39.

———. 1998. Negative Social Capital: State Breakdown and Social Destitution in America's Urban Core. *Netherlands Journal of Housing and the Built Environment* 13, no. 1:25–39.

Wacquant, L. J. D., and Craig Calhoun. 1991. Interesse, racionalidade, e cultura. *Revista brasileira de ciencias sociais* 15, no. 6:23–48.

Walter, Richard. 1985. *The Province of Buenos Aires and Argentine Politics, 1912–1943.* Cambridge: Cambridge University Press.

Walzer, Susan. 1996. Thinking about the Baby: Gender and Divisions of Infant Care. *Social Problems* 43, no. 2:219–33.

Weber, Max. 1949. *The Methodology of the Social Sciences.* New York: Free Press.

———. 1968. *Economy and Society.* Berkeley: University of California Press.

Weingrod, Alex. 1977. Patrons, Patronage, and Political Parties. In *Friends, Followers, and Factions: A Reader in Political Clientelism,* ed. Steffen Schmidt, Laura Guasti, Carl Landé, and James Scott. Berkeley: University of California Press.

Wellman, B., and S. Berkowitz. 1988. *Social Structures: A Network Approach.* Cambridge: Cambridge University Press.

West, Candace, and Don Zimmerman. 1987. Doing Gender. *Gender and Society* 1, no. 2:125–51.

Whyte, William Foote. 1943. *Street Corner Society: The Social Structure of an Italian Slum.* Chicago: University of Chicago Press.

Williams, Raymond. 1977. *Marxism and Literature.* New York: Oxford University Press.

Williams, Terry. 1989. *The Cocaine Kids.* New York: Addison-Wesley.

———. 1992. *Crackhouse: Notes from the End of the Line.* New York: Penguin.

Willis, Paul. 1981. *Learning to Labor: How Working-Class Kids Get Working-Class Jobs.* New York: Columbia University Press.

Wilson, William Julius. 1997. *When Work Disappears.* New York: Knopf.

Wittgenstein, Ludwig. 1953. *Philosophical Investigations.* New York: Macmillan.

Wolf, Eric. 1977. Kinship, Friendship, and Patron-Client Relations in Complex Societies. In *Friends, Followers, and Factions: A Reader in Political Cli-*

entelism, ed. Steffen Schmidt, Laura
Guasti, Carl Landé, and James Scott.
Berkeley: University of California
Press.

Yujnovsky, Oscar. 1984. *Las claves políticas*
del problema habitacional argentino. Buenos
Aires: Grupo Editor Latinoamericano.

Zerubavel, Eviatar. 1996. Social Memories: Steps to a Sociology of the Past.
Qualitative Sociology 19, no. 3:283–99.

Index

flexibilization and, 36–7; and income reduction, 35; inequality and, 38–41; poverty and, 33; structural character of, 34; the unemployed and, 33

Unmet basic needs, 67

Ward boss, 83, 90, 117

Weber, Max: on domination, 115–16; on ideal types, 210–14

Wright Mills, C., 18, 203

Javier Auyero is Assistant Professor in
the Department of Sociology at the State
University of New York at Stony Brook.

Library of Congress Cataloging-in-Publication Data
Auyero, Javier.
Poor people's politics : Peronist survival networks
and the legacy of Evita / Javier Auyero.
p. cm.
Includes bibliographical references and indexes.
ISBN 0-8223-2627-2 (cloth : alk. paper)
ISBN 0-8223-2621-3 (pbk. : alk. paper)
1. Poor—Argentina—Buenos Aires—Political
activity.   2. Patronage, Political—Argentina—
Buenos Aires.   3. Peronism.   I. Title.
HC177.B82 A89 2000   322.4'4'0982—dc21   00-037115